CSS Crash Course for Beginners in 10 Hours or Less

(Book 1)

This book may be purchased in bulk for educational, business, fundraising, or sales promotional use.

ISBN:

Published by: Ekesy In-Outdoor Company

10B, Mufutau Opeifa Street, Oke-Odo, Ile-Epo B/Stop, Alimosho, Lagos, Nigeria

Email: dev@israeljoshua.com.ng

Tel: +234 803 815 4459, +234 813 2228 534

For information, please contact us @

dev@israeljoshua.com.ng

www.israeljoshua.com.ng

Call: +234 803 815 4459

Whatsapp: +234 813 2228 534

TABLE OF CONTENT

DEDICATION

I, **Israel Joshua Chukwubueze**, formerly known as **Christopher Ekene Okade**, write this book with a full heart and a grateful soul. I dedicate this work, *"CSS Crash Course for Beginners in 10 Hours or Less,"* to the ones who have continuously shaped, supported, and inspired my journey.

To Almighty God

First and foremost, **I give all glory, honor, and praise to Almighty God**, the source of my knowledge, strength, and purpose. Without God's divine guidance and wisdom, this book would never have come to life. Through every page, every chapter, and every line of code, His presence has been constant. He is my ultimate teacher, counselor, and light. I am deeply humbled by the grace that keeps me moving forward in all my pursuits, especially in empowering others through education and creativity.

To My Beautiful Kids

To my incredible daughters — **you are my daily motivation and inspiration**. Every lesson I teach, every book I write, every piece of knowledge I share, I do it with you in mind. I want you to grow in a world where learning is exciting, where your creativity has no limits, and where your voice matters. I hope that when you see my work, it reminds you that **you can learn anything, build anything, and become anything** with faith, discipline, and love. You are my legacy, and I am proud of the amazing individuals you are becoming.

To My Dear Mother

To my beloved mum — **thank you for your unwavering love, prayers, and resilience**. Your sacrifices, patience, and nurturing spirit have laid the foundation upon which I stand today. You have taught me the value of hard work, humility, and perseverance. Your encouragement during moments of doubt and your joyful spirit in times of success have always lifted me higher. This book is a product of your selflessness, and I honor you with every word written in it.

To My Readers Around the World

To **you, the reader** — this book is **for you, because of you, and dedicated to your growth**. Whether you are just starting your journey into the world of web development or you are looking to strengthen your foundation in CSS, I wrote this with your learning style, challenges, and success in mind. You're not just reading a book — **you're gaining a skill that can change your life**. Every line of instruction, every layout strategy, and every example in this course has been carefully designed to make your learning smoother, more practical, and easier to understand.

Your time is precious, and I do not take it for granted. **Thank you for choosing to learn from me**. I promise to always give you my best, and to be a voice of clarity in a world full of complexity. Keep building. Keep learning. Keep moving forward.

With all my heart,
Israel Joshua Chukwubueze

PREFACE

My name is **Israel Joshua Chukwubueze**, formerly known as **Christopher Ekene Okade**, and I welcome you to *CSS Crash Course for Beginners in 10 Hours or Less*. Writing and teaching have always been more than just professional pursuits for me — they are part of who I am. I've always believed that knowledge should not remain locked behind complicated explanations or unreachable terms. It should be passed on with simplicity, joy, and practical clarity.

This book was born from that belief. Over the years, I've mentored countless students one-on-one, taught online and offline, published hundreds of resources, and continued to see a common challenge — many beginners are discouraged by how hard CSS seems at the start. The syntax looks strange, the layout feels confusing, and the visual results don't always match expectations. I've been there, and I get it.

That's why this book exists.

Why CSS Matters

CSS — short for *Cascading Style Sheets* — is the language that **brings beauty, structure, and interactivity to websites**. It takes the raw content written in HTML and gives it life. Fonts, colors, spacing, animations, layouts — all of that comes from CSS. Without it, the web would be plain, lifeless, and hard to navigate.

In this book, **you'll learn how to style web pages with confidence and clarity**. Whether you're a total beginner or someone who needs a refresher, I've structured this crash course in a way that cuts out confusion and replaces it with hands-on practice and real-world examples. You don't need any fancy tools or advanced background. You only need your curiosity, a browser, a code editor, and a willingness to learn one step at a time.

What This Book Offers You

This crash course is divided into **30 digestible chapters**, each designed to build your skills in small but meaningful steps. You won't be overwhelmed. Each chapter tackles specific, practical CSS topics like fonts, margins, flexbox, grid, media queries, animations, and more — and it does so with **clear explanations, simple code samples, and guided exercises**.

Here's how I structured the learning experience for you:

- **Bold Concepts, Simple Explanations:** You'll get the why and how behind every concept without the clutter.
- **Quick Wins:** You'll see results early. From the first few chapters, you'll start styling basic web pages and feel the reward of what you're learning.
- **Visual Thinking:** CSS is visual by nature, so you'll think in terms of space, layout, and color as you code.
- **10-Hour Path:** I kept your time in mind. In 10 hours or less, you'll gain a strong foundation you can build on for future skills like responsive design, frameworks, or even advanced UI development.

How to Use This Book

To get the most out of this crash course:

- **Start Small, Keep Going:** Don't rush. Focus on each chapter and try out the examples before moving to the next.
- **Code Along:** Reading is helpful, but CSS is best learned by **doing**. Copy the examples, change them, break them, and see what happens.
- **Experiment:** Try things outside the book. Once you understand a property or concept, test it in your own small projects.
- **Ask Questions:** Don't be afraid to not know everything. Learning means figuring things out little by little.

My Promise to You

I didn't write this book to impress anyone. I wrote it to **help people** — people like you who want to understand how websites are styled and structured. I want you to feel like CSS is something **you can do, not something reserved for the experts**. I believe that with the right guide, clear examples, and just a bit of practice, anyone can learn to write clean, effective CSS.

Throughout these pages, you'll see a lot of my personality — straightforward, practical, and committed to your progress. My goal is that when you finish this book, you won't just know what CSS is, but you'll know **how to use it to create your own beautiful, responsive websites**.

A Personal Note

This book is not just a technical manual. It's also a reflection of my journey — from student to teacher, from curiosity to clarity, from trial and error to guiding others. I've made many mistakes along the way, and I've turned those lessons into wisdom you'll find in this course. You're not alone on this path, and you don't need to be perfect. **You just need to start.**

Thank you for letting me be a part of your learning. Thank you for opening this book, and for choosing to grow your skill. Whether you're building a career in tech or simply picking up a new hobby, I believe in your ability to learn CSS — clearly, confidently, and completely.

Let's get started.

With gratitude and purpose,
Israel Joshua Chukwubueze

Chapter 1: Introduction to CSS

1.1 What is CSS?

Understanding Cascading Style Sheets

CSS stands for Cascading Style Sheets, a powerful styling language that transforms plain HTML documents into visually appealing and professionally designed web pages. CSS serves as the presentation layer of web development, controlling how HTML elements appear on screen, in print, or when spoken aloud by screen readers.

The term "cascading" refers to the hierarchical nature of CSS rules, where styles flow down from parent elements to their children, and multiple style rules can apply to the same element. When conflicts arise between different CSS rules targeting the same element, CSS follows a specific order of priority to determine which styles take precedence.

The Role of CSS in Web Development

CSS operates independently from HTML content, allowing developers to separate structure from presentation. This separation provides numerous advantages including easier maintenance, consistent styling across multiple pages, and the ability to completely change a website's appearance without modifying the underlying HTML structure.

Modern CSS has evolved far beyond simple color and font styling. Today's CSS includes advanced features such as animations, transitions, grid layouts, flexbox positioning, custom properties (variables), and responsive design capabilities that adapt to different screen sizes and devices.

CSS Syntax Structure

CSS follows a straightforward syntax pattern consisting of selectors, properties, and values:

#css

```
selector {
```

```
    property: value;
    property: value;
}
```

Each CSS rule begins with a selector that identifies which HTML elements to style, followed by a declaration block enclosed in curly braces. Within the declaration block, individual declarations consist of a property name, a colon, and a value, terminated by a semicolon.

Types of CSS Selectors

CSS offers various selector types to target HTML elements:

Element Selectors target HTML tags directly:

#css

```
h1 {
    color: blue;
}
```

Class Selectors target elements with specific class attributes:

#css

```
.highlight {
    background-color: yellow;
}
```

ID Selectors target elements with unique ID attributes:

#css

```css
#header {
    font-size: 24px;
}
```

Attribute Selectors target elements based on their attributes:

#css

```css
input[type="text"] {
    border: 1px solid gray;
}
```

1.2 History and Evolution of CSS

The Pre-CSS Era

Before CSS existed, web developers had limited options for styling HTML documents. Early web pages relied heavily on HTML attributes like `bgcolor`, `font`, and `center` tags for presentation. This approach created several problems: mixing content with presentation, code duplication across pages, and difficulty maintaining consistent styling across large websites.

CSS Level 1 (CSS1) - 1996

The World Wide Web Consortium (W3C) introduced CSS1 in December 1996, establishing the foundation for web styling. CSS1 included basic features such as font properties, color control, text alignment, margin and padding control, and background styling. Despite its limitations, CSS1 provided the crucial separation of content and presentation that would become fundamental to modern web development.

CSS Level 2 (CSS2) - 1998

CSS2 arrived in May 1998, introducing significant enhancements including positioning properties (absolute, relative, fixed), z-index for layer control, media types for different output devices, and improved selector options. CSS2 also introduced the box model concept, which remains central to CSS layout understanding today.

CSS 2.1 - 2004-2011

CSS 2.1 represented a refinement of CSS2, removing poorly supported features and clarifying specifications. This version became the stable foundation that most browsers implemented consistently, leading to better cross-browser compatibility.

CSS Level 3 (CSS3) - 2001-Present

Unlike previous versions, CSS3 development followed a modular approach, with different features developing independently. This approach allowed faster implementation of individual features without waiting for the entire specification to complete.

Key CSS3 modules include:

- **Selectors Level 3**: Advanced pseudo-selectors like `:nth-child()` and `:not()`
- **Media Queries**: Responsive design capabilities
- **Flexbox**: Flexible box layout model
- **Grid Layout**: Two-dimensional layout system
- **Animations and Transitions**: Motion and interaction effects
- **Custom Properties**: CSS variables for reusable values

Modern CSS (CSS4 and Beyond)

Current CSS development continues the modular approach, with new features constantly being proposed, tested, and implemented. Modern CSS includes advanced features like container queries, cascade layers, and improved logical properties that adapt to different writing modes.

1.3 How CSS Works with HTML

The Document Structure Relationship

HTML provides the structural foundation of web pages through semantic markup, while CSS applies styling rules to transform that structure into visually appealing presentations. This relationship follows the separation of concerns principle, where each technology handles its specific responsibility.

The Rendering Process

When a browser loads a web page, it follows a specific process:

1. **HTML Parsing**: The browser reads and parses the HTML document, creating a Document Object Model (DOM) tree
2. **CSS Parsing**: The browser reads and parses CSS stylesheets, creating a CSS Object Model (CSSOM)
3. **Render Tree Construction**: The browser combines the DOM and CSSOM to create a render tree
4. **Layout Calculation**: The browser calculates the exact position and size of each element
5. **Painting**: The browser renders the visual representation on screen

Linking CSS to HTML

CSS connects to HTML through several methods, each serving different purposes and use cases. The relationship between HTML and CSS occurs through selectors that match HTML elements based on their tag names, attributes, positions, or states.

The Cascade and Specificity

The "cascading" nature of CSS means that multiple rules can apply to the same element. When conflicts occur, CSS uses specificity calculations to determine which rules take precedence:

- **Inline styles**: 1000 points
- **IDs**: 100 points
- **Classes, attributes, pseudo-classes**: 10 points

- **Elements and pseudo-elements**: 1 point

#css

```css
/* Specificity: 1 (element) */
p {
    color: blue;
}

/* Specificity: 10 (class) */
.special {
    color: red;
}

/* Specificity: 11 (element + class) */
p.special {
    color: green;
}
```

Inheritance in CSS

Many CSS properties inherit values from parent elements to their children, creating consistent styling throughout the document hierarchy. Properties like `color`, `font-family`, and `line-height` inherit by default, while properties like `border`, `margin`, and `padding` do not.

#css

```css
body {
    font-family: Arial, sans-serif;
    color: #333;
}
```

```
/* All text within body inherits the font-family and
color */
```

1.4 Inline, Internal, and External CSS

Inline CSS

Inline CSS applies styles directly to individual HTML elements using the `style` attribute. This method provides the highest specificity and overrides other CSS rules, but should be used sparingly due to maintenance and scalability concerns.

Syntax:

#html

```
<p style="color: red; font-size: 18px;">This paragraph
has inline styling.</p>
```

Advantages of Inline CSS:

- Immediate application without external dependencies
- Highest specificity for overriding other styles
- Useful for quick testing and debugging
- Dynamic styling through JavaScript manipulation

Disadvantages of Inline CSS:

- Mixes content with presentation
- Difficult to maintain across multiple elements
- Increases HTML file size
- Cannot use advanced CSS features like media queries
- Poor reusability

When to Use Inline CSS: Inline CSS works best for unique, one-time styling needs, email templates (where external stylesheets may not load), and temporary styling during development and testing.

Internal CSS

Internal CSS places style rules within the HTML document's `<head>` section using `<style>` tags. This method keeps all styling for a single page contained within that page's HTML file.

Syntax:

#html

```
<!DOCTYPE html>
<html>
<head>
    <style>
        body {
            background-color: #f0f0f0;
            font-family: 'Helvetica', sans-serif;
        }

        .header {
            background-color: #333;
            color: white;
            padding: 20px;
            text-align: center;
        }

        .content {
            margin: 20px;
            line-height: 1.6;
        }
```

```
    </style>
</head>
<body>
    <div class="header">
        <h1>Welcome to My Website</h1>
    </div>
    <div class="content">
        <p>This is styled with internal CSS.</p>
    </div>
</body>
</html>
```

Advantages of Internal CSS:

- All styles for a page contained in one file
- Faster loading than external stylesheets for single pages
- Can override external stylesheet rules
- Useful for page-specific styling

Disadvantages of Internal CSS:

- Styles cannot be shared across multiple pages
- Increases HTML file size
- Makes HTML less readable
- Requires duplication for consistent multi-page styling

When to Use Internal CSS: Internal CSS suits single-page websites, page-specific styles that won't be reused, and situations where external file loading may be problematic.

External CSS

External CSS stores style rules in separate `.css` files that link to HTML documents. This method provides the best separation of concerns and scalability for multi-page websites.

Creating an External CSS File: Create a file named `styles.css`:

#css

```css
/* styles.css */
* {
    margin: 0;
    padding: 0;
    box-sizing: border-box;
}

body {
    font-family: 'Georgia', serif;
    background-color: #ffffff;
    color: #333333;
    line-height: 1.8;
}

.container {
    max-width: 1200px;
    margin: 0 auto;
    padding: 20px;
}

.navigation {
    background-color: #2c3e50;
    padding: 15px 0;
}
```

```css
.navigation ul {
    list-style: none;
    display: flex;
    justify-content: center;
}

.navigation li {
    margin: 0 20px;
}

.navigation a {
    color: white;
    text-decoration: none;
    font-weight: bold;
    transition: color 0.3s ease;
}

.navigation a:hover {
    color: #3498db;
}
```

Linking External CSS to HTML:

#html

```html
<!DOCTYPE html>
<html>
<head>
    <meta charset="UTF-8">
    <meta name="viewport" content="width=device-width,
initial-scale=1.0">
```

```
    <title>My Website</title>
    <link rel="stylesheet" href="styles.css">
</head>
<body>
    <nav class="navigation">
        <ul>
            <li><a href="#home">Home</a></li>
            <li><a href="#about">About</a></li>
            <li><a href="#contact">Contact</a></li>
        </ul>
    </nav>
    <div class="container">
        <h1>Welcome to My Website</h1>
        <p>This page uses external CSS styling.</p>
    </div>
</body>
</html>
```

Advantages of External CSS:

- Complete separation of content and presentation
- Styles can be shared across multiple pages
- Easier maintenance and updates
- Smaller HTML file sizes
- Browser caching improves performance
- Better organization for large projects

Disadvantages of External CSS:

- Requires additional HTTP requests
- Potential render blocking
- Dependency on external file loading

Multiple External Stylesheets: You can link multiple external CSS files to a single HTML document:

#html

```
<head>
    <link rel="stylesheet" href="reset.css">
    <link rel="stylesheet" href="typography.css">
    <link rel="stylesheet" href="layout.css">
    <link rel="stylesheet" href="components.css">
</head>
```

1.5 Setting Up Your First CSS File

Project Structure Planning

Before creating your first CSS file, establish a logical project structure that will scale as your website grows. A well-organized project structure improves maintainability and collaboration.

Basic Project Structure:

```
my-website/
├── index.html
├── about.html
├── contact.html
├── css/
│   ├── styles.css
│   ├── reset.css
│   └── responsive.css
├── images/
│   ├── logo.png
│   └── background.jpg
```

```
└── js/
    └── script.js
```

Advanced Project Structure:

```
my-website/
├── index.html
├── pages/
│   ├── about.html
│   └── contact.html
├── assets/
│   ├── css/
│   │   ├── main.css
│   │   ├── components/
│   │   │   ├── header.css
│   │   │   ├── navigation.css
│   │   │   └── footer.css
│   │   └── utilities/
│   │       ├── reset.css
│   │       └── helpers.css
│   ├── images/
│   └── fonts/
└── js/
```

Creating Your First CSS File

Step 1: Create the CSS File Create a new file named `styles.css` in your project directory or css folder.

Step 2: Start with a CSS Reset Begin your CSS file with a reset to ensure consistent styling across different browsers:

```
#css
```

```css
/* CSS Reset */
* {
    margin: 0;
    padding: 0;
    box-sizing: border-box;
}

html {
    font-size: 16px;
    scroll-behavior: smooth;
}

body {
    font-family: -apple-system, BlinkMacSystemFont,
'Segoe UI', Roboto, sans-serif;
    line-height: 1.6;
    color: #333;
    background-color: #fff;
}

img {
    max-width: 100%;
    height: auto;
}

a {
    text-decoration: none;
    color: inherit;
}

ul, ol {
```

```
    list-style: none;
}
```

Step 3: Define Your Color Palette Establish a consistent color scheme using CSS custom properties (variables):

#css

```
/* Color Palette */
:root {
    --primary-color: #3498db;
    --secondary-color: #2ecc71;
    --accent-color: #e74c3c;
    --text-color: #333333;
    --text-light: #666666;
    --background-color: #ffffff;
    --background-light: #f8f9fa;
    --border-color: #dee2e6;
}
```

Step 4: Set Up Typography Define your typography system with consistent font sizes and spacing:

#css

```
/* Typography */
h1, h2, h3, h4, h5, h6 {
    font-weight: 600;
    line-height: 1.3;
    margin-bottom: 0.5em;
    color: var(--text-color);
```

```css
}

h1 { font-size: 2.5rem; }
h2 { font-size: 2rem; }
h3 { font-size: 1.75rem; }
h4 { font-size: 1.5rem; }
h5 { font-size: 1.25rem; }
h6 { font-size: 1rem; }

p {
    margin-bottom: 1rem;
    color: var(--text-color);
}

.lead {
    font-size: 1.25rem;
    font-weight: 300;
    color: var(--text-light);
}
```

Step 5: Create Layout Components Build reusable layout components:

#css

```css
/* Layout Components */
.container {
    max-width: 1200px;
    margin: 0 auto;
    padding: 0 20px;
}
```

```css
.section {
    padding: 60px 0;
}

.grid {
    display: grid;
    gap: 2rem;
}

.grid-2 { grid-template-columns: repeat(2, 1fr); }
.grid-3 { grid-template-columns: repeat(3, 1fr); }
.grid-4 { grid-template-columns: repeat(4, 1fr); }

.flex {
    display: flex;
}

.flex-center {
    display: flex;
    justify-content: center;
    align-items: center;
}

.text-center { text-align: center; }
.text-left { text-align: left; }
.text-right { text-align: right; }
```

Step 6: Add Component Styles Create specific component styles:

#css

```css
/* Header Component */
.header {
    background-color: var(--background-light);
    padding: 1rem 0;
    border-bottom: 1px solid var(--border-color);
}

.nav {
    display: flex;
    justify-content: space-between;
    align-items: center;
}

.nav-links {
    display: flex;
    gap: 2rem;
}

.nav-link {
    color: var(--text-color);
    font-weight: 500;
    transition: color 0.3s ease;
}

.nav-link:hover {
    color: var(--primary-color);
}

/* Button Component */
.btn {
```

```css
    display: inline-block;
    padding: 12px 24px;
    border: none;
    border-radius: 6px;
    font-size: 1rem;
    font-weight: 600;
    text-align: center;
    cursor: pointer;
    transition: all 0.3s ease;
    text-decoration: none;
}

.btn-primary {
    background-color: var(--primary-color);
    color: white;
}

.btn-primary:hover {
    background-color: #2980b9;
    transform: translateY(-2px);
}

.btn-secondary {
    background-color: transparent;
    color: var(--primary-color);
    border: 2px solid var(--primary-color);
}

.btn-secondary:hover {
    background-color: var(--primary-color);
    color: white;
```

```
}
```

Linking Your CSS File to HTML

Create a corresponding HTML file that uses your CSS:

#html

```
<!DOCTYPE html>
<html lang="en">
<head>
    <meta charset="UTF-8">
    <meta name="viewport" content="width=device-width,
initial-scale=1.0">
    <title>My First CSS Project</title>
    <link rel="stylesheet" href="styles.css">
</head>
<body>
    <header class="header">
        <div class="container">
            <nav class="nav">
                <div class="logo">
                    <h2>My Website</h2>
                </div>
                <ul class="nav-links">
                    <li><a href="#" class="nav-
link">Home</a></li>
                    <li><a href="#" class="nav-
link">About</a></li>
                    <li><a href="#" class="nav-
link">Services</a></li>
```

```
                    <li><a href="#" class="nav-
link">Contact</a></li>
                </ul>
            </nav>
        </div>
    </header>

    <main>
        <section class="section">
            <div class="container">
                <div class="text-center">
                    <h1>Welcome to My Website</h1>
                    <p class="lead">This is my first CSS-
styled webpage</p>
                    <a href="#" class="btn btn-
primary">Get Started</a>
                    <a href="#" class="btn btn-
secondary">Learn More</a>
                </div>
            </div>
        </section>

        <section class="section">
            <div class="container">
                <div class="grid grid-3">
                    <div>
                        <h3>Feature One</h3>
                        <p>Description of the first
feature with some detailed information.</p>
                    </div>
                    <div>
                        <h3>Feature Two</h3>
```

```
                        <p>Description of the second
feature with some detailed information.</p>
                    </div>
                    <div>
                        <h3>Feature Three</h3>
                        <p>Description of the third
feature with some detailed information.</p>
                    </div>
                </div>
            </div>
        </section>
    </main>
</body>
</html>
```

CSS Organization Best Practices

Comment Your Code:

#css

```
/*
=========================================================
=================
   HEADER COMPONENTS

=========================================================
================= */


/* Main navigation bar */
.nav {
    /* styles here */
}
```

```css
/* Navigation links */
.nav-link {
    /* styles here */
}
```

Use Consistent Naming Conventions: Follow BEM (Block, Element, Modifier) methodology:

#css

```css
/* Block */
.card { }

/* Element */
.card__title { }
.card__content { }

/* Modifier */
.card--featured { }
.card--large { }
```

Group Related Styles: Organize your CSS file into logical sections:

1. CSS Reset/Normalize
2. Variables and Custom Properties
3. Base Typography
4. Layout Components
5. UI Components
6. Utilities
7. Media Queries

Essential Tips

- Always use semantic HTML as the foundation for your CSS styling, as clean markup makes CSS more effective and maintainable.
- Start with a CSS reset or normalize stylesheet to ensure consistent rendering across different browsers and eliminate default styling inconsistencies.
- Organize your CSS file with clear comments and consistent indentation, grouping related styles together for easier navigation and maintenance.
- Use CSS custom properties (variables) for colors, fonts, and commonly used values to maintain consistency and make global changes effortless.
- Test your CSS across multiple browsers and devices regularly during development rather than waiting until the end of the project.

Actionable Strategies

- Create a systematic approach to CSS development by starting with mobile-first design principles and progressively enhancing for larger screens.
- Develop a personal CSS framework or library of commonly used components that you can reuse across projects to speed up development time.
- Use browser developer tools extensively to inspect elements, test changes in real-time, and understand how CSS rules are being applied or overridden.
- Implement a CSS methodology like BEM, OOCSS, or SMACSS to maintain consistent naming conventions and code organization as projects grow.
- Practice CSS specificity management by keeping selectors as simple as possible and avoiding overly complex or deeply nested rules.
- Set up a CSS linting tool in your development environment to catch syntax errors and enforce coding standards automatically.
- Build a collection of CSS snippets and code examples that you can reference and adapt for future projects, creating your own personal knowledge base.

Chapter 2: CSS Syntax and Selectors

2.1 Understanding CSS Syntax Structure

CSS (Cascading Style Sheets) operates on a fundamental principle of rules and declarations that define how HTML elements should appear and behave on web pages. The syntax structure forms the backbone of every CSS implementation, and mastering this foundation is essential for creating effective stylesheets.

The Anatomy of CSS Rules

Every CSS rule consists of two primary components: a selector and a declaration block. The selector identifies which HTML elements the rule should target, while the declaration block contains one or more property-value pairs that define the styling instructions.

#css

```
selector {
    property: value;
    property: value;
}
```

The declaration block is enclosed within curly braces `{}`, and each declaration consists of a property name followed by a colon `:`, then the property value, and finally terminated with a semicolon `;`. This semicolon is crucial as it separates multiple declarations within the same rule.

CSS Property-Value Pairs

Properties represent the specific aspects of an element that you want to modify, such as color, font-size, margin, or background. Values define how these properties should be set. CSS supports various value types including keywords, numbers, percentages, lengths, colors, and URLs.

#css

```
h1 {
    color: blue;
    font-size: 24px;
    margin: 10px 0;
    background-color: #f0f0f0;
}
```

In this example, `color`, `font-size`, `margin`, and `background-color` are properties, while `blue`, `24px`, `10px 0`, and `#f0f0f0` are their corresponding values.

Comments in CSS

CSS supports single-line and multi-line comments using the `/* */` syntax. Comments are invaluable for documenting your code, explaining complex rules, or temporarily disabling certain styles during development.

#css

```
/* This is a single-line comment */

/*
This is a multi-line comment
that spans several lines
*/

.header {
    background-color: navy; /* Primary brand color */
    /* font-weight: bold; This line is commented out */
}
```

CSS Cascade and Inheritance

The "Cascading" in CSS refers to how styles are applied when multiple rules target the same element. The cascade follows specific rules of precedence: inline styles override internal styles, internal styles override external stylesheets, and later rules override earlier ones when specificity is equal.

Inheritance allows certain properties to pass from parent elements to their children automatically. Properties like `color`, `font-family`, and `line-height` inherit by default, while others like `margin`, `padding`, and `border` do not.

#css

```
body {
    font-family: Arial, sans-serif;
    color: #333;
}

p {
    /* Inherits font-family and color from body */
    margin: 15px 0; /* This does not inherit */
}
```

2.2 Selectors: Basic, Grouping, and Universal

Selectors are the foundation of CSS targeting, allowing you to specify which HTML elements should receive particular styling. Understanding different selector types and their applications is crucial for efficient CSS development.

Element Selectors

Element selectors target HTML elements directly by their tag name. These selectors apply styles to all instances of the specified element throughout the document.

#css

```
h1 {
    color: darkblue;
    font-weight: bold;
}

p {
    line-height: 1.6;
    margin-bottom: 15px;
}

img {
    max-width: 100%;
    height: auto;
}
```

Element selectors are broad in scope and useful for establishing baseline styles across your website. They form the foundation upon which more specific selectors build.

Grouping Selectors

When multiple elements require identical styling, grouping selectors eliminates code repetition and improves maintainability. Separate multiple selectors with commas to apply the same rule set to all listed elements.

#css

```
h1, h2, h3, h4, h5, h6 {
```

```
    font-family: 'Georgia', serif;
    margin-top: 0;
    margin-bottom: 20px;
}

header, footer, aside {
    background-color: #f8f9fa;
    padding: 20px;
    border: 1px solid #dee2e6;
}
```

Grouping selectors streamlines CSS maintenance because changes to grouped properties automatically apply to all listed selectors, reducing the likelihood of inconsistencies.

Universal Selector

The universal selector * targets every element in the document. While powerful, it should be used judiciously due to performance implications and potential unintended consequences.

#css

```
* {
    margin: 0;
    padding: 0;
    box-sizing: border-box;
}
```

This CSS reset removes default margins and paddings from all elements and applies consistent box-sizing behavior. The universal selector is commonly used for CSS resets and establishing global defaults.

Descendant Selectors

Descendant selectors target elements that are nested within other elements, regardless of how deeply nested they are. Use a space to separate the ancestor and descendant selectors.

#css

```
article p {
    font-size: 16px;
    text-align: justify;
}

nav ul {
    list-style: none;
    display: flex;
}

.sidebar img {
    border-radius: 8px;
    box-shadow: 0 2px 4px rgba(0,0,0,0.1);
}
```

Child Selectors

Child selectors use the > symbol to target direct children only, not deeper descendants. This provides more precise control than descendant selectors.

#css

```css
ul > li {
    margin-bottom: 10px;
}

.menu > a {
    display: block;
    padding: 8px 12px;
    text-decoration: none;
}
```

Adjacent Sibling Selectors

The adjacent sibling selector + targets an element that immediately follows another element at the same level in the HTML structure.

#css

```css
h2 + p {
    font-weight: bold;
    margin-top: 0;
}

img + figcaption {
    font-style: italic;
    text-align: center;
}
```

General Sibling Selectors

The general sibling selector ~ targets all siblings that follow a specified element, not just the immediately adjacent one.

#css

```
h3 ~ p {
    color: #666;
}

.featured ~ .article {
    border-left: 3px solid #007bff;
}
```

2.3 Class vs. ID Selectors

Class and ID selectors provide precise targeting mechanisms for specific elements, but they serve different purposes and have distinct characteristics that affect their usage patterns and specificity.

Class Selectors

Class selectors begin with a period `.` followed by the class name. They target elements with matching class attributes and can be applied to multiple elements throughout a document.

#css

```
.highlight {
    background-color: yellow;
    padding: 2px 4px;
}

.button {
```

```
    display: inline-block;
    padding: 10px 20px;
    background-color: #007bff;
    color: white;
    text-decoration: none;
    border-radius: 4px;
    transition: background-color 0.3s ease;
}

.button:hover {
    background-color: #0056b3;
}
```

HTML implementation:

#html

```
<p>This text contains a <span
class="highlight">highlighted section</span>.</p>
<a href="#" class="button">Click Me</a>
<button class="button">Submit Form</button>
```

Classes excel at creating reusable styles that can be applied consistently across multiple elements. They promote modular CSS architecture and maintainable code structures.

Multiple Classes

Elements can have multiple classes by separating class names with spaces in the HTML class attribute. This allows for combining different styling behaviors on a single element.

#css

```
.box {
    padding: 20px;
    border: 1px solid #ccc;
}

.rounded {
    border-radius: 8px;
}

.shadow {
    box-shadow: 0 2px 8px rgba(0,0,0,0.1);
}

.large {
    font-size: 1.2em;
}
```

HTML usage:

#html

```
<div class="box rounded shadow">Basic box with rounded corners and shadow</div>
<div class="box large">Large text box</div>
<div class="box rounded shadow large">Box with all enhancements</div>
```

ID Selectors

ID selectors begin with a hash symbol # followed by the ID name. They target elements with matching ID attributes, and each ID should be unique within a document.

#css

```
#header {
    background-color: #2c3e50;
    color: white;
    padding: 20px 0;
    position: fixed;
    top: 0;
    width: 100%;
    z-index: 1000;
}

#navigation {
    background-color: #34495e;
    padding: 10px 0;
}

#main-content {
    margin-top: 120px;
    padding: 20px;
    max-width: 1200px;
    margin-left: auto;
    margin-right: auto;
}

#footer {
    background-color: #7f8c8d;
    color: white;
```

```
    text-align: center;
    padding: 30px 0;
    margin-top: 50px;
}
```

HTML structure:

#html

```
<header id="header">
    <nav id="navigation">
        <!-- Navigation content -->
    </nav>
</header>
<main id="main-content">
    <!-- Main page content -->
</main>
<footer id="footer">
    <!-- Footer content -->
</footer>
```

Specificity Differences

ID selectors have higher specificity than class selectors, meaning ID styles will override class styles when both target the same element. Understanding specificity is crucial for predicting which styles will apply.

#css

```
.text-blue {
    color: blue;
```

```
}

#special-text {
    color: red; /* This will override the blue color */
}
```

HTML:

#html

```
<p class="text-blue" id="special-text">This text will be red, not blue</p>
```

Best Practices for Classes vs. IDs

Use classes for styling purposes and when you need to apply the same styles to multiple elements. Classes promote reusability and modular CSS architecture. Reserve IDs for unique page sections, JavaScript targeting, and anchor links. Avoid using IDs primarily for styling due to their high specificity, which can make CSS harder to maintain and override.

2.4 Attribute and Pseudo-class Selectors

Attribute and pseudo-class selectors provide advanced targeting capabilities that go beyond basic element, class, and ID selection. These selectors enable dynamic styling based on element states, user interactions, and HTML attributes.

Attribute Selectors

Attribute selectors target elements based on their HTML attributes and attribute values, offering flexible selection criteria that complement traditional selectors.

Basic Attribute Presence

The simplest attribute selector targets elements that have a specific attribute, regardless of its value.

#css

```
[title] {
    border-bottom: 1px dotted #666;
    cursor: help;
}

[disabled] {
    opacity: 0.5;
    cursor: not-allowed;
}

[required] {
    border-left: 3px solid #dc3545;
}
```

Exact Attribute Value Matching

Target elements with specific attribute values using the equals operator =.

#css

```
[type="email"] {
    background-image: url('email-icon.svg');
    background-repeat: no-repeat;
    background-position: right 10px center;
    padding-right: 35px;
}
```

```
[lang="en"] {
    font-family: "Helvetica Neue", Arial, sans-serif;
}

[data-status="active"] {
    background-color: #28a745;
    color: white;
}
```

Partial Attribute Value Matching

CSS provides several operators for partial attribute value matching:

#css

```
/* Contains word */
[class~="highlight"] {
    background-color: yellow;
}

/* Starts with */
[href^="https://"] {
    color: green;
}

[href^="mailto:"] {
    color: blue;
}

/* Ends with */
[href$=".pdf"] {
```

```css
    background-image: url('pdf-icon.svg');
    padding-left: 20px;
}

[src$=".jpg"], [src$=".png"], [src$=".gif"] {
    border: 2px solid #ccc;
    border-radius: 4px;
}

/* Contains substring */
[href*="github"] {
    background-color: #333;
    color: white;
    padding: 2px 6px;
    border-radius: 3px;
}
```

Language and Direction Attributes

Attribute selectors are particularly useful for internationalization and accessibility features.

#css

```css
[lang^="ar"] {
    direction: rtl;
    text-align: right;
}

[dir="rtl"] {
    padding-right: 20px;
    padding-left: 0;
```

```
}
```

Pseudo-class Selectors

Pseudo-classes select elements based on their state or position rather than their attributes or content. They begin with a colon : and provide dynamic styling capabilities.

Link and Interaction States

The most common pseudo-classes handle link states and user interactions.

#css

```css
a:link {
    color: #007bff;
    text-decoration: none;
}

a:visited {
    color: #6f42c1;
}

a:hover {
    color: #0056b3;
    text-decoration: underline;
}

a:active {
    color: #dc3545;
}
```

```
button:hover {
    background-color: #e0e0e0;
    cursor: pointer;
}

input:focus {
    outline: 2px solid #007bff;
    outline-offset: 2px;
    border-color: #007bff;
}
```

Form Element States

Pseudo-classes provide excellent styling opportunities for form elements based on their validation states and user interaction.

#css

```
input:valid {
    border-color: #28a745;
    background-color: #f8f9fa;
}

input:invalid {
    border-color: #dc3545;
    background-color: #fff5f5;
}

input:required {
    border-left: 3px solid #ffc107;
}
```

```css
input:optional {
    border-left: 3px solid #6c757d;
}

input:disabled {
    background-color: #e9ecef;
    cursor: not-allowed;
    opacity: 0.6;
}

input:checked + label {
    font-weight: bold;
    color: #007bff;
}
```

Structural Pseudo-classes

Structural pseudo-classes select elements based on their position within their parent element.

#css

```css
li:first-child {
    border-top: 2px solid #007bff;
}

li:last-child {
    border-bottom: 2px solid #007bff;
}

tr:nth-child(even) {
    background-color: #f8f9fa;
```

```
}

tr:nth-child(odd) {
    background-color: white;
}

p:nth-child(3n) {
    font-weight: bold;
}

article > p:first-of-type {
    font-size: 1.2em;
    font-weight: 500;
}

section > h2:only-child {
    text-align: center;
    margin: 40px 0;
}
```

Advanced Structural Selectors

More complex structural relationships can be targeted with advanced pseudo-classes.

#css

```
/* Every third paragraph starting from the second */
p:nth-child(3n+2) {
    margin-left: 20px;
    border-left: 3px solid #17a2b8;
    padding-left: 15px;
```

```
}

/* Last two items */
li:nth-last-child(-n+2) {
    font-weight: bold;
}

/* Empty elements */
p:empty {
    display: none;
}

/* Elements with no siblings */
img:only-child {
    display: block;
    margin: 20px auto;
    max-width: 100%;
}
```

Negation Pseudo-class

The `:not()` pseudo-class selects elements that do not match the specified selector.

#css

```
input:not([type="submit"]) {
    border: 1px solid #ced4da;
    padding: 8px 12px;
}

p:not(.special) {
    color: #6c757d;
```

```
}

li:not(:first-child) {
    margin-top: 10px;
}

a:not([href^="http"]) {
    color: #28a745;
}
```

2.5 Best Practices in Selector Usage

Effective selector usage forms the foundation of maintainable, performant, and scalable CSS. Following established best practices ensures your stylesheets remain manageable as projects grow in complexity and team size.

Selector Specificity Management

Understanding and managing selector specificity prevents common CSS conflicts and makes stylesheets more predictable. Specificity is calculated based on the types of selectors used: inline styles (1000), IDs (100), classes/attributes/pseudo-classes (10), and elements (1).

#css

```
/* Low specificity - easily overridden */
p {
    color: black;
}

/* Medium specificity */
.content p {
```

```css
    color: gray;
}

/* Higher specificity */
.sidebar .content p {
    color: blue;
}

/* Very high specificity - difficult to override */
#main .sidebar .content p {
    color: red;
}
```

Instead of increasing specificity to override styles, consider refactoring selectors or using more specific classes.

#css

```css
/* Better approach - use specific classes */
.content-text {
    color: gray;
}

.sidebar-text {
    color: blue;
}

.featured-text {
    color: red;
}
```

Performance Considerations

CSS selector performance varies significantly based on how browsers parse them. Browsers read selectors from right to left, making the rightmost selector (key selector) most important for performance.

#css

```
/* Inefficient - browser must check every div for
.content class */
.content div {
    padding: 10px;
}

/* More efficient - specific key selector */
.content-block {
    padding: 10px;
}

/* Inefficient - universal selector as key selector */
.sidebar * {
    margin: 0;
}

/* Better - target specific elements */
.sidebar p,
.sidebar h1,
.sidebar h2,
.sidebar ul {
    margin: 0;
}
```

Maintainable Selector Patterns

Create selector patterns that remain maintainable as projects evolve. Avoid overly complex selectors and deeply nested structures.

#css

```css
/* Complex and fragile */
.header .navigation ul li a.active {
    color: #007bff;
}

/* Simpler and more maintainable */
.nav-link-active {
    color: #007bff;
}

/* Component-based approach */
.navigation {
    /* Navigation container styles */
}

.navigation__list {
    list-style: none;
    display: flex;
}

.navigation__item {
    margin-right: 20px;
}
```

```
.navigation__link {
    color: #333;
    text-decoration: none;
}

.navigation__link--active {
    color: #007bff;
    font-weight: bold;
}
```

Semantic and Accessible Selectors

Write selectors that enhance rather than conflict with semantic HTML and accessibility features.

#css

```
/* Leverage semantic HTML */
main {
    max-width: 1200px;
    margin: 0 auto;
}

article header {
    border-bottom: 1px solid #eee;
    margin-bottom: 20px;
}

aside {
    background-color: #f8f9fa;
    padding: 20px;
```

```css
}

/* Support accessibility attributes */
[aria-hidden="true"] {
    display: none;
}

[aria-expanded="true"] + .dropdown-menu {
    display: block;
}

/* Focus indicators for keyboard navigation */
button:focus,
input:focus,
select:focus,
textarea:focus {
    outline: 2px solid #007bff;
    outline-offset: 2px;
}
```

Modular and Reusable Selectors

Design selectors for reusability across different contexts while maintaining specificity control.

#css

```css
/* Utility classes for common patterns */
.text-center { text-align: center; }
.text-right { text-align: right; }
.text-bold { font-weight: bold; }
```

```css
.margin-bottom { margin-bottom: 20px; }
.padding-large { padding: 30px; }

/* Component-based selectors */
.card {
    border: 1px solid #dee2e6;
    border-radius: 8px;
    padding: 20px;
    background-color: white;
    box-shadow: 0 2px 4px rgba(0,0,0,0.1);
}

.card__header {
    border-bottom: 1px solid #dee2e6;
    margin-bottom: 15px;
    padding-bottom: 15px;
}

.card__title {
    margin: 0;
    font-size: 1.25em;
    color: #2c3e50;
}

.card__content {
    line-height: 1.6;
}

.card__footer {
    margin-top: 15px;
    padding-top: 15px;
```

```
    border-top: 1px solid #dee2e6;
    text-align: right;
}
```

Selector Organization and Documentation

Organize selectors logically and document complex selector patterns for team collaboration.

#css

```css
/* ========================================
   TYPOGRAPHY
   ======================================== */

h1, h2, h3, h4, h5, h6 {
    font-family: 'Georgia', serif;
    line-height: 1.3;
    margin-bottom: 20px;
}

/* ========================================
   LAYOUT COMPONENTS
   ======================================== */

.container {
    max-width: 1200px;
    margin: 0 auto;
    padding: 0 20px;
}
```

```css
.grid {
    display: grid;
    gap: 20px;
}

/* Two-column grid for tablet and up */
@media (min-width: 768px) {
    .grid--two-col {
        grid-template-columns: 1fr 1fr;
    }
}

/* ========================================
   INTERACTIVE ELEMENTS
   ======================================== */

/* Button component with variants */
.btn {
    display: inline-block;
    padding: 10px 20px;
    border: none;
    border-radius: 4px;
    text-decoration: none;
    cursor: pointer;
    transition: all 0.3s ease;
}

.btn--primary {
    background-color: #007bff;
    color: white;
}
```

```css
.btn--primary:hover {
    background-color: #0056b3;
}

.btn--secondary {
    background-color: #6c757d;
    color: white;
}

.btn--secondary:hover {
    background-color: #545b62;
}
```

Mobile-First and Responsive Selectors

Design selectors with mobile-first responsive design principles, ensuring styles work effectively across all device sizes.

#css

```css
/* Mobile-first approach */
.navigation {
    display: block;
}

.navigation__list {
    flex-direction: column;
}

.navigation__item {
```

```
    width: 100%;
    border-bottom: 1px solid #eee;
}

/* Tablet and up */
@media (min-width: 768px) {
    .navigation__list {
        flex-direction: row;
    }

    .navigation__item {
        width: auto;
        border-bottom: none;
        margin-right: 30px;
    }
}

/* Desktop enhancements */
@media (min-width: 1024px) {
    .navigation {
        display: flex;
        justify-content: space-between;
        align-items: center;
    }
}
```

Essential Tips

- **Keep specificity low and consistent**: Avoid using IDs for styling and minimize deeply nested selectors. This makes your CSS more flexible and easier to maintain. Use classes as your primary styling mechanism and reserve IDs for JavaScript hooks and unique page sections.

- **Use meaningful and descriptive class names**: Choose class names that describe the purpose or content rather than appearance. Names like `.primary-navigation` or `.article-content` are more maintainable than `.blue-text` or `.big-font` because they remain relevant even when visual designs change.
- **Leverage attribute selectors for form styling**: Take advantage of HTML5 form attributes like `[required]`, `[type="email"]`, and `:invalid` to create dynamic form styling that responds to user input and validation states without requiring additional JavaScript.
- **Combine multiple selector types strategically**: Mix element, class, attribute, and pseudo-class selectors to create precise targeting while maintaining readable code. For example, `input[type="text"]:focus:invalid` provides specific styling for text inputs that are focused and contain invalid data.
- **Test selector performance with complex layouts**: In large applications, monitor how selector choices affect rendering performance. Avoid universal selectors in performance-critical areas and prefer class-based targeting over complex descendant selectors when possible.

Actionable Strategies

- **Implement a consistent naming convention**: Adopt a methodology like BEM (Block Element Modifier) or create your own consistent system for naming classes. This prevents naming conflicts and makes your CSS more predictable for team members working on the same project.
- **Create a selector complexity budget**: Establish rules for maximum selector specificity and nesting depth in your projects. For example, limit selectors to three levels deep and avoid combining more than two IDs or complex pseudo-selectors in a single rule.
- **Build a utility-first foundation**: Create a library of single-purpose utility classes for common properties like margins, padding, colors, and typography. This reduces the need for complex selectors and promotes consistent design patterns across your application.
- **Use CSS custom properties with selectors**: Combine CSS variables with attribute selectors to create themeable components. For example, use `[data-theme="dark"]` selectors to switch entire color schemes by changing a single HTML attribute.

- **Practice progressive enhancement with pseudo-classes**: Start with basic element styling and layer on enhancements using pseudo-classes like `:hover`, `:focus`, and `:active`. This ensures your interface remains functional even when advanced CSS features aren't supported.
- **Document complex selector patterns**: Create comments or external documentation explaining why specific selector combinations were chosen, especially for complex structural pseudo-classes or attribute selectors that might not be immediately obvious to other developers.
- **Regularly audit and refactor selectors**: Periodically review your CSS to identify unused selectors, overly specific rules, or patterns that could be simplified. Tools like CSS analyzers can help identify specificity issues and unused styles that bloat your stylesheets.

Chapter 3: Colors and Backgrounds

Color serves as one of the most powerful tools in web design, capable of evoking emotions, establishing brand identity, and guiding user attention. Understanding how to effectively implement colors and backgrounds in CSS transforms static web pages into visually compelling experiences that engage users and communicate your intended message.

3.1 Color Models: HEX, RGB, HSL

Understanding Color Theory in Digital Design

Digital displays create colors by combining red, green, and blue light in varying intensities. This additive color model forms the foundation for all color systems used in CSS. Unlike traditional painting where mixing colors creates darker results, digital colors become brighter when combined, with all three primary colors at full intensity producing white light.

HEX Color Notation

HEX (hexadecimal) notation represents colors using a six-character code preceded by a hash symbol. Each pair of characters corresponds to red, green, and blue values, ranging from 00 (no intensity) to FF (maximum intensity).

#css

```
/* Basic HEX colors */
.red-text {
    color: #FF0000; /* Pure red */
}

.green-background {
    background-color: #00FF00; /* Pure green */
}

.blue-border {
```

```
    border: 2px solid #0000FF; /* Pure blue */
}

/* Common HEX colors */
.header {
    background-color: #333333; /* Dark gray */
    color: #FFFFFF; /* White text */
}

.accent {
    color: #FF6B35; /* Orange accent */
}

.muted {
    background-color: #F8F9FA; /* Light gray background
*/
}
```

Three-Character HEX Shorthand

When both characters in each color pair are identical, you can use shorthand notation:

#css

```
/* Shorthand HEX examples */
.shorthand-red {
    color: #F00; /* Equivalent to #FF0000 */
}

.shorthand-white {
```

```
    background-color: #FFF; /* Equivalent to #FFFFFF */
}

.shorthand-black {
    color: #000; /* Equivalent to #000000 */
}
```

RGB Color Model

RGB notation explicitly defines red, green, and blue values using decimal numbers from 0 to 255. This system provides intuitive control over individual color channels and makes color adjustments more predictable.

#css

```
/* RGB color examples */
.rgb-header {
    background-color: rgb(51, 51, 51); /* Same as #333333
*/
    color: rgb(255, 255, 255); /* Same as #FFFFFF */
}

.rgb-accent {
    color: rgb(255, 107, 53); /* Same as #FF6B35 */
}

/* Creating color variations */
.light-blue {
    background-color: rgb(173, 216, 230);
}

.medium-blue {
```

```
    background-color: rgb(100, 149, 237);
}

.dark-blue {
    background-color: rgb(25, 25, 112);
}
```

RGBA for Transparency

RGBA extends RGB by adding an alpha channel for transparency control, with values from 0 (completely transparent) to 1 (completely opaque).

#css

```
/* RGBA transparency examples */
.overlay {
    background-color: rgba(0, 0, 0, 0.5); /* 50%
transparent black */
    position: absolute;
    top: 0;
    left: 0;
    width: 100%;
    height: 100%;
}

.glass-effect {
    background-color: rgba(255, 255, 255, 0.2); /* 20%
opaque white */
    backdrop-filter: blur(10px);
    border: 1px solid rgba(255, 255, 255, 0.3);
}
```

```
.notification {
    background-color: rgba(76, 175, 80, 0.9); /* 90%
opaque green */
    color: rgba(255, 255, 255, 1); /* Fully opaque white
*/
}
```

HSL Color Model

HSL (Hue, Saturation, Lightness) provides an intuitive approach to color selection that mirrors how humans naturally perceive color relationships. Hue represents the color wheel position (0-360 degrees), saturation controls color intensity (0-100%), and lightness determines brightness (0-100%).

#css

```
/* HSL color examples */
.hsl-primary {
    color: hsl(220, 100%, 50%); /* Pure blue */
}

.hsl-secondary {
    color: hsl(220, 75%, 40%); /* Darker, less saturated
blue */
}

.hsl-tertiary {
    color: hsl(220, 50%, 80%); /* Light, muted blue */
}

/* Creating color schemes with HSL */
.complementary-colors {
```

```
    background: linear-gradient(
        45deg,
        hsl(0, 100%, 50%),     /* Red */
        hsl(180, 100%, 50%)    /* Cyan (opposite on color
wheel) */
    );
}
```

HSLA for HSL with Transparency

HSLA combines HSL color definition with alpha transparency control:

#css

```
/* HSLA transparency examples */
.card {
    background-color: hsla(210, 100%, 97%, 0.8); /* Light
blue with transparency */
    border: 1px solid hsla(210, 50%, 80%, 0.6);
}

.warning-banner {
    background-color: hsla(45, 100%, 85%, 0.9); /* Semi-
transparent yellow */
    border-left: 4px solid hsla(45, 100%, 50%, 1); /*
Solid yellow border */
}
```

Color Model Comparison and Selection

Each color model offers distinct advantages for different scenarios. HEX provides compact notation ideal for static colors and design systems. RGB offers precise control over individual color channels, making it perfect for programmatic color manipulation. HSL excels in creating harmonious color schemes and maintaining consistent relationships between related colors.

3.2 Applying Color to Text, Backgrounds, and Borders

Text Color Properties

The `color` property controls text color and serves as the foundation for readable, accessible typography. Proper contrast ratios between text and background colors ensure content remains legible across different devices and viewing conditions.

#css

```css
/* Basic text coloring */
.primary-heading {
    color: #2C3E50; /* Dark blue-gray */
    font-size: 2.5rem;
    font-weight: bold;
}

.secondary-text {
    color: #7F8C8D; /* Medium gray */
    font-size: 1.1rem;
    line-height: 1.6;
}

.error-message {
    color: #E74C3C; /* Red for errors */
    font-weight: 500;
}
```

```css
.success-message {
    color: #27AE60; /* Green for success */
    font-weight: 500;
}
```

Link Color States

Links require multiple color states to provide clear user feedback and maintain usability standards:

#css

```css
/* Comprehensive link styling */
a {
    color: #3498DB; /* Default link color */
    text-decoration: none;
    transition: color 0.3s ease;
}

a:visited {
    color: #9B59B6; /* Purple for visited links */
}

a:hover {
    color: #2980B9; /* Darker blue on hover */
    text-decoration: underline;
}

a:focus {
    color: #2980B9;
```

```
    outline: 2px solid #3498DB;
    outline-offset: 2px;
}

a:active {
    color: #1F4E79; /* Even darker when clicked */
}
```

Background Color Applications

Background colors create visual hierarchy, define sections, and establish the overall aesthetic of your design. Strategic background color usage guides user attention and improves content organization.

#css

```
/* Section-based background colors */
.hero-section {
    background-color: #34495E; /* Dark background */
    color: #FFFFFF; /* White text for contrast */
    padding: 4rem 2rem;
    text-align: center;
}

.content-section {
    background-color: #FFFFFF; /* White background */
    color: #2C3E50; /* Dark text */
    padding: 3rem 2rem;
}

.sidebar {
```

```css
    background-color: #ECF0F1; /* Light gray */
    padding: 2rem;
    border-radius: 8px;
}

/* Card-based layouts */
.card {
    background-color: #FFFFFF;
    border-radius: 12px;
    box-shadow: 0 4px 6px rgba(0, 0, 0, 0.1);
    padding: 1.5rem;
    margin-bottom: 1.5rem;
}

.card-header {
    background-color: #F8F9FA;
    padding: 1rem 1.5rem;
    border-bottom: 1px solid #DEE2E6;
    border-radius: 12px 12px 0 0;
}
```

Border Color Techniques

Border colors define boundaries, create emphasis, and add visual polish to design elements. Understanding border color applications enhances the professional appearance of your layouts.

#css

```css
/* Basic border coloring */
.input-field {
```

```
    border: 2px solid #BDC3C7; /* Light gray border */
    padding: 0.75rem;
    border-radius: 4px;
    transition: border-color 0.3s ease;
}

.input-field:focus {
    border-color: #3498DB; /* Blue when focused */
    outline: none;
}

.input-field.error {
    border-color: #E74C3C; /* Red for validation errors
*/
}

.input-field.success {
    border-color: #27AE60; /* Green for successful
validation */
}

/* Decorative borders */
.quote-block {
    border-left: 4px solid #F39C12; /* Orange accent
border */
    padding-left: 1.5rem;
    margin: 2rem 0;
    font-style: italic;
    color: #7F8C8D;
}
```

```css
.highlight-box {
    border: 3px solid #9B59B6; /* Purple border */
    border-radius: 8px;
    padding: 2rem;
    background-color: rgba(155, 89, 182, 0.05);
}
```

Multi-Side Border Colors

CSS allows different colors for each border side, enabling creative design solutions:

#css

```css
/* Individual border side colors */
.multi-border {
    border-top: 3px solid #E74C3C;    /* Red top */
    border-right: 3px solid #F39C12;  /* Orange right */
    border-bottom: 3px solid #27AE60; /* Green bottom */
    border-left: 3px solid #3498DB;   /* Blue left */
    padding: 2rem;
}

/* Asymmetric border designs */
.accent-card {
    border: 1px solid #DEE2E6;
    border-top: 4px solid #9B59B6; /* Purple accent top
*/
    padding: 1.5rem;
    background-color: #FFFFFF;
}
```

3.3 Using Transparent Colors and Opacity

Understanding Opacity vs Alpha Transparency

Transparency in CSS can be achieved through two primary methods: the `opacity` property affects entire elements including their children, while alpha channels in color values provide selective transparency without inheritance issues.

#css

```css
/* Opacity property - affects entire element */
.fade-overlay {
    background-color: #000000;
    opacity: 0.7; /* 70% opaque, affects all child elements */
    position: absolute;
    top: 0;
    left: 0;
    width: 100%;
    height: 100%;
}

/* Alpha transparency - affects only the specified property */
.selective-transparency {
    background-color: rgba(0, 0, 0, 0.7); /* Only background is transparent */
    color: rgb(255, 255, 255); /* Text remains fully opaque */
    padding: 2rem;
}
```

Layered Transparency Effects

Combining multiple transparent elements creates sophisticated visual depth and modern design aesthetics:

#css

```
/* Layered transparency example */
.glass-card {
    background-color: rgba(255, 255, 255, 0.25);
    backdrop-filter: blur(10px);
    border: 1px solid rgba(255, 255, 255, 0.18);
    border-radius: 16px;
    padding: 2rem;
    box-shadow: 0 8px 32px rgba(31, 38, 135, 0.37);
}

.nested-transparency {
    background-color: rgba(52, 152, 219, 0.1);
    padding: 1.5rem;
    border-radius: 8px;
}

.nested-transparency .inner-element {
    background-color: rgba(52, 152, 219, 0.2);
    padding: 1rem;
    border-radius: 4px;
}
```

Hover and Transition Transparency

Dynamic transparency changes provide engaging user interactions and feedback:

#css

```css
/* Interactive transparency */
.hover-card {
    background-color: rgba(255, 255, 255, 0.9);
    transition: all 0.3s ease;
    padding: 2rem;
    border-radius: 12px;
    cursor: pointer;
}

.hover-card:hover {
    background-color: rgba(255, 255, 255, 1);
    transform: translateY(-4px);
    box-shadow: 0 12px 24px rgba(0, 0, 0, 0.15);
}

/* Button transparency states */
.transparent-button {
    background-color: transparent;
    border: 2px solid rgba(52, 152, 219, 0.8);
    color: rgba(52, 152, 219, 0.8);
    padding: 0.75rem 1.5rem;
    border-radius: 6px;
    transition: all 0.3s ease;
}

.transparent-button:hover {
    background-color: rgba(52, 152, 219, 0.1);
```

```
    border-color: rgba(52, 152, 219, 1);
    color: rgba(52, 152, 219, 1);
}
```

Transparency for Accessibility

Proper transparency implementation maintains accessibility while creating visual appeal:

#css

```
/* Accessible transparency examples */
.accessible-overlay {
    background-color: rgba(0, 0, 0, 0.8); /* High
contrast overlay */
    color: #FFFFFF;
    padding: 2rem;
}

.low-contrast-element {
    background-color: rgba(108, 117, 125, 0.1); /* Subtle
background */
    color: #212529; /* High contrast text */
    padding: 1rem;
}

/* Focus indicators with transparency */
.focus-element:focus {
    outline: 3px solid rgba(52, 152, 219, 0.6);
    outline-offset: 2px;
    background-color: rgba(52, 152, 219, 0.05);
}
```

3.4 Background Properties (Image, Repeat, Size)

Background Image Implementation

Background images add visual richness and personality to web designs. Proper implementation ensures images enhance rather than hinder content readability and user experience.

#css

```css
/* Basic background image setup */
.hero-banner {
    background-image: url('images/hero-background.jpg');
    background-color: #2C3E50; /* Fallback color */
    height: 500px;
    display: flex;
    align-items: center;
    justify-content: center;
    color: #FFFFFF;
    text-align: center;
}

/* Multiple background images */
.layered-background {
    background-image:
        url('images/overlay-pattern.png'),
        url('images/main-background.jpg');
    background-position: center, center;
    background-repeat: repeat, no-repeat;
    background-size: 50px 50px, cover;
}
```

Background Repeat Control

The `background-repeat` property determines how background images tile across elements, offering precise control over pattern creation and image display:

#css

```
/* Background repeat variations */
.no-repeat {
    background-image: url('images/logo.png');
    background-repeat: no-repeat; /* Display once */
    background-position: center;
    height: 200px;
}

.repeat-x {
    background-image: url('images/horizontal-
pattern.png');
    background-repeat: repeat-x; /* Repeat horizontally
only */
    height: 100px;
}

.repeat-y {
    background-image: url('images/vertical-pattern.png');
    background-repeat: repeat-y; /* Repeat vertically
only */
    width: 200px;
}
```

```
.repeat-pattern {
    background-image: url('images/tile-pattern.png');
    background-repeat: repeat; /* Repeat in both
directions */
    min-height: 300px;
}

/* Space and round repeat values */
.spaced-repeat {
    background-image: url('images/icon.svg');
    background-repeat: space; /* Distribute with equal
spacing */
    background-size: 50px 50px;
    height: 300px;
}

.rounded-repeat {
    background-image: url('images/pattern.png');
    background-repeat: round; /* Scale to fit without
cutting */
    height: 250px;
}
```

Background Size Properties

Background size control ensures images display appropriately across different viewport sizes and design requirements:

#css

```
/* Background size options */
.cover-background {
```

```
    background-image: url('images/landscape.jpg');
    background-size: cover; /* Scale to cover entire area
*/
    background-position: center;
    height: 400px;
}

.contain-background {
    background-image: url('images/portrait.jpg');
    background-size: contain; /* Scale to fit entirely
within area */
    background-repeat: no-repeat;
    background-position: center;
    height: 400px;
    background-color: #F8F9FA;
}

.specific-size {
    background-image: url('images/icon.svg');
    background-size: 64px 64px; /* Exact dimensions */
    background-repeat: no-repeat;
    background-position: top left;
    padding-left: 80px;
    min-height: 64px;
}

.percentage-size {
    background-image: url('images/texture.png');
    background-size: 50% 75%; /* Percentage-based sizing
*/
    background-repeat: no-repeat;
```

```
    background-position: center;
    height: 300px;
}
```

Background Position Control

Precise background positioning enables fine-tuned image placement and creates sophisticated compositional effects:

#css

```
/* Background position examples */
.top-left-position {
    background-image: url('images/corner-
decoration.svg');
    background-position: top left;
    background-repeat: no-repeat;
    background-size: 100px 100px;
}

.center-position {
    background-image: url('images/centered-logo.png');
    background-position: center center; /* Same as
'center' */
    background-repeat: no-repeat;
    height: 200px;
}

.offset-position {
    background-image: url('images/accent.png');
    background-position: 20px 30px; /* Specific pixel
offset */
```

```
    background-repeat: no-repeat;
    background-size: 50px 50px;
}

.percentage-position {
    background-image: url('images/element.svg');
    background-position: 75% 25%; /* Percentage
positioning */
    background-repeat: no-repeat;
    background-size: 80px 80px;
}
```

Background Attachment Effects

Background attachment controls how images behave during scrolling, creating engaging parallax and fixed background effects:

#css

```
/* Background attachment options */
.fixed-background {
    background-image: url('images/parallax-bg.jpg');
    background-attachment: fixed; /* Fixed during scroll
*/
    background-size: cover;
    background-position: center;
    height: 100vh;
    display: flex;
    align-items: center;
    justify-content: center;
}
```

```css
.scroll-background {
    background-image: url('images/texture.png');
    background-attachment: scroll; /* Scrolls with content (default) */
    background-repeat: repeat;
    min-height: 500px;
    padding: 2rem;
}

.local-background {
    background-image: url('images/pattern.svg');
    background-attachment: local; /* Scrolls with element content */
    background-repeat: repeat;
    height: 300px;
    overflow-y: scroll;
    padding: 2rem;
}
```

Comprehensive Background Shorthand

The background shorthand property combines all background properties into a single, efficient declaration:

#css

```css
/* Background shorthand examples */
.shorthand-example {
    /* background: color image repeat position/size attachment */
    background: #F8F9FA url('images/bg.jpg') no-repeat center/cover fixed;
```

```
    height: 500px;
}

.complex-shorthand {
    background:
        linear-gradient(rgba(0,0,0,0.4),
rgba(0,0,0,0.4)),
        url('images/hero.jpg') no-repeat center/cover;
    color: #FFFFFF;
    padding: 4rem 2rem;
    text-align: center;
}
```

3.5 Gradient Backgrounds: Linear and Radial

Linear Gradient Fundamentals

Linear gradients create smooth color transitions along straight lines, providing modern alternatives to solid colors and background images. Understanding gradient syntax and color stop placement enables sophisticated visual effects.

#css

```
/* Basic linear gradients */
.simple-linear {
    background: linear-gradient(to right, #FF6B6B,
#4ECDC4);
    height: 200px;
    border-radius: 8px;
}

.vertical-gradient {
```

```
    background: linear-gradient(to bottom, #667eea,
#764ba2);
    height: 300px;
}

.diagonal-gradient {
    background: linear-gradient(45deg, #f093fb, #f5576c);
    height: 250px;
}

/* Degree-based directions */
.angled-gradient {
    background: linear-gradient(135deg, #667eea, #764ba2,
#f093fb);
    height: 300px;
}

.precise-angle {
    background: linear-gradient(27deg, #13547a, #80d0c7);
    height: 200px;
}
```

Advanced Linear Gradient Techniques

Multi-stop gradients and strategic color placement create complex visual effects and sophisticated design solutions:

#css

```
/* Multi-stop gradients */
.sunset-gradient {
    background: linear-gradient(
```

```
        to bottom,
        #ff9a9e 0%,
        #fecfef 25%,
        #fecfef 50%,
        #a8edea 75%,
        #fed6e3 100%
    );
    height: 400px;
}

.rainbow-gradient {
    background: linear-gradient(
        90deg,
        #ff0000 0%,
        #ff8000 16.66%,
        #ffff00 33.33%,
        #00ff00 50%,
        #0080ff 66.66%,
        #8000ff 83.33%,
        #ff0080 100%
    );
    height: 100px;
}

/* Gradient overlays */
.gradient-overlay {
    background:
        linear-gradient(
            to bottom,
            rgba(0, 0, 0, 0) 0%,
            rgba(0, 0, 0, 0.3) 50%,
```

```
            rgba(0, 0, 0, 0.8) 100%
        ),
        url('images/background.jpg') center/cover;
    height: 500px;
    color: #FFFFFF;
    display: flex;
    align-items: flex-end;
    padding: 2rem;
}
```

Radial Gradient Applications

Radial gradients emanate from central points, creating circular or elliptical color transitions perfect for spotlight effects, buttons, and decorative elements:

#css

```
/* Basic radial gradients */
.simple-radial {
    background: radial-gradient(circle, #ff9a9e,
#fad0c4);
    height: 300px;
    border-radius: 50%;
}

.elliptical-radial {
    background: radial-gradient(ellipse, #667eea,
#764ba2);
    height: 200px;
    width: 400px;
    border-radius: 12px;
}
```

```css
/* Positioned radial gradients */
.positioned-radial {
    background: radial-gradient(
        circle at top left,
        #ff9a9e,
        #fecfef,
        #a8edea
    );
    height: 300px;
}

.offset-radial {
    background: radial-gradient(
        ellipse at 70% 30%,
        #667eea 0%,
        #764ba2 50%,
        #f093fb 100%
    );
    height: 350px;
}
```

Complex Radial Gradient Effects

Advanced radial gradient techniques create sophisticated visual effects and modern design elements:

#css

```css
/* Multi-layer radial gradients */
.layered-radial {
```

```
    background:
        radial-gradient(circle at 25% 25%, rgba(255, 0,
150, 0.5) 0%, transparent 50%),
        radial-gradient(circle at 75% 75%, rgba(0, 150,
255, 0.5) 0%, transparent 50%),
        linear-gradient(45deg, #667eea, #764ba2);
    height: 400px;
}

/* Spotlight effect */
.spotlight {
    background: radial-gradient(
        circle at center,
        rgba(255, 255, 255, 0.8) 0%,
        rgba(255, 255, 255, 0.4) 30%,
        rgba(255, 255, 255, 0.1) 60%,
        transparent 100%
    );
    height: 500px;
    background-color: #2C3E50;
}

/* Button gradients */
.gradient-button {
    background: radial-gradient(ellipse at center,
#667eea 0%, #764ba2 100%);
    border: none;
    color: #FFFFFF;
    padding: 1rem 2rem;
    border-radius: 25px;
    cursor: pointer;
```

```
    transition: transform 0.2s ease;
}

.gradient-button:hover {
    transform: scale(1.05);
    background: radial-gradient(ellipse at center,
#5a6fd8 0%, #6a4190 100%);
}
```

Conic Gradients for Modern Effects

Conic gradients rotate around a central point, creating pie-chart effects and modern geometric patterns:

#css

```
/* Conic gradient examples */
.pie-gradient {
    background: conic-gradient(
        from 0deg,
        #ff6b6b 0deg 90deg,
        #4ecdc4 90deg 180deg,
        #45b7d1 180deg 270deg,
        #96ceb4 270deg 360deg
    );
    width: 300px;
    height: 300px;
    border-radius: 50%;
}

.rainbow-wheel {
```

```
    background: conic-gradient(
        hsl(0, 100%, 50%),
        hsl(60, 100%, 50%),
        hsl(120, 100%, 50%),
        hsl(180, 100%, 50%),
        hsl(240, 100%, 50%),
        hsl(300, 100%, 50%),
        hsl(360, 100%, 50%)
    );
    width: 200px;
    height: 200px;
    border-radius: 50%;
}
```

Gradient Animation Techniques

Animated gradients create dynamic, engaging visual effects that capture user attention:

#css

```
/* Animated gradient backgrounds */
@keyframes gradientShift {
    0% {
        background-position: 0% 50%;
    }
    50% {
        background-position: 100% 50%;
    }
    100% {
        background-position: 0% 50%;
```

```
    }
}

.animated-gradient {
    background: linear-gradient(-45deg, #ee7752, #e73c7e,
#23a6d5, #23d5ab);
    background-size: 400% 400%;
    animation: gradientShift 4s ease infinite;
    height: 300px;
}

/* Rotating conic gradient */
@keyframes rotate {
    from {
        transform: rotate(0deg);
    }
    to {
        transform: rotate(360deg);
    }
}

.rotating-gradient {
    background: conic-gradient(#667eea, #764ba2,
#667eea);
    width: 200px;
    height: 200px;
    border-radius: 50%;
    animation: rotate 3s linear infinite;
}
```

Essential Tips

- **Maintain consistent color ratios throughout your design** by establishing a primary color palette with 3-5 core colors and using them in consistent proportions across all elements. This creates visual harmony and professional cohesion that users unconsciously recognize and appreciate.
- **Test color combinations across multiple devices and lighting conditions** since colors appear differently on various screens and under different ambient lighting. Use tools like contrast checkers and view your designs on mobile devices, tablets, and desktop monitors to ensure consistent visual quality.
- **Create depth with layered transparency effects** by combining multiple semi-transparent elements with different opacity levels. This technique adds sophisticated visual hierarchy without overwhelming users, making interfaces feel modern and professionally polished.
- **Use HSL values for systematic color scheme development** because HSL makes it intuitive to create harmonious color relationships by adjusting hue, saturation, and lightness independently. This approach ensures your color schemes feel intentional rather than randomly assembled.
- **Implement gradients as texture replacements** to reduce image file sizes and improve loading performance while maintaining visual richness. Gradients load instantly and scale perfectly across all screen sizes, making them ideal for background textures and decorative elements.

Actionable Strategies

- **Establish a semantic color system** where specific colors consistently represent the same meanings throughout your site (red for errors, green for success, blue for information). Document these relationships in a style guide to maintain consistency across all pages and components.
- **Create hover state variations using CSS filters** like `brightness()`, `contrast()`, and `saturate()` instead of defining entirely new colors. This approach maintains color relationships while providing clear interactive feedback, and it automatically adapts if you change your base colors.
- **Implement progressive image enhancement** by setting background colors that match the average color of your background images. This

ensures smooth visual transitions while images load and provides fallback colors for users with slow connections or disabled images.

- **Use gradient overlays to improve text readability** over background images by applying semi-transparent linear gradients that darken the background behind text areas. This technique maintains image visibility while ensuring text meets accessibility contrast requirements.
- **Build responsive color schemes using CSS custom properties** that automatically adjust based on user preferences and device capabilities. Define color variables that change based on media queries for light/dark modes, high contrast needs, and different screen types.
- **Optimize gradient performance** by using simpler gradients with fewer color stops on mobile devices and more complex gradients on desktop. This approach maintains visual quality while ensuring smooth performance across all device types and processing capabilities.
- **Create visual rhythm with alternating background colors** in content sections, list items, or card layouts. Use subtle color variations (like alternating between white and very light gray) to help users track information and create natural reading flow without adding visual noise.

Chapter 4: Typography and Fonts

Typography forms the backbone of web design, serving as the primary medium through which users consume content. Understanding how to manipulate text appearance, readability, and visual hierarchy through CSS typography properties transforms ordinary web pages into polished, professional presentations. This chapter provides comprehensive coverage of CSS typography fundamentals, from basic font selection to advanced spacing techniques.

4.1 Font-Family and Web-safe Fonts

Understanding Font-Family Property

The `font-family` property defines which typeface browsers should use to display text content. This property accepts multiple font names as fallback options, creating a font stack that ensures consistent rendering across different devices and operating systems.

#css

```
body {
    font-family: "Helvetica Neue", Helvetica, Arial,
sans-serif;
}
```

Font Stack Hierarchy

Font stacks operate on a priority system where browsers attempt to load the first specified font. If unavailable, they move to the next option in the list. This cascading approach prevents typography failures when specific fonts aren't installed on user devices.

#css

```
.heading {
```

```
    font-family: "Times New Roman", Times, serif;
}

.body-text {
    font-family: Georgia, "Times New Roman", serif;
}

.modern-text {
    font-family: "Segoe UI", Tahoma, Geneva, Verdana,
sans-serif;
}
```

Generic Font Families

CSS recognizes five generic font families that serve as ultimate fallbacks:

- **serif**: Fonts with decorative strokes extending from letter forms
- **sans-serif**: Clean fonts without decorative strokes
- **monospace**: Fixed-width fonts where each character occupies equal space
- **cursive**: Fonts mimicking handwritten or script styles
- **fantasy**: Decorative fonts for display purposes

#css

```
.serif-example {
    font-family: "Times New Roman", serif;
}

.sans-serif-example {
    font-family: Arial, sans-serif;
}
```

```
.monospace-example {
    font-family: "Courier New", monospace;
}

.cursive-example {
    font-family: "Brush Script MT", cursive;
}

.fantasy-example {
    font-family: Impact, fantasy;
}
```

Web-Safe Font Categories

Web-safe fonts guarantee consistent appearance across different platforms and browsers. These fonts are commonly installed on most operating systems, reducing the risk of font substitution.

Serif Web-Safe Fonts

Serif fonts enhance readability in printed materials and formal digital content. Common web-safe serif fonts include:

#css

```
.times-font {
    font-family: "Times New Roman", Times, serif;
}

.georgia-font {
    font-family: Georgia, serif;
}
```

```
.palatino-font {
    font-family: "Palatino Linotype", "Book Antiqua",
Palatino, serif;
}
```

Sans-Serif Web-Safe Fonts

Sans-serif fonts provide clean, modern aesthetics ideal for digital screens and contemporary designs:

#css

```
.arial-font {
    font-family: Arial, Helvetica, sans-serif;
}

.helvetica-font {
    font-family: Helvetica, Arial, sans-serif;
}

.verdana-font {
    font-family: Verdana, Geneva, sans-serif;
}

.trebuchet-font {
    font-family: "Trebuchet MS", Helvetica, sans-serif;
}
```

Monospace Web-Safe Fonts

Monospace fonts serve technical content, code displays, and situations requiring precise character alignment:

#css

```css
.courier-font {
    font-family: "Courier New", Courier, monospace;
}

.lucida-console {
    font-family: "Lucida Console", Monaco, monospace;
}
```

Font Selection Best Practices

Effective font selection considers readability, brand consistency, and technical compatibility. Limit font varieties within single projects to maintain visual cohesion while ensuring adequate contrast between headings and body text.

#css

```css
/* Consistent font hierarchy */
h1, h2, h3, h4, h5, h6 {
    font-family: "Helvetica Neue", Arial, sans-serif;
}

p, li, td {
    font-family: Georgia, "Times New Roman", serif;
}
```

```
code, pre {
    font-family: "Consolas", "Monaco", monospace;
}
```

4.2 Font Size, Weight, Style, and Variant

Font Size Control

The `font-size` property controls text size using various measurement units. Each unit type offers different advantages depending on the design context and responsive requirements.

Absolute Units

Absolute units maintain consistent sizes regardless of parent element dimensions:

#css

```
.pixel-sizing {
    font-size: 16px; /* Fixed pixel size */
}

.point-sizing {
    font-size: 12pt; /* Print-oriented point size */
}

.inch-sizing {
    font-size: 0.2in; /* Physical inch measurement */
}
```

Relative Units

Relative units scale proportionally to parent elements or root settings, enabling flexible responsive designs:

#css

```
.em-sizing {
    font-size: 1.2em; /* 120% of parent element size */
}

.rem-sizing {
    font-size: 1.5rem; /* 150% of root element size */
}

.percentage-sizing {
    font-size: 110%; /* 110% of parent element size */
}

.viewport-sizing {
    font-size: 4vw; /* 4% of viewport width */
}
```

Keyword Values

CSS provides keyword values for common font sizes:

#css

```
.keyword-sizes {
    font-size: xx-small; /* Smallest keyword size */
    font-size: x-small;
    font-size: small;
```

```
    font-size: medium; /* Default browser size */
    font-size: large;
    font-size: x-large;
    font-size: xx-large; /* Largest keyword size */
}

.relative-keywords {
    font-size: smaller; /* Smaller than parent */
    font-size: larger; /* Larger than parent */
}
```

Font Weight Management

The `font-weight` property controls text thickness, accepting both numeric values and descriptive keywords:

#css

```
.weight-keywords {
    font-weight: normal; /* Default weight (400) */
    font-weight: bold; /* Bold weight (700) */
    font-weight: bolder; /* Bolder than parent */
    font-weight: lighter; /* Lighter than parent */
}

.weight-numeric {
    font-weight: 100; /* Thin */
    font-weight: 200; /* Extra Light */
    font-weight: 300; /* Light */
    font-weight: 400; /* Normal */
    font-weight: 500; /* Medium */
```

```
    font-weight: 600; /* Semi Bold */
    font-weight: 700; /* Bold */
    font-weight: 800; /* Extra Bold */
    font-weight: 900; /* Black */
}
```

Font Style Variations

The `font-style` property modifies text appearance through stylistic variations:

#css

```
.style-variations {
    font-style: normal; /* Standard upright text */
    font-style: italic; /* Slanted text */
    font-style: oblique; /* Artificially slanted text */
}

.oblique-angle {
    font-style: oblique 15deg; /* Custom oblique angle */
}
```

Font Variant Properties

Font variants enable typographic refinements through alternative character forms:

#css

```
.small-caps {
```

```
    font-variant: small-caps; /* Uppercase letters in
smaller size */
}

.normal-variant {
    font-variant: normal; /* Default variant */
}

/* Advanced font variant properties */
.advanced-variants {
    font-variant-caps: small-caps;
    font-variant-numeric: lining-nums;
    font-variant-ligatures: common-ligatures;
}
```

Combining Typography Properties

The `font` shorthand property combines multiple typography settings in a single declaration:

#css

```
.shorthand-font {
    /* font: style variant weight size/line-height family
*/
    font: italic small-caps bold 16px/1.4 Arial, sans-
serif;
}

.minimal-shorthand {
    font: 14px "Helvetica Neue", sans-serif;
}
```

```
.comprehensive-shorthand {
    font: normal normal 400 18px/1.6 Georgia, serif;
}
```

4.3 Line Height, Letter Spacing, and Word Spacing

Line Height Fundamentals

Line height determines the vertical space between text lines, significantly impacting readability and visual rhythm. Proper line height creates comfortable reading experiences while maintaining design harmony.

#css

```
.line-height-examples {
    line-height: 1.5; /* Unitless multiplier
(recommended) */
    line-height: 24px; /* Fixed pixel value */
    line-height: 150%; /* Percentage of font size */
    line-height: 1.5em; /* Em-based value */
}
```

Optimal Line Height Ratios

Different content types benefit from specific line height ratios:

#css

```
.headings {
    line-height: 1.2; /* Tighter spacing for large text
*/
}
```

```
.body-text {
    line-height: 1.6; /* Comfortable reading spacing */
}

.small-text {
    line-height: 1.4; /* Slightly tighter for small fonts
*/
}

.display-text {
    line-height: 1.1; /* Very tight for large display
text */
}
```

Letter Spacing Control

The `letter-spacing` property adjusts horizontal space between individual characters, enabling fine typography control:

#css

```
.letter-spacing-examples {
    letter-spacing: normal; /* Default spacing */
    letter-spacing: 0.1em; /* Slight expansion */
    letter-spacing: 2px; /* Fixed pixel spacing */
    letter-spacing: -0.05em; /* Tighter spacing */
}

.tracking-variations {
    letter-spacing: 0.2em; /* Loose tracking */
```

```
    letter-spacing: 0.1em; /* Open tracking */
    letter-spacing: 0; /* Normal tracking */
    letter-spacing: -0.02em; /* Tight tracking */
}
```

Contextual Letter Spacing

Different text contexts require adjusted letter spacing for optimal readability:

#css

```
.uppercase-text {
    text-transform: uppercase;
    letter-spacing: 0.1em; /* Uppercase needs more
spacing */
}

.small-caps-text {
    font-variant: small-caps;
    letter-spacing: 0.05em; /* Small caps benefit from
slight spacing */
}

.logo-text {
    letter-spacing: 0.2em; /* Brand names often use loose
spacing */
}
```

Word Spacing Adjustments

The `word-spacing` property controls horizontal space between words, useful for fine-tuning text flow:

#css

```
.word-spacing-examples {
    word-spacing: normal; /* Default word spacing */
    word-spacing: 0.2em; /* Increased word spacing */
    word-spacing: 5px; /* Fixed pixel spacing */
    word-spacing: -0.1em; /* Reduced word spacing */
}
```

Creating Typographic Rhythm

Combining line height, letter spacing, and word spacing creates consistent typographic rhythm throughout designs:

#css

```
.typographic-rhythm {
    font-family: Georgia, serif;
    font-size: 18px;
    line-height: 1.6;
    letter-spacing: 0.01em;
    word-spacing: 0.05em;
}

.compact-rhythm {
    font-family: Arial, sans-serif;
    font-size: 14px;
    line-height: 1.4;
    letter-spacing: normal;
    word-spacing: normal;
}
```

```css
.expanded-rhythm {
    font-family: "Helvetica Neue", sans-serif;
    font-size: 16px;
    line-height: 1.8;
    letter-spacing: 0.05em;
    word-spacing: 0.1em;
}
```

4.4 Text Align, Indentation, and Decoration

Text Alignment Options

The `text-align` property controls horizontal text positioning within container elements:

#css

```css
.alignment-options {
    text-align: left; /* Left alignment (default) */
    text-align: right; /* Right alignment */
    text-align: center; /* Center alignment */
    text-align: justify; /* Justified alignment */
}

.advanced-alignment {
    text-align: start; /* Start edge (respects text direction) */
    text-align: end; /* End edge (respects text direction) */
    text-align: match-parent; /* Inherits parent alignment */
}
```

Contextual Text Alignment

Different content types benefit from specific alignment strategies:

#css

```
.article-title {
    text-align: center;
    margin-bottom: 1em;
}

.article-body {
    text-align: left;
    text-align: justify; /* For formal documents */
}

.sidebar-content {
    text-align: right;
}

.quote-text {
    text-align: center;
    font-style: italic;
}
```

Text Indentation Techniques

The `text-indent` property creates first-line indentation for paragraph formatting:

#css

```
.indentation-examples {
    text-indent: 2em; /* Standard paragraph indentation */
    text-indent: 30px; /* Fixed pixel indentation */
    text-indent: 5%; /* Percentage-based indentation */
}

.hanging-indent {
    text-indent: -2em;
    padding-left: 2em; /* Creates hanging indent effect */
}

.no-indent {
    text-indent: 0; /* Removes indentation */
}
```

Special Indentation Patterns

Creative indentation enhances document structure and visual hierarchy:

#css

```
.poetry-format {
    text-indent: 2em;
    line-height: 1.8;
}

.bibliography-entry {
    text-indent: -2em;
    padding-left: 2em;
    margin-bottom: 0.5em;
```

```
}

.dialogue-format {
    text-indent: 1em;
    margin-left: 2em;
}
```

Text Decoration Properties

Text decoration adds visual emphasis through underlines, overlines, and strikethrough effects:

#css

```
.decoration-types {
    text-decoration: none; /* No decoration */
    text-decoration: underline; /* Underline text */
    text-decoration: overline; /* Overline text */
    text-decoration: line-through; /* Strikethrough text
*/
}

.combined-decorations {
    text-decoration: underline overline; /* Multiple
decorations */
}
```

Advanced Text Decoration

Modern CSS provides detailed decoration control:

#css

```
.decoration-details {
    text-decoration-line: underline;
    text-decoration-color: red;
    text-decoration-style: solid;
    text-decoration-thickness: 2px;
}

.decoration-styles {
    text-decoration: underline wavy blue;
    text-decoration: line-through double green;
    text-decoration: overline dotted purple;
}

.link-decorations {
    text-decoration: none;
    border-bottom: 1px solid currentColor;
    transition: border-bottom-color 0.3s ease;
}

.link-decorations:hover {
    border-bottom-color: transparent;
}
```

Text Transform Effects

The `text-transform` property modifies text capitalization:

#css

```
.transform-options {
```

```
    text-transform: none; /* No transformation */
    text-transform: uppercase; /* ALL UPPERCASE */
    text-transform: lowercase; /* all lowercase */
    text-transform: capitalize; /* Title Case Words */
}

.contextual-transforms {
    text-transform: uppercase;
    letter-spacing: 0.1em; /* Uppercase often needs
letter spacing */
}
```

4.5 Importing Google Fonts in Your Projects

Google Fonts Integration Methods

Google Fonts provides extensive typography options through multiple integration approaches. Each method offers different advantages for various project requirements and performance considerations.

HTML Link Method

The simplest integration approach involves adding link elements to HTML document heads:

#html

```
<!DOCTYPE html>
<html>
<head>
    <link rel="preconnect"
href="https://fonts.googleapis.com">
```

```
    <link rel="preconnect"
href="https://fonts.gstatic.com" crossorigin>
    <link
href="https://fonts.googleapis.com/css2?family=Roboto:wgh
t@300;400;700&display=swap" rel="stylesheet">
</head>
<body>
    <!-- Page content -->
</body>
</html>
css
body {
    font-family: 'Roboto', sans-serif;
}

.light-text {
    font-weight: 300;
}

.normal-text {
    font-weight: 400;
}

.bold-text {
    font-weight: 700;
}
```

CSS @import Method

The @import rule enables font loading directly within CSS files:

#css

```
@import
url('https://fonts.googleapis.com/css2?family=Open+Sans:i
tal,wght@0,300;0,400;0,600;1,300;1,400&display=swap');

body {
    font-family: 'Open Sans', sans-serif;
}

.italic-light {
    font-style: italic;
    font-weight: 300;
}

.italic-normal {
    font-style: italic;
    font-weight: 400;
}
```

Multiple Font Family Integration

Projects often require multiple font families for different content types:

#html

```
<link
href="https://fonts.googleapis.com/css2?family=Merriweath
er:wght@300;400;700&family=Source+Sans+Pro:wght@300;400;6
00;700&display=swap" rel="stylesheet">
```

#css

```
/* Serif font for body text */
```

```
.serif-content {
    font-family: 'Merriweather', serif;
}

/* Sans-serif font for headings */
.sans-serif-headings {
    font-family: 'Source Sans Pro', sans-serif;
}

h1, h2, h3, h4, h5, h6 {
    font-family: 'Source Sans Pro', sans-serif;
    font-weight: 600;
}

p, li, td {
    font-family: 'Merriweather', serif;
    font-weight: 400;
}
```

Font Display Optimization

The `font-display` parameter controls font loading behavior and prevents layout shifts:

#html

```
<!-- Swap display for immediate text rendering -->
<link
href="https://fonts.googleapis.com/css2?family=Lato:wght@
300;400;700&display=swap" rel="stylesheet">
```

```
<!-- Optional display for enhanced performance -->
<link
href="https://fonts.googleapis.com/css2?family=Playfair+Display:wght@400;700&display=optional" rel="stylesheet">
```

Performance Optimization Strategies

Font Preloading

Preloading critical fonts improves perceived performance:

#html

```
<link rel="preload"
href="https://fonts.gstatic.com/s/roboto/v30/KFOmCnqEu92Fr1Mu4mxK.woff2" as="font" type="font/woff2" crossorigin>
```

Selective Font Weight Loading

Loading only necessary font weights reduces bandwidth usage:

#html

```
<!-- Load only required weights -->
<link
href="https://fonts.googleapis.com/css2?family=Nunito:wght@400;600&display=swap" rel="stylesheet">
css
.regular-text {
    font-family: 'Nunito', sans-serif;
    font-weight: 400; /* Only load weight 400 */
}

.semibold-text {
```

```
    font-family: 'Nunito', sans-serif;
    font-weight: 600; /* Only load weight 600 */
}
```

Variable Fonts Implementation

Variable fonts provide multiple font variations in single files:

#html

```
<link
href="https://fonts.googleapis.com/css2?family=Inter:wght@100..900&display=swap" rel="stylesheet">
css
.variable-font {
    font-family: 'Inter', sans-serif;
    font-weight: 350; /* Any value between 100-900 */
}

.dynamic-weight {
    font-family: 'Inter', sans-serif;
    font-weight: 425;
    transition: font-weight 0.3s ease;
}

.dynamic-weight:hover {
    font-weight: 600;
}
```

Fallback Font Strategies

Robust font stacks ensure consistent typography when Google Fonts fail to load:

#css

```
.robust-typography {
    font-family: 'Roboto', -apple-system,
BlinkMacSystemFont, 'Segoe UI', Helvetica, Arial, sans-
serif;
}

.serif-stack {
    font-family: 'Crimson Text', Georgia, 'Times New
Roman', Times, serif;
}

.monospace-stack {
    font-family: 'Fira Code', 'Consolas', 'Monaco',
'Courier New', monospace;
}
```

Custom Font Loading with JavaScript

Advanced font loading control using the Font Loading API:

#html

```
<script>
if ('fonts' in document) {
    const roboto = new FontFace('Roboto',
'url(https://fonts.gstatic.com/s/roboto/v30/KFOmCnqEu92Fr
1Mu4mxK.woff2)');

    roboto.load().then(function(loadedFont) {
```

```
        document.fonts.add(loadedFont);
        document.documentElement.classList.add('roboto-
loaded');
    });
}
</script>
```

#css

```
body {
    font-family: Arial, sans-serif; /* Fallback font */
}

.roboto-loaded body {
    font-family: 'Roboto', Arial, sans-serif; /* Applied
after loading */
}
```

Essential Tips

- **Start with a solid font hierarchy** - Establish clear visual relationships between headings, subheadings, and body text using consistent font sizes, weights, and spacing. This creates intuitive content structure that guides readers through your content naturally.
- **Prioritize readability over aesthetics** - Choose font combinations that maintain excellent legibility across different devices and screen sizes. Test your typography choices on various devices to ensure optimal reading experiences for all users.
- **Limit font variety within projects** - Restrict yourself to 2-3 font families maximum to maintain visual cohesion and prevent design chaos. Too many fonts create confusion and diminish the professional appearance of your website.
- **Pay attention to line length and spacing** - Keep text lines between 45-75 characters for optimal readability, and use appropriate line height

(typically 1.4-1.6) to create comfortable reading rhythm without cramped or excessive spacing.

- **Consider loading performance implications** - Only load font weights and styles you actually use in your design. Each additional font variant increases page load time, so be selective about which Google Fonts variations you include.

Actionable Strategies

- **Implement a modular scale system** - Use mathematical ratios (like 1.25 or 1.414) to create harmonious font size relationships throughout your design. This ensures consistent visual rhythm and professional typography hierarchy.
- **Test font combinations before committing** - Create style tiles or mockups testing different font pairings to see how they work together across various content types. Consider contrast between serif and sans-serif combinations for visual interest.
- **Optimize for mobile-first typography** - Design your typography system starting with mobile devices, then enhance for larger screens. This ensures excellent readability on smaller screens where most users will access your content.
- **Create consistent spacing patterns** - Establish standardized margin and padding measurements that complement your typography choices. Use rem or em units for scalable spacing that maintains proportional relationships.
- **Leverage CSS custom properties for typography systems** - Define font sizes, weights, and spacing as CSS variables to create maintainable typography systems that can be easily updated across entire projects.
- **Implement progressive font loading strategies** - Use font-display: swap and preload critical fonts to prevent invisible text and layout shifts. Consider using system fonts as immediate fallbacks for better perceived performance.
- **Document your typography decisions** - Create a style guide documenting your font choices, sizes, weights, and spacing decisions. This ensures consistency across team members and future project development phases.

Chapter 5: The Box Model Explained

5.1 What is the CSS Box Model?

The CSS Box Model forms the fundamental foundation of how web browsers calculate space, positioning, and layout for every element on a webpage. Every HTML element, whether it's a paragraph, heading, image, or div, exists as a rectangular box that follows specific rules for spacing and dimensions.

The Four Components of the Box Model

The Box Model consists of four distinct layers that wrap around your content like nested boxes:

- **Content Area**: The innermost area containing your actual text, images, or other media
- **Padding**: The transparent space immediately surrounding the content
- **Border**: The line that can surround the padding and content
- **Margin**: The outermost transparent space that separates the element from neighboring elements

Visual Representation

Imagine looking at a framed picture on a wall. The picture itself represents the content area. The matting around the picture acts like padding, creating breathing room. The physical frame resembles the border, providing a visible boundary. Finally, the space between this framed picture and other wall decorations functions as the margin.

How Browsers Calculate Total Element Size

When a browser renders an element, it calculates the total space occupied using this formula:

Total Width = Content Width + Left Padding + Right Padding + Left Border + Right Border + Left Margin + Right Margin

Total Height = Content Height + Top Padding + Bottom Padding + Top Border + Bottom Border + Top Margin + Bottom Margin

Default Box Model Behavior

By default, browsers use the "content-box" model, meaning when you set width and height properties, you're only specifying the content area dimensions. All padding, borders, and margins add to these base dimensions, potentially making elements larger than expected.

#css

```css
.example-box {
    width: 200px;
    height: 100px;
    padding: 20px;
    border: 5px solid black;
    margin: 15px;
}
/* Total width: 200 + 40 + 10 + 30 = 280px */
/* Total height: 100 + 40 + 10 + 30 = 180px */
```

5.2 Understanding Content, Padding, Border, and Margin

Content Area Deep Dive

The content area represents the actual space where your text, images, videos, or other media appears. This area's dimensions are controlled by the `width` and `height` properties, along with their minimum and maximum variants.

Content Area Properties

#css

```
.content-example {
    width: 300px;            /* Fixed width */
    height: 200px;           /* Fixed height */
    min-width: 250px;        /* Minimum width constraint */
    max-width: 400px;        /* Maximum width constraint */
    min-height: 150px;       /* Minimum height constraint
*/
    max-height: 300px;       /* Maximum height constraint
*/
}
```

Content can overflow its designated area when it's too large to fit. The `overflow` property controls this behavior:

#css

```
.overflow-example {
    width: 200px;
    height: 100px;
    overflow: hidden;        /* Hide overflowing content */
    overflow: scroll;        /* Add scrollbars */
    overflow: auto;          /* Add scrollbars only when
needed */
    overflow: visible;       /* Show overflowing content
(default) */
}
```

Padding: Creating Internal Breathing Room

Padding creates space between your content and the element's border. Unlike margins, padding is part of the element itself and inherits the element's background color or image.

Padding Syntax Variations

#css

```css
/* Individual sides */
.padding-individual {
    padding-top: 10px;
    padding-right: 15px;
    padding-bottom: 20px;
    padding-left: 25px;
}

/* Shorthand - all sides same */
.padding-uniform {
    padding: 15px;
}

/* Shorthand - vertical and horizontal */
.padding-two-values {
    padding: 10px 20px; /* top/bottom: 10px, left/right: 20px */
}

/* Shorthand - top, horizontal, bottom */
.padding-three-values {
    padding: 5px 15px 25px; /* top: 5px, left/right: 15px, bottom: 25px */
}
```

```css
/* Shorthand - clockwise from top */
.padding-four-values {
    padding: 5px 10px 15px 20px; /* top, right, bottom, left */
}
```

Practical Padding Applications

#css

```css
.button-padding {
    background-color: #007bff;
    color: white;
    padding: 12px 24px; /* Comfortable click area */
    border: none;
    border-radius: 4px;
}

.article-padding {
    background-color: #f8f9fa;
    padding: 30px; /* Generous reading space */
    margin-bottom: 20px;
}

.navigation-item {
    padding: 8px 16px; /* Balanced spacing for nav links */
    display: inline-block;
}
```

Border: Defining Element Boundaries

Borders create visible boundaries around elements, sitting between padding and margin. Borders can be styled with different widths, styles, and colors.

Border Properties Breakdown

#css

```css
/* Individual border properties */
.border-detailed {
    border-width: 2px;
    border-style: solid;
    border-color: #333333;
}

/* Shorthand syntax */
.border-shorthand {
    border: 2px solid #333333;
}

/* Individual sides */
.border-sides {
    border-top: 1px solid red;
    border-right: 2px dashed blue;
    border-bottom: 3px dotted green;
    border-left: 4px double orange;
}
```

Border Style Options

#css

```css
.border-styles {
    border: 3px solid black;    /* Solid line */
```

```
    border: 3px dashed black;   /* Dashed line */
    border: 3px dotted black;   /* Dotted line */
    border: 3px double black;   /* Double line */
    border: 3px groove black;   /* 3D grooved effect
*/
    border: 3px ridge black;    /* 3D ridged effect
*/
    border: 3px inset black;    /* 3D inset effect
*/
    border: 3px outset black;   /* 3D outset effect
*/
    border: none;               /* No border */
    border: hidden;             /* Hidden border */
}

    border-image: url('border-pattern.png') 10
repeat;
}


/* Partial borders */
.partial-border {
    border-bottom: 2px solid #e74c3c; /* Only bottom
border */
    padding-bottom: 10px;
}
```

Advanced Border Techniques

#css

```
/* Rounded corners */
.rounded-borders {
    border: 2px solid #007bff;
```

```
    border-radius: 8px; /* All corners */
    border-radius: 10px 5px; /* top-left/bottom-right,
top-right/bottom-left */
    border-radius: 10px 5px 15px 20px; /* clockwise from
top-left */
}

/* Border images */
.border-image-example {
    border: 10px solid transparent;
```

Margin: Creating External Space

Margins create space outside the element's border, separating it from neighboring elements. Unlike padding, margins are transparent and don't inherit background colors.

Margin Syntax and Behavior

#css

```
/* Same syntax patterns as padding */
.margin-examples {
    margin: 20px;              /* All sides */
    margin: 10px 20px;         /* Vertical, horizontal */
    margin: 5px 10px 15px;     /* Top, horizontal, bottom
*/
    margin: 5px 10px 15px 20px; /* Clockwise from top */
}

/* Individual sides */
.margin-individual {
```

```
    margin-top: 10px;
    margin-right: 15px;
    margin-bottom: 20px;
    margin-left: 25px;
}
```

Margin Collapse

One of the most important concepts in CSS is margin collapse, where vertical margins between adjacent elements combine rather than add together.

#css

```
.first-element {
    margin-bottom: 30px;
}

.second-element {
    margin-top: 20px;
}
/* The space between these elements is 30px, not 50px */
```

Centering with Margins

#css

```
.centered-element {
    width: 300px;
    margin: 0 auto; /* Centers horizontally */
}

.centered-with-spacing {
    width: 80%;
```

```
    max-width: 600px;
    margin: 20px auto; /* Centers with top/bottom margin
*/
}
```

Negative Margins

#css

```
.negative-margin {
    margin-top: -10px;    /* Pulls element upward */
    margin-left: -15px;   /* Pulls element leftward */
}

.overlap-effect {
    background-color: rgba(255, 0, 0, 0.7);
    margin-left: -20px;   /* Creates overlapping effect
*/
}
```

5.3 Setting Width and Height

Understanding how to control element dimensions forms a crucial part of layout design. Width and height properties interact directly with the box model, and their behavior changes based on the box-sizing property.

Basic Width and Height Properties

#css

```
/* Fixed dimensions */
.fixed-size {
```

```css
    width: 300px;
    height: 200px;
}

/* Percentage-based dimensions */
.percentage-size {
    width: 50%;      /* 50% of parent element */
    height: 75%;     /* 75% of parent element */
}

/* Viewport-based dimensions */
.viewport-size {
    width: 50vw;     /* 50% of viewport width */
    height: 100vh;   /* 100% of viewport height */
}
```

Minimum and Maximum Constraints

#css

```css
.responsive-container {
    width: 100%;
    min-width: 320px;     /* Never smaller than 320px */
    max-width: 1200px;    /* Never larger than 1200px */
    height: auto;
    min-height: 400px;    /* Minimum height maintained */
    max-height: 800px;    /* Maximum height constraint */
}
```

Height Calculation Challenges

Height calculation in CSS often proves more complex than width due to the nature of content flow:

#css

```
.height-auto {
    height: auto; /* Adjusts to content (default) */
}

.full-height-container {
    height: 100vh; /* Full viewport height */
    overflow-y: auto; /* Scroll if content overflows */
}

.percentage-height-child {
    height: 100%; /* Only works if parent has defined
height */
}
```

Intrinsic and Extrinsic Sizing

#css

```
.intrinsic-sizing {
    width: max-content;  /* Width of longest line */
    width: min-content;  /* Width of longest word */
    width: fit-content;  /* Shrinks to content, respects
max-width */
}

.flexible-sizing {
```

```
    width: 100%;
    max-width: fit-content;
    margin: 0 auto;
}
```

Box Sizing Impact on Dimensions

#css

```
/* Content-box (default) */
.content-box-example {
    box-sizing: content-box;
    width: 200px;
    padding: 20px;
    border: 5px solid black;
    /* Total width: 200 + 40 + 10 = 250px */
}

/* Border-box */
.border-box-example {
    box-sizing: border-box;
    width: 200px;
    padding: 20px;
    border: 5px solid black;
    /* Total width: 200px (padding and border included)
*/
    /* Content width: 200 - 40 - 10 = 150px */
}
```

5.4 Box Sizing: Content-Box vs Border-Box

The `box-sizing` property fundamentally changes how browsers calculate element dimensions, making it one of the most important properties for layout control.

Content-Box: The Default Behavior

Content-box represents the traditional CSS box model where width and height only apply to the content area:

#css

```css
.content-box-demo {
    box-sizing: content-box; /* Default value */
    width: 300px;
    height: 200px;
    padding: 25px;
    border: 5px solid #333;
    margin: 15px;

    /* Calculations:
       Content area: 300px × 200px
       Total width: 300 + 50 + 10 = 360px
       Total height: 200 + 50 + 10 = 260px
       Space occupied: 390px × 290px (including margins)
    */
}
```

Border-Box: The Intuitive Alternative

Border-box includes padding and border within the specified width and height:

#css

```
.border-box-demo {
    box-sizing: border-box;
    width: 300px;
    height: 200px;
    padding: 25px;
    border: 5px solid #333;
    margin: 15px;

    /* Calculations:
       Total width: 300px (as specified)
       Total height: 200px (as specified)
       Content area: 300 - 50 - 10 = 240px × 200 - 50 -
10 = 140px
       Space occupied: 330px × 230px (including margins)
    */
}
```

Universal Border-Box Reset

Many developers apply border-box to all elements for more predictable sizing:

#css

```
/* Universal box-sizing reset */
*, *::before, *::after {
    box-sizing: border-box;
}

/* Alternative inheritance method */
html {
```

```
    box-sizing: border-box;
}

*, *::before, *::after {
    box-sizing: inherit;
}
```

Practical Applications

#css

```css
/* Form styling with predictable sizing */
.form-input {
    box-sizing: border-box;
    width: 100%;
    padding: 12px;
    border: 2px solid #ddd;
    border-radius: 4px;
    /* Width remains 100% regardless of padding/border */
}

/* Grid layout with consistent columns */
.grid-item {
    box-sizing: border-box;
    width: 33.333%;
    padding: 10px;
    border: 1px solid #ccc;
    float: left;
    /* Each item exactly 1/3 width including
padding/border */
```

```
}

/* Card components with predictable dimensions */
.card {
    box-sizing: border-box;
    width: 300px;
    height: 400px;
    padding: 20px;
    border: 1px solid #e1e1e1;
    border-radius: 8px;
    /* Card always exactly 300×400px */
}
```

Box Sizing and Responsive Design

#css

```
.responsive-container {
    box-sizing: border-box;
    width: 100%;
    max-width: 1200px;
    padding: 0 20px;
    margin: 0 auto;
    /* Padding included in width calculations */
}

@media (max-width: 768px) {
    .responsive-container {
        padding: 0 15px; /* Smaller padding on mobile */
        /* Width calculations remain predictable */
```

```
    }
}
```

5.5 Debugging Layouts Using Dev Tools

Browser Developer Tools provide powerful features for visualizing and debugging the box model, making layout issues much easier to identify and resolve.

Accessing Developer Tools

Most modern browsers offer similar developer tools:

- **Chrome/Edge**: F12 or Right-click → Inspect
- **Firefox**: F12 or Right-click → Inspect Element
- **Safari**: Enable Developer Menu, then Option+Cmd+I

Elements Panel Box Model Visualization

The Elements panel shows a visual representation of the box model for any selected element:

- **Color-coded visualization**: Content (blue), padding (green), border (yellow), margin (orange)
- **Numerical values**: Exact pixel measurements for each layer
- **Interactive editing**: Click values to modify them in real-time

Console Box Model Inspection

#javascript

```javascript
// Get computed styles for any element
const element = document.querySelector('.my-element');
```

```
const styles = window.getComputedStyle(element);

console.log('Width:', styles.width);
console.log('Padding:', styles.padding);
console.log('Border:', styles.borderWidth);
console.log('Margin:', styles.margin);
console.log('Box Sizing:', styles.boxSizing);
```

Layout Tab Features

Modern browsers include specialized layout debugging tools:

Grid and Flexbox Overlays

#css

```css
.debug-grid {
    display: grid;
    grid-template-columns: repeat(3, 1fr);
    gap: 20px;
    /* Enable grid overlay in dev tools */
}

.debug-flex {
    display: flex;
    justify-content: space-between;
    align-items: center;
    /* Enable flexbox overlay in dev tools */
}
```

Box Model Highlighting

Developer tools can highlight different box model layers:

- Hover over elements to see box model visualization
- Toggle specific layers (content, padding, border, margin)
- Measure distances between elements

Common Layout Debugging Scenarios

Unexpected Element Sizes

#css

```css
/* Problem: Element larger than expected */
.unexpected-size {
    width: 200px;
    padding: 50px;    /* Adds 100px to width */
    border: 10px solid black; /* Adds 20px to width */
    /* Total width: 320px in content-box model */
}

/* Solution: Use border-box or adjust measurements */
.corrected-size {
    box-sizing: border-box;
    width: 200px;
    padding: 50px;
    border: 10px solid black;
    /* Total width: 200px as expected */
}
```

Margin Collapse Issues

#css

```css
/* Problem: Unexpected spacing between elements */
.first-section {
    margin-bottom: 40px;
}

.second-section {
    margin-top: 30px;
}
/* Actual space: 40px (margins collapse to larger value)
*/

/* Debug: Check computed margins in dev tools */
/* Solution: Use padding or single-direction margins */
.corrected-sections {
    margin-bottom: 40px;
    margin-top: 0; /* Prevent collapse */
}
```

Overflow Problems

#css

```css
/* Problem: Content overflowing container */
.overflow-container {
    width: 300px;
    height: 200px;
    padding: 20px;
    /* Content area only 260×160px */
}

/* Debug: Check element dimensions vs content size */
/* Solution: Adjust dimensions or overflow handling */
```

```css
.overflow-fixed {
    width: 300px;
    height: 200px;
    padding: 20px;
    box-sizing: border-box; /* Full 300×200px available
*/
    overflow: auto; /* Add scrollbars if needed */
}
```

Performance Debugging

#css

```css
/* Identify expensive layout operations */
.performance-conscious {
    /* Avoid properties that trigger layout recalculation
*/
    transform: translateX(10px); /* Better than left:
10px; */
    opacity: 0.8; /* Better than visibility changes */
}

/* Use containment for isolated components */
.contained-component {
    contain: layout style; /* Isolate layout calculations
*/
}
```

Mobile Debugging Techniques

#css

```css
/* Debug responsive layouts */
.mobile-debug {
    /* Add temporary borders to visualize layout */
    border: 1px solid red;
}

@media (max-width: 768px) {
    .mobile-debug {
        /* Check calculations on mobile */
        font-size: 16px; /* Ensure readable text */
        padding: 10px; /* Sufficient touch targets */
        min-height: 44px; /* iOS touch target minimum */
    }
}
```

Essential Tips

- **Always set `box-sizing: border-box`** on all elements using the universal selector. This makes width and height calculations much more intuitive and predictable, especially when working with percentages and responsive designs.
- **Use browser developer tools religiously** when debugging layout issues. The visual box model representation shows exactly how space is being calculated and can immediately reveal why elements don't appear where expected.
- **Learn margin collapse behavior** to avoid frustrating spacing issues. Vertical margins between adjacent elements collapse to the larger value, not the sum. Use padding instead of margins when you need additive spacing.
- **Establish a consistent spacing system** using CSS custom properties for margins and padding values. This creates visual harmony and makes global adjustments much easier to implement across your entire project.

- **Test your layouts with extreme content** to ensure robustness. Try very long text strings, large images, and empty elements to see how your box model implementations handle edge cases and prevent layout breaks.

Actionable Strategies

- **Create a comprehensive CSS reset** that includes `box-sizing: border-box` for all elements, removes default margins and padding from key elements, and establishes consistent baseline styles across different browsers.
- **Build a spacing utility class system** with predefined margin and padding classes (like `.m-1`, `.p-2`, `.mx-3`) that correspond to your design system's spacing scale, making layout implementation faster and more consistent.
- **Implement a container query approach** for component-based designs where elements adapt based on their container size rather than viewport size, giving you more granular control over how the box model behaves in different contexts.
- **Master the relationship between display properties and box model behavior** by understanding how `block`, `inline`, `inline-block`, `flex`, and `grid` affect width, height, margin, and padding calculations differently.
- **Develop debugging workflows** that include systematic checking of computed styles, using temporary background colors or borders to visualize element boundaries, and creating isolated test cases for complex layout problems.
- **Optimize for performance** by understanding which box model changes trigger layout recalculation versus simple repaints, and structure your CSS to minimize expensive operations during animations and interactions.
- **Document your box model decisions** in component libraries or style guides, including rationale for border-box usage, spacing system choices, and common patterns that other developers can reference and maintain consistently.

Chapter 6: Display and Visibility

Understanding how elements appear and behave on a webpage forms the foundation of effective CSS layout design. The display property controls the fundamental rendering behavior of HTML elements, while visibility properties determine whether elements remain visible to users. This chapter provides comprehensive coverage of display types, visibility controls, and modern layout techniques that enable precise control over element presentation.

6.1 Display Property: Block, Inline, Inline-Block

The display property serves as the cornerstone of CSS layout control, determining how elements interact with surrounding content and occupy space within the document flow. Every HTML element possesses a default display value, but CSS allows complete override of these behaviors to achieve desired layouts.

Understanding Block Elements

Block elements represent the most fundamental display type, creating rectangular boxes that occupy the full available width of their container. These elements naturally stack vertically, with each block element forcing subsequent content to appear on new lines.

#css

```
.block-element {
    display: block;
    width: 100%;
    height: 50px;
    background-color: #3498db;
    margin: 10px 0;
    padding: 15px;
}
```

Block elements accept all CSS properties including width, height, margin, and padding. The browser calculates their width based on the containing element, automatically expanding to fill available horizontal space unless explicitly constrained.

#html

```
<div class="block-element">Block Element 1</div>
<div class="block-element">Block Element 2</div>
<p class="block-element">Block Paragraph</p>
```

Common block elements include `div`, `p`, `h1-h6`, `section`, `article`, and `footer`. These elements provide structural foundation for webpage layouts, acting as containers for other content.

Block Element Characteristics and Behavior

Block elements possess several defining characteristics that influence layout behavior:

Full Width Occupation: Block elements automatically expand to consume their parent container's entire width, unless constrained by explicit width declarations or other CSS properties.

Vertical Stacking: Multiple block elements stack vertically in document order, with each element appearing below the previous one in the normal document flow.

Margin Collapse: Adjacent block elements experience margin collapse, where vertical margins between elements merge rather than add together. The larger margin value takes precedence.

#css

```
.margin-example {
    display: block;
    margin-bottom: 20px;
```

```
    margin-top: 30px;
    background-color: #e74c3c;
    padding: 10px;
}
```

Dimensional Control: Block elements respond to width, height, min-width, max-width, min-height, and max-height properties, providing precise control over element dimensions.

Inline Elements and Their Limitations

Inline elements flow within text content, appearing alongside other inline elements on the same line until line wrapping occurs. These elements respect the text baseline and integrate seamlessly with textual content.

#css

```
.inline-element {
    display: inline;
    background-color: #f39c12;
    padding: 5px 10px;
    margin: 0 5px;
    color: white;
    font-weight: bold;
}
```

#html

```
<p>This paragraph contains <span class="inline-
element">inline elements</span> that flow with the text.
Here's <a href="#" class="inline-element">another inline
element</a> in the same line.</p>
```

Inline elements possess significant limitations that affect layout flexibility:

No Dimensional Control: Width and height properties have no effect on inline elements. The element's dimensions depend entirely on content size and font properties.

Limited Vertical Spacing: Top and bottom margins do not affect inline elements. Only left and right margins apply, creating horizontal spacing between adjacent inline elements.

Padding Behavior: While inline elements accept padding values, vertical padding may overlap adjacent line content without affecting line height or spacing.

Inline-Block: The Hybrid Solution

Inline-block elements combine the flowing behavior of inline elements with the dimensional control of block elements, creating versatile layout components.

#css

```
.inline-block-element {
    display: inline-block;
    width: 150px;
    height: 100px;
    background-color: #9b59b6;
    margin: 10px;
    padding: 15px;
    vertical-align: top;
    text-align: center;
    color: white;
}
```

#html

```
<div class="inline-block-element">Box 1</div>
```

```
<div class="inline-block-element">Box 2</div>
<div class="inline-block-element">Box 3</div>
```

Inline-block elements enable creation of horizontal layouts without floating or complex positioning, making them ideal for navigation menus, button groups, and grid-like arrangements.

Vertical Alignment in Inline-Block

The vertical-align property becomes crucial when working with inline-block elements, controlling how elements align relative to the text baseline or each other.

#css

```
.alignment-demo {
    display: inline-block;
    width: 100px;
    margin: 5px;
    background-color: #1abc9c;
    color: white;
    text-align: center;
}

.align-top { vertical-align: top; height: 60px; }
.align-middle { vertical-align: middle; height: 80px; }
.align-bottom { vertical-align: bottom; height: 100px; }
```

Common Display Property Values

Beyond the primary display types, CSS provides additional display values for specialized layout needs:

display: table: Creates table-like layout behavior without using HTML table elements, useful for equal-height columns and complex alignment scenarios.

display: list-item: Generates list item markers (bullets or numbers) and creates block-level behavior, typically used with `ul` and `ol` elements.

display: contents: Removes the element's box from the layout while preserving its children, effectively making the element transparent to layout calculations.

#css

```
.table-display {
    display: table;
    width: 100%;
    border-collapse: separate;
    border-spacing: 10px;
}

.table-cell {
    display: table-cell;
    background-color: #34495e;
    padding: 20px;
    color: white;
    vertical-align: top;
}
```

6.2 None vs Visibility Hidden

Understanding the distinction between `display: none` and `visibility: hidden` prevents common layout issues and ensures proper element hiding behavior. Both properties hide elements from view, but their impact on document layout differs significantly.

Display None: Complete Removal

The `display: none` declaration completely removes elements from the document flow, as if they never existed in the HTML structure. The browser allocates no space for hidden elements, causing surrounding content to reflow and fill the vacated area.

#css

```
.display-none {
    display: none;
}

.toggle-visibility {
    background-color: #e67e22;
    padding: 20px;
    margin: 10px 0;
    transition: all 0.3s ease;
}

.visible {
    display: block;
}
```

#html

```
<div class="toggle-visibility visible">Visible
Element</div>
<div class="toggle-visibility display-none">Hidden
Element</div>
<div class="toggle-visibility visible">Another Visible
Element</div>
```

When elements use `display: none`, they become completely inaccessible to screen readers and assistive technologies, effectively removing them from the accessibility tree. This behavior suits scenarios where content should be conditionally rendered based on user interactions or device characteristics.

Visibility Hidden: Space Preservation

The `visibility: hidden` property hides elements while maintaining their allocated space in the document layout. Hidden elements remain part of the document flow, preserving the original layout structure.

#css

```
.visibility-hidden {
    visibility: hidden;
}

.space-demo {
    background-color: #2ecc71;
    padding: 30px;
    margin: 15px 0;
    text-align: center;
    color: white;
}
```

#html

```
<div class="space-demo">Element Before</div>
<div class="space-demo visibility-hidden">Hidden But
Space Reserved</div>
<div class="space-demo">Element After</div>
```

Elements with `visibility: hidden` maintain their dimensions, margins, padding, and position within the layout. This preservation prevents layout shifting when toggling element visibility, creating smoother user experiences.

Opacity: Transparency Control

The opacity property provides another method for hiding elements, creating transparency effects while maintaining full layout participation and user interaction capabilities.

#css

```
.opacity-demo {
    opacity: 0;
    background-color: #8e44ad;
    padding: 25px;
    margin: 10px 0;
    transition: opacity 0.4s ease;
    color: white;
}

.opacity-demo:hover {
    opacity: 1;
}

.semi-transparent {
    opacity: 0.5;
}
```

Unlike `visibility: hidden`, elements with `opacity: 0` remain interactive and accessible to assistive technologies, making them suitable for fade-in animations and hover effects.

Performance Considerations

Different hiding methods impact browser rendering performance differently:

Display None Performance: Completely hidden elements skip rendering calculations, potentially improving performance for complex layouts with many hidden elements.

Visibility Hidden Performance: Hidden elements participate in layout calculations but skip painting operations, offering moderate performance benefits.

Opacity Performance: Transparent elements undergo full rendering processes, including layout, painting, and compositing operations.

#css

```
.performance-comparison {
    width: 200px;
    height: 150px;
    background: linear-gradient(45deg, #3498db, #e74c3c);
    margin: 10px;
    display: inline-block;
}

.gpu-accelerated {
    will-change: opacity;
    transform: translateZ(0); /* Force GPU acceleration
*/
}
```

Conditional Visibility Techniques

Responsive design often requires showing or hiding elements based on screen size or device capabilities. Media queries combined with display properties enable sophisticated conditional visibility.

#css

```
.mobile-only {
    display: block;
}

.desktop-only {
    display: none;
}

@media (min-width: 768px) {
    .mobile-only {
        display: none;
    }

    .desktop-only {
        display: block;
    }
}

.print-hidden {
    display: block;
}

@media print {
    .print-hidden {
        display: none;
    }
```

```
}
```

6.3 Display Flex and Grid Basics

Modern CSS layout systems revolutionize how developers approach complex layouts, moving beyond traditional float-based techniques to more intuitive and powerful solutions. Flexbox and Grid represent the current standard for professional web development.

Flexbox Fundamentals

Flexbox creates one-dimensional layouts, organizing elements along either horizontal or vertical axes. The flex container defines the layout context, while flex items adapt to available space according to specified rules.

#css

```css
.flex-container {
    display: flex;
    background-color: #ecf0f1;
    padding: 20px;
    margin: 20px 0;
    border-radius: 8px;
}

.flex-item {
    background-color: #3498db;
    color: white;
    padding: 20px;
    margin: 10px;
    flex: 1;
    text-align: center;
    border-radius: 4px;
```

```
}
```

#html

```
<div class="flex-container">
    <div class="flex-item">Item 1</div>
    <div class="flex-item">Item 2</div>
    <div class="flex-item">Item 3</div>
</div>
```

Flex Direction and Wrap

The flex-direction property controls the main axis orientation, while flex-wrap determines whether items wrap to new lines when space becomes insufficient.

#css

```
.flex-row {
    display: flex;
    flex-direction: row;
    flex-wrap: wrap;
    gap: 15px;
}

.flex-column {
    display: flex;
    flex-direction: column;
    height: 300px;
    justify-content: space-between;
}
```

```
.flex-item-sized {
    background-color: #e74c3c;
    color: white;
    padding: 15px;
    margin: 5px;
    min-width: 150px;
    text-align: center;
}
```

Flex Item Properties

Individual flex items can control their growth, shrinkage, and base size through dedicated properties:

#css

```
.flex-grow-demo {
    display: flex;
    height: 100px;
    background-color: #f8f9fa;
    padding: 10px;
    gap: 10px;
}

.grow-1 { flex-grow: 1; background-color: #28a745; }
.grow-2 { flex-grow: 2; background-color: #17a2b8; }
.grow-0 { flex-grow: 0; width: 100px; background-color:
#6c757d; }

.shrink-demo {
    display: flex;
```

```
    width: 300px;
    background-color: #f8f9fa;
    padding: 10px;
    gap: 10px;
}

.no-shrink { flex-shrink: 0; width: 200px; background-
color: #dc3545; }
.can-shrink { flex-shrink: 1; width: 200px; background-
color: #ffc107; }
```

Alignment in Flexbox

Flexbox provides powerful alignment capabilities through justify-content and align-items properties:

#css

```
.alignment-demo {
    display: flex;
    height: 200px;
    background-color: #e9ecef;
    margin: 20px 0;
    border: 2px dashed #6c757d;
}

.center-all {
    justify-content: center;
    align-items: center;
}

.space-between {
```

```
    justify-content: space-between;
    align-items: flex-end;
}

.flex-align-item {
    background-color: #007bff;
    color: white;
    padding: 15px 25px;
    border-radius: 4px;
}
```

CSS Grid Introduction

CSS Grid creates two-dimensional layouts, providing precise control over both rows and columns simultaneously. Grid surpasses flexbox for complex layouts requiring exact positioning and spanning capabilities.

#css

```
.grid-container {
    display: grid;
    grid-template-columns: repeat(3, 1fr);
    grid-template-rows: repeat(3, 100px);
    gap: 15px;
    background-color: #f8f9fa;
    padding: 20px;
    border-radius: 8px;
}

.grid-item {
    background-color: #28a745;
```

```
    color: white;
    display: flex;
    align-items: center;
    justify-content: center;
    border-radius: 4px;
    font-weight: bold;
}

.grid-item:nth-child(1) {
    grid-column: 1 / 3;
    background-color: #dc3545;
}

.grid-item:nth-child(4) {
    grid-row: 2 / 4;
    background-color: #17a2b8;
}
```

Grid Template Areas

Named grid areas provide intuitive layout definition, making complex grid structures more maintainable and readable:

#css

```
.layout-grid {
    display: grid;
    grid-template-areas:
        "header header header"
        "sidebar main main"
        "footer footer footer";
```

```
    grid-template-columns: 200px 1fr 1fr;
    grid-template-rows: 80px 1fr 60px;
    gap: 20px;
    height: 100vh;
    padding: 20px;
}

.header { grid-area: header; background-color: #343a40; }
.sidebar { grid-area: sidebar; background-color: #6c757d;
}
.main { grid-area: main; background-color: #e9ecef; }
.footer { grid-area: footer; background-color: #495057; }
```

Responsive Grid Layouts

Grid provides powerful responsive capabilities through auto-fit, auto-fill, and minmax functions:

#css

```
.responsive-grid {
    display: grid;
    grid-template-columns: repeat(auto-fit, minmax(250px,
1fr));
    gap: 20px;
    padding: 20px;
}

.responsive-item {
    aspect-ratio: 1;
    background: linear-gradient(135deg, #667eea 0%,
#764ba2 100%);
```

```
    border-radius: 8px;
    display: flex;
    align-items: center;
    justify-content: center;
    color: white;
    font-size: 18px;
    font-weight: bold;
}
```

6.4 Hiding Elements Responsibly

Responsible element hiding considers accessibility, performance, and user experience implications. Different hiding methods serve distinct purposes and should be chosen based on specific requirements and contexts.

Accessibility Considerations

Screen readers and assistive technologies interact differently with various hiding methods, making accessibility impact a crucial consideration:

#css

```
.screen-reader-only {
    position: absolute;
    left: -10000px;
    width: 1px;
    height: 1px;
    overflow: hidden;
}

.aria-hidden-example {
    display: block;
```

```
    /* Use aria-hidden="true" in HTML for decorative elements */
}

.focus-visible-hidden {
    opacity: 0;
    pointer-events: none;
    transition: opacity 0.3s ease;
}

.focus-visible-hidden:focus {
    opacity: 1;
    pointer-events: auto;
}
```

Progressive Enhancement

Hiding elements should support progressive enhancement, ensuring content remains accessible when CSS fails to load or JavaScript is disabled:

#css

```
.js-enhanced {
    display: none;
}

.no-js .js-enhanced {
    display: block;
}

.css-supported {
```

```
    display: none;
}

@supports (display: grid) {
    .css-supported {
        display: block;
    }
}
```

Animation-Friendly Hiding

Modern interfaces require smooth transitions when showing or hiding elements. Opacity and transform-based hiding enables fluid animations:

#css

```css
.fade-transition {
    opacity: 1;
    transform: translateY(0);
    transition: opacity 0.4s ease, transform 0.4s ease;
}

.fade-transition.hidden {
    opacity: 0;
    transform: translateY(-20px);
    pointer-events: none;
}

.slide-transition {
    max-height: 500px;
    overflow: hidden;
```

```
    transition: max-height 0.5s ease;
}

.slide-transition.collapsed {
    max-height: 0;
}
```

Performance-Optimized Hiding

Large applications with many hidden elements benefit from performance-conscious hiding strategies:

#css

```
.lazy-load-hidden {
    display: none;
    contain: layout style paint;
}

.lazy-load-hidden.loaded {
    display: block;
}

.gpu-optimized-hide {
    opacity: 0;
    transform: translateZ(0);
    will-change: opacity;
    transition: opacity 0.3s ease;
}
```

Context-Aware Hiding

Different contexts require different hiding approaches. Print styles, mobile interfaces, and touch devices may need specialized hiding rules:

#css

```css
.touch-hidden {
    display: block;
}

@media (hover: hover) and (pointer: fine) {
    .touch-hidden {
        display: none;
    }
}

.print-only {
    display: none;
}

@media print {
    .print-only {
        display: block;
    }

    .no-print {
        display: none !important;
    }
}

.reduced-motion {
    transition: none !important;
```

```
    animation: none !important;
}

@media (prefers-reduced-motion: reduce) {
    .motion-sensitive {
        display: none;
    }
}
```

6.5 Combining Display Types for Layouts

Sophisticated layouts often require combining multiple display types to achieve desired results. Understanding how different display values interact enables creation of complex, responsive layouts that work across devices and contexts.

Flex and Grid Hybrid Layouts

Combining flexbox and grid creates powerful layout systems that leverage each technology's strengths:

#css

```
.hybrid-layout {
    display: grid;
    grid-template-columns: 1fr 3fr 1fr;
    grid-template-rows: auto 1fr auto;
    min-height: 100vh;
    gap: 20px;
}

.header-flex {
    grid-column: 1 / -1;
```

```
    display: flex;
    justify-content: space-between;
    align-items: center;
    background-color: #2c3e50;
    padding: 1rem 2rem;
    color: white;
}

.sidebar-flex {
    display: flex;
    flex-direction: column;
    gap: 1rem;
    background-color: #ecf0f1;
    padding: 1rem;
}

.main-grid {
    display: grid;
    grid-template-columns: repeat(auto-fit, minmax(300px,
1fr));
    gap: 1rem;
    padding: 1rem;
}
```

Nested Display Contexts

Display contexts can be nested to create hierarchical layouts with different behaviors at each level:

#css

```css
.outer-flex {
    display: flex;
    flex-direction: column;
    height: 100vh;
}

.header-section {
    flex: 0 0 auto;
    display: flex;
    justify-content: space-between;
    background-color: #34495e;
    padding: 1rem;
}

.content-section {
    flex: 1;
    display: grid;
    grid-template-columns: 250px 1fr;
    overflow: hidden;
}

.navigation {
    display: flex;
    flex-direction: column;
    background-color: #2c3e50;
    padding: 1rem;
    overflow-y: auto;
}

.main-content {
```

```
    display: grid;
    grid-template-rows: auto 1fr;
    overflow: hidden;
}

.content-grid {
    display: grid;
    grid-template-columns: repeat(auto-fill,
minmax(250px, 1fr));
    gap: 1rem;
    padding: 1rem;
    overflow-y: auto;
}
```

Responsive Display Switching

Modern responsive design often requires changing display types at different breakpoints:

#css

```
.responsive-layout {
    display: block;
}

@media (min-width: 768px) {
    .responsive-layout {
        display: flex;
        gap: 2rem;
    }
}
```

```css
@media (min-width: 1024px) {
    .responsive-layout {
        display: grid;
        grid-template-columns: repeat(3, 1fr);
        gap: 2rem;
    }
}

.adaptive-card {
    background-color: white;
    border-radius: 8px;
    box-shadow: 0 2px 10px rgba(0,0,0,0.1);
    padding: 1.5rem;
    margin-bottom: 1rem;
    display: block;
}

@media (min-width: 768px) {
    .adaptive-card {
        display: flex;
        align-items: center;
        margin-bottom: 0;
    }
}
```

Component-Based Display Patterns

Modern web development benefits from reusable display patterns that can be applied across different components:

#css

```
.card-component {
    display: flex;
    flex-direction: column;
    background-color: white;
    border-radius: 12px;
    box-shadow: 0 4px 6px rgba(0, 0, 0, 0.1);
    overflow: hidden;
    transition: transform 0.2s ease, box-shadow 0.2s
ease;
}

.card-component:hover {
    transform: translateY(-2px);
    box-shadow: 0 8px 25px rgba(0, 0, 0, 0.15);
}

.card-header {
    display: flex;
    align-items: center;
    justify-content: space-between;
    padding: 1rem 1.5rem;
    background-color: #f8f9fa;
    border-bottom: 1px solid #dee2e6;
}

.card-body {
    flex: 1;
    padding: 1.5rem;
    display: flex;
```

```
    flex-direction: column;
    gap: 1rem;
}

.card-footer {
    display: flex;
    justify-content: flex-end;
    gap: 0.5rem;
    padding: 1rem 1.5rem;
    background-color: #f8f9fa;
    border-top: 1px solid #dee2e6;
}
```

Advanced Layout Techniques

Sophisticated layouts may require advanced techniques that push the boundaries of CSS display capabilities:

#css

```
.masonry-layout {
    display: grid;
    grid-template-columns: repeat(auto-fill,
minmax(300px, 1fr));
    grid-auto-rows: 10px;
    gap: 1rem;
}

.masonry-item {
    background-color: white;
    border-radius: 8px;
```

```
    box-shadow: 0 2px 8px rgba(0,0,0,0.1);
    padding: 1rem;
    break-inside: avoid;
}

.masonry-item:nth-child(1) { grid-row-end: span 20; }
.masonry-item:nth-child(2) { grid-row-end: span 30; }
.masonry-item:nth-child(3) { grid-row-end: span 25; }

.sticky-layout {
    display: grid;
    grid-template-columns: 250px 1fr;
    gap: 2rem;
    max-width: 1200px;
    margin: 0 auto;
    padding: 2rem;
}

.sticky-sidebar {
    position: sticky;
    top: 2rem;
    height: fit-content;
    display: flex;
    flex-direction: column;
    gap: 1rem;
}
```

Essential Tips

- Master the default display values of HTML elements to avoid unnecessary CSS declarations and maintain cleaner, more efficient stylesheets that work with browser defaults rather than against them.
- Always test element hiding with screen readers and keyboard navigation to ensure accessibility compliance, particularly when using display:none versus visibility:hidden, as these properties affect assistive technology differently.
- Use CSS containment properties (contain: layout, style, paint) when hiding complex elements to improve rendering performance and prevent unnecessary style calculations on hidden content.
- Implement progressive enhancement by designing layouts that work without CSS first, then adding display properties to enhance the experience, ensuring content remains accessible even when styles fail to load.
- Combine transform and opacity for smooth show/hide animations instead of toggling display values, as transforms can be hardware-accelerated and provide better performance for interactive transitions.

Actionable Strategies

- Create a systematic approach to responsive display by establishing breakpoint-specific display patterns that consistently apply across your entire project, using CSS custom properties to maintain consistency.
- Build reusable component classes that combine multiple display contexts, such as cards that use flexbox internally while participating in grid layouts externally, maximizing layout flexibility.
- Implement performance-conscious hiding strategies by using will-change property judiciously and removing it after animations complete to prevent unnecessary GPU layer creation and memory usage.
- Establish clear naming conventions for display-related classes that indicate both the display type and responsive behavior, making your CSS more maintainable and self-documenting for team collaboration.
- Use CSS Grid for two-dimensional layouts and Flexbox for one-dimensional layouts as the primary rule, falling back to older display methods only when necessary for browser support requirements.
- Create comprehensive fallback strategies for modern display properties by providing alternative layouts using older display methods, ensuring compatibility across different browser versions and capabilities.

Chapter 7: Positioning Elements

Understanding how to position elements on a webpage is fundamental to creating sophisticated layouts and interactive designs. CSS positioning allows you to control exactly where elements appear on the page, how they relate to other elements, and how they behave when users scroll or interact with your content.

7.1 Static, Relative, Absolute, Fixed

Static Positioning

Static positioning is the default position value for all HTML elements. Elements with static positioning follow the normal document flow, appearing one after another in the order they appear in your HTML markup. Static positioned elements ignore any top, right, bottom, left, or z-index properties you might apply to them.

#css

```
.static-element {
    position: static;
    /* These properties will be ignored */
    top: 50px;
    left: 100px;
}
```

Static positioning is useful when you want elements to behave naturally within the document flow. Most text content, paragraphs, and basic layout elements work perfectly with static positioning.

Understanding Document Flow

Before diving into other positioning types, it's crucial to understand the normal document flow. Block-level elements stack vertically, taking up the full width of their container, while inline elements flow horizontally until they wrap to the next line. This natural flow forms the foundation for all other positioning methods.

Relative Positioning

Relative positioning moves an element from its normal position in the document flow while maintaining its original space. Other elements behave as if the relatively positioned element is still in its original location, even though it visually appears elsewhere.

#css

```
.relative-element {
    position: relative;
    top: 20px;
    left: 30px;
    background-color: lightblue;
}
```

#html

```
<div class="container">
    <p>This paragraph comes before the relatively positioned element.</p>
    <div class="relative-element">
        This div is moved 20px down and 30px right from its normal position.
    </div>
    <p>This paragraph comes after, but notice the gap where the div originally was.</p>
</div>
```

Relative positioning creates a positioning context for absolutely positioned child elements. This makes it invaluable for creating complex layouts where you need precise control over child element placement.

Practical Applications of Relative Positioning

Relative positioning excels in scenarios where you need subtle adjustments to element placement without disrupting the overall layout flow. Common use cases include:

- Fine-tuning the position of icons next to text
- Creating hover effects that slightly move elements
- Establishing positioning contexts for absolutely positioned children
- Making minor layout adjustments without affecting surrounding elements

Absolute Positioning

Absolute positioning removes an element completely from the normal document flow. The element positions itself relative to its nearest positioned ancestor (an ancestor with position set to anything other than static). If no positioned ancestor exists, the element positions itself relative to the initial containing block, typically the viewport.

#css

```
.container {
    position: relative;
    width: 400px;
    height: 300px;
    border: 2px solid black;
}

.absolute-element {
    position: absolute;
    top: 50px;
```

```
    right: 20px;
    width: 100px;
    height: 80px;
    background-color: red;
}
```

#html

```
<div class="container">
    <p>This is normal content in the container.</p>
    <div class="absolute-element">
        This div is positioned absolutely within the container.
    </div>
    <p>Notice how this text flows as if the absolute element doesn't exist.</p>
</div>
```

Absolutely positioned elements don't affect the position of other elements, and other elements don't affect their position. This makes them perfect for overlays, tooltips, dropdown menus, and other interface elements that need to appear above or alongside existing content.

Advanced Absolute Positioning Techniques

You can use combinations of offset properties to create flexible positioning:

#css

```
.full-overlay {
    position: absolute;
    top: 0;
```

```
    right: 0;
    bottom: 0;
    left: 0;
    background-color: rgba(0, 0, 0, 0.5);
}

.center-absolute {
    position: absolute;
    top: 50%;
    left: 50%;
    transform: translate(-50%, -50%);
    width: 200px;
    height: 100px;
}
```

Fixed Positioning

Fixed positioning removes an element from the document flow and positions it relative to the viewport. Fixed elements remain in the same position even when the page is scrolled, making them ideal for navigation bars, floating action buttons, and persistent UI elements.

#css

```
.fixed-header {
    position: fixed;
    top: 0;
    left: 0;
    width: 100%;
    height: 60px;
    background-color: navy;
    color: white;
```

```
    z-index: 1000;
}

.fixed-sidebar {
    position: fixed;
    top: 60px;
    right: 0;
    width: 200px;
    height: calc(100vh - 60px);
    background-color: lightgray;
    overflow-y: auto;
}
```

#html

```html
<header class="fixed-header">
    <h1>Fixed Navigation</h1>
</header>
<aside class="fixed-sidebar">
    <nav>Fixed Sidebar Content</nav>
</aside>
<main style="margin-top: 60px; margin-right: 200px;">
    <p>Main content that scrolls normally...</p>
</main>
```

Fixed positioning is powerful for creating persistent user interface elements, but use it judiciously to avoid cluttering the viewport or interfering with content accessibility.

7.2 Z-index and Overlapping Elements

Understanding Stacking Context

When elements overlap, CSS determines their stacking order through stacking contexts. Every positioned element (except static) can have a z-index value that determines its position in the stacking order. Higher z-index values appear in front of lower values.

#css

```
.background-layer {
    position: absolute;
    top: 50px;
    left: 50px;
    width: 200px;
    height: 200px;
    background-color: blue;
    z-index: 1;
}

.middle-layer {
    position: absolute;
    top: 100px;
    left: 100px;
    width: 200px;
    height: 200px;
    background-color: green;
    z-index: 2;
}

.front-layer {
    position: absolute;
    top: 150px;
    left: 150px;
```

```
    width: 200px;
    height: 200px;
    background-color: red;
    z-index: 3;
}
```

Natural Stacking Order

Without explicit z-index values, elements stack according to these rules:

- Non-positioned elements appear behind positioned elements
- Among positioned elements, those appearing later in the HTML appear in front
- Child elements appear in front of their parents

Complex Stacking Scenarios

Understanding stacking contexts becomes crucial when dealing with complex layouts:

#css

```css
.modal-backdrop {
    position: fixed;
    top: 0;
    left: 0;
    width: 100%;
    height: 100%;
    background-color: rgba(0, 0, 0, 0.5);
    z-index: 1000;
}
```

```css
.modal-content {
    position: fixed;
    top: 50%;
    left: 50%;
    transform: translate(-50%, -50%);
    width: 400px;
    height: 300px;
    background-color: white;
    border-radius: 8px;
    box-shadow: 0 4px 20px rgba(0, 0, 0, 0.3);
    z-index: 1001;
}

.tooltip {
    position: absolute;
    bottom: 100%;
    left: 50%;
    transform: translateX(-50%);
    padding: 8px 12px;
    background-color: black;
    color: white;
    border-radius: 4px;
    z-index: 1002;
}
```

Negative Z-index Values

Negative z-index values push elements behind their stacking context:

#css

```
.background-decoration {
    position: absolute;
    top: 0;
    left: 0;
    width: 100%;
    height: 100%;
    background-image: linear-gradient(45deg, #f0f0f0,
#e0e0e0);
    z-index: -1;
}
```

7.3 Positioning Context and Offset Values

Establishing Positioning Context

The positioning context determines what an absolutely positioned element positions itself relative to. Any element with position set to relative, absolute, fixed, or sticky creates a positioning context for its absolutely positioned descendants.

#css

```
.card {
    position: relative;
    width: 300px;
    height: 200px;
    border: 1px solid #ccc;
    border-radius: 8px;
}

.badge {
    position: absolute;
```

```
    top: -10px;
    right: -10px;
    width: 30px;
    height: 30px;
    background-color: red;
    border-radius: 50%;
    display: flex;
    align-items: center;
    justify-content: center;
    color: white;
    font-weight: bold;
}
```

Understanding Offset Properties

The top, right, bottom, and left properties define how far an element should be from the edges of its positioning context:

#css

```
.corner-elements {
    position: relative;
    width: 400px;
    height: 300px;
    border: 2px solid black;
}

.top-left {
    position: absolute;
    top: 10px;
    left: 10px;
```

```
    width: 50px;
    height: 50px;
    background-color: red;
}

.top-right {
    position: absolute;
    top: 10px;
    right: 10px;
    width: 50px;
    height: 50px;
    background-color: blue;
}

.bottom-left {
    position: absolute;
    bottom: 10px;
    left: 10px;
    width: 50px;
    height: 50px;
    background-color: green;
}

.bottom-right {
    position: absolute;
    bottom: 10px;
    right: 10px;
    width: 50px;
    height: 50px;
    background-color: yellow;
}
```

Percentage Values in Positioning

Percentage values in positioning are calculated relative to the containing block's dimensions:

#css

```
.percentage-positioned {
    position: absolute;
    top: 25%;          /* 25% of container height from top
*/
    left: 50%;         /* 50% of container width from left
*/
    width: 30%;        /* 30% of container width */
    height: 40%;       /* 40% of container height */
    transform: translateX(-50%); /* Center horizontally
*/
}
```

Auto Values and Centering

Using auto values with positioning can create interesting centering effects:

#css

```
.horizontal-center {
    position: absolute;
    left: 0;
    right: 0;
    margin: 0 auto;
    width: 200px;
    height: 100px;
```

```
}

.vertical-center {
    position: absolute;
    top: 0;
    bottom: 0;
    margin: auto 0;
    width: 200px;
    height: 100px;
}

.full-center {
    position: absolute;
    top: 0;
    right: 0;
    bottom: 0;
    left: 0;
    margin: auto;
    width: 200px;
    height: 100px;
}
```

7.4 Sticky Position Explained

Basic Sticky Positioning

Sticky positioning combines aspects of relative and fixed positioning. A sticky element starts as relatively positioned but becomes fixed when it reaches a specified scroll position. This creates effects where elements "stick" to the viewport while scrolling.

#css

```css
.sticky-header {
    position: sticky;
    top: 0;
    background-color: white;
    border-bottom: 1px solid #ccc;
    padding: 10px 0;
}

.sticky-sidebar {
    position: sticky;
    top: 20px;
    height: fit-content;
}
```

#html

```html
<div class="container">
    <header class="sticky-header">
        <h2>This header sticks to the top when
scrolling</h2>
    </header>
    <div class="content-layout">
        <main class="main-content">
            <p>Long content that scrolls...</p>
            <!-- More content -->
        </main>
        <aside class="sticky-sidebar">
            <nav>Navigation that sticks while
scrolling</nav>
        </aside>
    </div>
```

```
</div>
```

Sticky Positioning Requirements

For sticky positioning to work effectively, several conditions must be met:

- The element must have at least one of top, right, bottom, or left specified
- The element's parent must have enough height for scrolling to occur
- The sticky element must not be clipped by an ancestor with overflow: hidden

Advanced Sticky Patterns

Creating multiple sticky elements with different stick points:

#css

```
.sticky-nav {
    position: sticky;
    top: 0;
    background-color: #333;
    color: white;
    padding: 15px 0;
    z-index: 100;
}

.sticky-subheader {
    position: sticky;
    top: 60px; /* Sticks below the main nav */
    background-color: #666;
    color: white;
```

```
    padding: 10px 0;
    z-index: 99;
}

.section-header {
    position: sticky;
    top: 120px; /* Sticks below both previous sticky elements */
    background-color: #999;
    padding: 8px 0;
    z-index: 98;
}
```

Sticky Table Headers

One of the most practical applications of sticky positioning is for table headers:

#css

```
.sticky-table {
    border-collapse: collapse;
    width: 100%;
    max-height: 400px;
    overflow-y: auto;
    display: block;
}

.sticky-table thead {
    position: sticky;
    top: 0;
    background-color: #f8f9fa;
```

```
    z-index: 10;
}

.sticky-table th,
.sticky-table td {
    padding: 12px;
    text-align: left;
    border-bottom: 1px solid #ddd;
}
```

7.5 Positioning Use Cases in Layouts

Modal and Dialog Creation

Positioning is essential for creating modal dialogs and overlay interfaces:

#css

```
.modal-overlay {
    position: fixed;
    top: 0;
    left: 0;
    width: 100%;
    height: 100%;
    background-color: rgba(0, 0, 0, 0.6);
    display: flex;
    align-items: center;
    justify-content: center;
    z-index: 1000;
}
```

```
.modal-dialog {
    position: relative;
    background-color: white;
    border-radius: 8px;
    box-shadow: 0 10px 30px rgba(0, 0, 0, 0.3);
    max-width: 500px;
    width: 90%;
    max-height: 80vh;
    overflow-y: auto;
}

.modal-close {
    position: absolute;
    top: 15px;
    right: 20px;
    background: none;
    border: none;
    font-size: 24px;
    cursor: pointer;
    z-index: 1;
}
```

Dropdown Menu Systems

Creating sophisticated dropdown menus using positioning:

#css

```
.dropdown-container {
    position: relative;
    display: inline-block;
```

```
}

.dropdown-trigger {
    padding: 10px 15px;
    background-color: #007bff;
    color: white;
    border: none;
    cursor: pointer;
}

.dropdown-menu {
    position: absolute;
    top: 100%;
    left: 0;
    min-width: 200px;
    background-color: white;
    border: 1px solid #ccc;
    border-radius: 4px;
    box-shadow: 0 4px 8px rgba(0, 0, 0, 0.1);
    z-index: 100;
    opacity: 0;
    visibility: hidden;
    transform: translateY(-10px);
    transition: all 0.3s ease;
}

.dropdown-container:hover .dropdown-menu {
    opacity: 1;
    visibility: visible;
    transform: translateY(0);
}
```

```
.dropdown-item {
    display: block;
    padding: 10px 15px;
    text-decoration: none;
    color: #333;
    border-bottom: 1px solid #eee;
}

.dropdown-item:hover {
    background-color: #f8f9fa;
}
```

Tooltip Implementation

Creating informative tooltips with positioning:

#css

```
.tooltip-container {
    position: relative;
    display: inline-block;
    cursor: help;
}

.tooltip-text {
    position: absolute;
    bottom: 125%;
    left: 50%;
    transform: translateX(-50%);
    background-color: black;
```

```
    color: white;
    padding: 8px 12px;
    border-radius: 4px;
    font-size: 14px;
    white-space: nowrap;
    opacity: 0;
    visibility: hidden;
    transition: opacity 0.3s ease;
    z-index: 1000;
}

.tooltip-text::after {
    content: '';
    position: absolute;
    top: 100%;
    left: 50%;
    transform: translateX(-50%);
    border: 5px solid transparent;
    border-top-color: black;
}

.tooltip-container:hover .tooltip-text {
    opacity: 1;
    visibility: visible;
}
```

Card Overlay Effects

Creating sophisticated card layouts with overlay information:

#css

```css
.card-container {
    position: relative;
    width: 300px;
    height: 200px;
    border-radius: 8px;
    overflow: hidden;
    cursor: pointer;
}

.card-image {
    width: 100%;
    height: 100%;
    object-fit: cover;
    transition: transform 0.3s ease;
}

.card-overlay {
    position: absolute;
    top: 0;
    left: 0;
    right: 0;
    bottom: 0;
    background: linear-gradient(
        to bottom,
        transparent 0%,
        rgba(0, 0, 0, 0.8) 100%
    );
    display: flex;
    align-items: flex-end;
```

```
    padding: 20px;
    color: white;
    opacity: 0;
    transition: opacity 0.3s ease;
}

.card-container:hover .card-image {
    transform: scale(1.1);
}

.card-container:hover .card-overlay {
    opacity: 1;
}
```

Floating Action Buttons

Creating modern floating action buttons:

#css

```
.fab-container {
    position: fixed;
    bottom: 30px;
    right: 30px;
    z-index: 1000;
}

.fab-main {
    width: 60px;
    height: 60px;
    border-radius: 50%;
```

```
    background-color: #ff4081;
    border: none;
    box-shadow: 0 4px 12px rgba(0, 0, 0, 0.3);
    cursor: pointer;
    display: flex;
    align-items: center;
    justify-content: center;
    color: white;
    font-size: 24px;
    transition: all 0.3s ease;
}

.fab-main:hover {
    transform: scale(1.1);
    box-shadow: 0 6px 16px rgba(0, 0, 0, 0.4);
}

.fab-actions {
    position: absolute;
    bottom: 70px;
    right: 0;
    display: flex;
    flex-direction: column;
    gap: 10px;
    opacity: 0;
    visibility: hidden;
    transform: translateY(20px);
    transition: all 0.3s ease;
}

.fab-container:hover .fab-actions {
```

```
    opacity: 1;
    visibility: visible;
    transform: translateY(0);
}

.fab-action {
    width: 48px;
    height: 48px;
    border-radius: 50%;
    background-color: white;
    border: none;
    box-shadow: 0 2px 8px rgba(0, 0, 0, 0.2);
    cursor: pointer;
    display: flex;
    align-items: center;
    justify-content: center;
    transition: all 0.2s ease;
}
```

Layout Grid Overlays

Creating debugging overlays for layout development:

#css

```css
.layout-overlay {
    position: fixed;
    top: 0;
    left: 0;
    width: 100%;
    height: 100%;
```

```
    pointer-events: none;
    z-index: 9999;
    opacity: 0.3;
}

.grid-overlay {
    position: absolute;
    top: 0;
    left: 0;
    width: 100%;
    height: 100%;
    background-image:
        linear-gradient(rgba(255, 0, 0, 0.1) 1px,
transparent 1px),
        linear-gradient(90deg, rgba(255, 0, 0, 0.1) 1px,
transparent 1px);
    background-size: 20px 20px;
}
```

Essential Tips

- Always establish a positioning context with relative positioning on parent containers when using absolute positioning on child elements. This prevents children from positioning relative to the viewport unexpectedly and gives you precise control over their placement within the intended container.
- Use z-index values strategically by creating a systematic numbering scheme rather than random high numbers. Reserve ranges like 1000-1999 for modals, 100-199 for dropdowns, and 10-99 for general overlays to maintain predictable stacking order across your entire project.
- Combine transform properties with positioning for pixel-perfect centering and smooth animations. Using `transform: translate(-50%, -50%)` with `top: 50%; left: 50%` creates

true center alignment regardless of element dimensions, while transform-based animations perform better than changing position values.

- Test sticky positioning thoroughly across different browsers and ensure parent containers have sufficient height and proper overflow settings. Sticky elements need adequate scroll space to function correctly and can behave unexpectedly when constrained by overflow: hidden ancestors.
- Consider the accessibility impact of fixed and absolute positioning, especially for keyboard navigation and screen readers. Ensure positioned elements maintain logical tab order and don't interfere with content accessibility by providing appropriate focus management and semantic markup.

Actionable Strategies

- Create a positioning hierarchy chart for complex projects that maps out z-index ranges, positioning contexts, and element relationships. This documentation prevents conflicts and makes it easier for team members to understand the layout structure when adding new positioned elements.
- Build reusable positioned component patterns like modals, tooltips, and dropdown menus that can be consistently applied across your project. Create CSS classes that handle the positioning logic separately from styling, making components more maintainable and reducing code duplication.
- Implement responsive positioning strategies using media queries to adjust element positions for different screen sizes. What works on desktop may create usability issues on mobile, so plan alternative positioning approaches for smaller viewports, including converting fixed elements to static or relative when appropriate.
- Use CSS custom properties (variables) to manage positioning values consistently across related elements. This approach makes it easier to adjust layouts globally and maintain consistent spacing relationships between positioned elements throughout your design system.
- Develop a testing methodology for positioned elements that includes checking behavior during window resizing, content length changes, and different viewport sizes. Positioned elements can behave unpredictably when content dimensions change, so thorough testing prevents layout breakage in production.

- Master the interaction between positioning and other layout methods like Flexbox and Grid. Understanding when to use positioning versus modern layout methods helps you choose the most appropriate solution for each design challenge and avoid overcomplicating layouts with unnecessary absolute positioning.
- Create performance-optimized positioning by minimizing layout thrashing through careful use of transform and opacity for animations instead of changing position values. Use will-change property judiciously on elements that will be animated, and consider using contain property to limit the scope of layout calculations for complex positioned elements.

Chapter 8: CSS Units and Measurements

Understanding CSS units and measurements forms the foundation of precise layout control and responsive design. This chapter provides comprehensive coverage of absolute and relative units, dynamic calculations, and strategic approaches to unit selection for modern web development.

8.1 Absolute Units: px, in, cm

Understanding Pixel Units (px)

Pixels represent the most commonly used absolute unit in CSS. A pixel corresponds to a single dot on a display screen, making it appear fixed and consistent across different viewing contexts. However, modern displays with varying pixel densities introduce complexity to this seemingly straightforward unit.

#css

```css
.container {
    width: 320px;
    height: 240px;
    border: 2px solid #333;
    margin: 10px;
    padding: 15px;
}

.button {
    width: 120px;
    height: 40px;
    font-size: 14px;
    border-radius: 4px;
}
```

Pixel units provide predictable sizing that remains constant regardless of parent element dimensions or user preferences. This consistency makes pixels ideal for elements requiring precise control, such as borders, small margins, and fixed-width layouts.

Device Pixels vs CSS Pixels

Modern devices distinguish between physical pixels and CSS pixels. High-resolution displays use multiple physical pixels to render a single CSS pixel, maintaining visual consistency across devices with different pixel densities.

#css

```css
.high-res-image {
    width: 200px; /* CSS pixels */
    height: 150px;
    background-image: url('image@2x.png');
    background-size: 200px 150px; /* Matches CSS pixel dimensions */
}

.precise-border {
    border: 1px solid #ddd; /* Always renders as thin line */
    box-shadow: 0 1px 3px rgba(0,0,0,0.1);
}
```

Physical Units: Inches and Centimeters

Physical units like inches (in) and centimeters (cm) provide real-world measurements, though their practical application in web development remains limited due to varying screen sizes and resolutions.

#css

```
.print-header {
    height: 1in; /* One inch tall */
    margin-bottom: 0.5in;
    font-size: 12pt; /* Point units for print */
}

.business-card {
    width: 3.5in; /* Standard business card width */
    height: 2in; /* Standard business card height */
    padding: 0.25in;
}
```

Physical units prove most valuable in print stylesheets where actual measurements matter:

#css

```
@media print {
    .document {
        width: 8.5in;
        height: 11in;
        margin: 1in;
        font-size: 12pt;
        line-height: 1.4;
    }

    .page-break {
        page-break-after: always;
        margin-bottom: 0;
    }
}
```

```
```

Point and Pica Units

Typography-focused units like points (pt) and picas (pc) derive from print design traditions. One point equals 1/72 of an inch, while one pica equals 12 points.

#css

```css
.print-document {
    font-size: 12pt;
    line-height: 14pt;
    margin: 72pt; /* One inch margin */
}

.heading-large {
    font-size: 24pt;
    margin-bottom: 12pt;
    letter-spacing: -0.5pt;
}
```

When to Use Absolute Units

Absolute units excel in specific scenarios:

- Fixed-width layouts requiring precise control
- Print stylesheets with exact measurements
- Small decorative elements like borders and dividers
- Icons and buttons with consistent sizing requirements

#css

```css
.icon-grid {
```

```
    display: grid;
    grid-template-columns: repeat(auto-fit, 48px);
    gap: 8px;
    padding: 16px;
}

.icon {
    width: 48px;
    height: 48px;
    border-radius: 8px;
    background-size: 24px 24px;
    background-position: center;
    background-repeat: no-repeat;
}
```

8.2 Relative Units: %, em, rem, vw, vh

Percentage Units (%)

Percentage units create relationships between child and parent elements, enabling flexible layouts that adapt to container dimensions. The percentage always refers to a property of the parent element.

#css

```
.sidebar {
    width: 25%; /* 25% of parent container width */
    height: 100%; /* Full height of parent */
    background-color: #f5f5f5;
    padding: 2%;
}
```

```css
.main-content {
    width: 75%; /* Remaining width after sidebar */
    padding: 3% 4%;
    margin-left: 25%; /* Same as sidebar width */
}
```

Different properties reference different parent dimensions:

#css

```css
.responsive-container {
    width: 90%; /* 90% of parent width */
    height: 60%; /* 60% of parent height */
    margin: 5% auto; /* 5% of parent width for top/bottom
*/
    padding: 3% 5%; /* 3% height, 5% width */
}

.flexible-image {
    width: 100%; /* Full container width */
    height: auto; /* Maintains aspect ratio */
    max-width: 800px; /* Prevents excessive scaling */
}
```

Em Units: Relative to Font Size

Em units scale relative to the current element's font size, creating typography-aware spacing and sizing. One em equals the computed font size of the element.

#css

```css
.article {
    font-size: 16px;
    line-height: 1.5em; /* 24px (16 × 1.5) */
    margin-bottom: 1em; /* 16px spacing */
    padding: 0.75em 1em; /* 12px top/bottom, 16px
left/right */
}

.article h2 {
    font-size: 1.5em; /* 24px (16 × 1.5) */
    margin: 1.5em 0 0.5em; /* 36px top, 12px bottom */
    padding-bottom: 0.25em; /* 6px */
    border-bottom: 1px solid #ddd;
}
```

Em units compound when nested, which can create unexpected results:

#css

```css
.parent {
    font-size: 18px;
}

.child {
    font-size: 1.2em; /* 21.6px (18 × 1.2) */
}

.grandchild {
    font-size: 1.2em; /* 25.92px (21.6 × 1.2) -
compounding effect */
}
```

Rem Units: Root-Relative Sizing

Rem units (root em) reference the root element's font size, eliminating compounding issues while maintaining scalability benefits.

#css

```
html {
    font-size: 16px; /* Base font size */
}

.component {
    font-size: 1.125rem; /* 18px */
    padding: 1rem 1.5rem; /* 16px 24px */
    margin-bottom: 2rem; /* 32px */
    border-radius: 0.5rem; /* 8px */
}

.large-heading {
    font-size: 2.5rem; /* 40px */
    line-height: 1.2;
    margin: 2rem 0 1rem; /* 32px top, 16px bottom */
}
```

Rem units provide consistent scaling across nested elements:

#css

```
.card {
    padding: 1.5rem;
```

```
    margin-bottom: 1rem;
    border-radius: 0.5rem;
}

.card-title {
    font-size: 1.25rem; /* Always 20px regardless of
nesting */
    margin-bottom: 0.75rem;
}

.card-content {
    font-size: 1rem; /* Always 16px */
    line-height: 1.6;
}
```

Viewport Units: vw, vh, vmin, vmax

Viewport units scale relative to the browser window dimensions, enabling true full-screen layouts and responsive typography.

#css

```
.hero-section {
    width: 100vw; /* Full viewport width */
    height: 100vh; /* Full viewport height */
    display: flex;
    align-items: center;
    justify-content: center;
    background: linear-gradient(45deg, #667eea 0%,
#764ba2 100%);
}
```

```
.hero-text {
    font-size: 4vw; /* Scales with viewport width */
    max-font-size: 3rem; /* Prevents excessive scaling */
    min-font-size: 1.5rem; /* Maintains readability */
    text-align: center;
    color: white;
}
```

Viewport units enable responsive spacing and sizing:

#css

```
.section {
    padding: 5vh 5vw; /* Responsive padding */
    min-height: 50vh; /* Minimum half-screen height */
}

.responsive-grid {
    display: grid;
    grid-template-columns: repeat(auto-fit, minmax(25vw,
300px));
    gap: 3vw;
    padding: 2vw;
}
```

Using vmin and vmax for balanced scaling:

#css

```
.square-element {
```

```
    width: 20vmin; /* 20% of smaller viewport dimension
*/
    height: 20vmin; /* Creates perfect square */
    border-radius: 50%;
    background-color: #3498db;
}

.wide-banner {
    width: 90vmax; /* 90% of larger viewport dimension */
    height: 10vmin;
    background-color: #e74c3c;
}
```

Container Query Units

Modern CSS introduces container query units that reference container dimensions rather than viewport:

#css

```
.card-container {
    container-type: inline-size;
    width: 100%;
    max-width: 800px;
}

.adaptive-card {
    padding: 2cqw; /* 2% of container width */
    font-size: calc(1rem + 1cqw); /* Responsive font size
*/
    border-radius: 1cqw;
}
```

```
```

8.3 Using calc() for Dynamic Values

Basic calc() Functionality

The calc() function performs mathematical calculations using different unit types, enabling dynamic sizing that combines fixed and flexible measurements.

#css

```css
.flexible-sidebar {
    width: calc(25% - 20px); /* Percentage minus fixed margin */
    padding: 15px;
    margin-right: 20px;
    background-color: #f8f9fa;
}

.main-content {
    width: calc(75% - 20px); /* Remaining space minus margin */
    padding: 20px;
    margin-left: 20px;
}
```

Complex Calculations

calc() supports addition, subtraction, multiplication, and division with proper operator spacing:

#css

```css
.responsive-container {
```

```
    width: calc(100% - 40px); /* Full width minus margins */
    max-width: calc(1200px - 4rem); /* Max width with padding consideration */
    margin: 0 auto;
    padding: calc(2rem + 1vw) calc(1rem + 2vw);
}

.dynamic-height {
    height: calc(100vh - 80px); /* Full height minus header */
    min-height: calc(400px + 5vh); /* Minimum plus viewport bonus */
    overflow-y: auto;
}
```

Combining Unit Types

calc() excels at mixing absolute and relative units for precise control:

#css

```
.header {
    height: 60px;
    position: fixed;
    top: 0;
    width: 100%;
    background-color: #333;
    z-index: 1000;
}

.content-wrapper {
```

```
    padding-top: calc(60px + 2rem); /* Header height plus
spacing */
    min-height: calc(100vh - 60px); /* Full height minus
header */
}

.flexible-columns {
    display: grid;
    grid-template-columns:
        250px /* Fixed sidebar */
        calc(100% - 250px - 2rem); /* Flexible main area
*/
    gap: 2rem;
}
```

Advanced calc() Techniques

Nested calculations and complex formulas create sophisticated layouts:

#css

```
.proportional-spacing {
    font-size: calc(1rem + 0.5vw);
    line-height: calc(1.4 + 0.2vw);
    margin-bottom: calc(1em + 0.5vh);
    padding: calc(1rem + 1vw) calc(1.5rem + 2vw);
}

.aspect-ratio-container {
    width: 100%;
    height: calc(100vw * 9 / 16); /* 16:9 aspect ratio */
```

```
    max-height: calc(100vh - 120px); /* Prevent overflow
*/
    background-color: #000;
    display: flex;
    align-items: center;
    justify-content: center;
}
```

calc() with CSS Custom Properties

Combining calc() with CSS variables creates maintainable, dynamic systems:

#css

```
:root {
    --header-height: 70px;
    --sidebar-width: 280px;
    --base-spacing: 1rem;
    --responsive-factor: 2vw;
}

.layout-container {
    margin-top: var(--header-height);
    padding-left: var(--sidebar-width);
    min-height: calc(100vh - var(--header-height));
}

.content-section {
    padding: calc(var(--base-spacing) + var(--responsive-
factor));
    margin-bottom: calc(var(--base-spacing) * 2);
```

```
    width: calc(100% - var(--sidebar-width) - var(--base-
spacing) * 2);
}
```

8.4 Best Practices for Responsive Design Units

Mobile-First Approach

Start with mobile-friendly units and enhance for larger screens:

#css

```
.container {
    width: 100%;
    padding: 1rem;
    font-size: 1rem;
    line-height: 1.5;
}

@media (min-width: 768px) {
    .container {
        max-width: 750px;
        margin: 0 auto;
        padding: 2rem;
        font-size: 1.125rem;
    }
}

@media (min-width: 1200px) {
    .container {
        max-width: 1140px;
        padding: 3rem;
```

```
        font-size: 1.25rem;
    }
}
```

Combining Unit Types Strategically

Different units serve different purposes in responsive design:

#css

```
.flexible-card {
    /* Use percentages for flexible widths */
    width: calc(100% - 2rem);
    max-width: 400px; /* Absolute maximum */

    /* Use rem for consistent spacing */
    padding: 1.5rem;
    margin-bottom: 2rem;

    /* Use em for typography-relative elements */
    border-radius: 0.5em;

    /* Use viewport units for responsive elements */
    min-height: 30vh;
}
```

Typography Scaling

Create responsive typography systems using multiple unit types:

#css

```css
:root {
    --font-size-small: clamp(0.875rem, 2vw, 1rem);
    --font-size-base: clamp(1rem, 2.5vw, 1.125rem);
    --font-size-large: clamp(1.25rem, 4vw, 1.75rem);
    --font-size-xl: clamp(1.875rem, 6vw, 3rem);
}

.heading-primary {
    font-size: var(--font-size-xl);
    line-height: 1.2;
    margin-bottom: calc(var(--font-size-base) * 0.75);
}

.body-text {
    font-size: var(--font-size-base);
    line-height: 1.6;
    margin-bottom: 1.5em;
}
```

Flexible Grid Systems

Create adaptable grid layouts using appropriate units:

#css

```css
.responsive-grid {
    display: grid;
    gap: clamp(1rem, 3vw, 2rem);
    grid-template-columns: repeat(auto-fit, minmax(250px,
1fr));
    padding: clamp(1rem, 5vw, 3rem);
```

```
}

.grid-item {
    background-color: #f8f9fa;
    padding: 1.5rem;
    border-radius: 0.5rem;
    min-height: 200px;
}
```

Accessible Unit Choices

Consider user preferences and accessibility requirements:

#css

```
@media (prefers-reduced-motion: reduce) {
    .animated-element {
        transition: none;
        transform: none;
    }
}

.accessible-text {
    font-size: max(1rem, 16px); /* Never smaller than
16px */
    line-height: max(1.5, 1.5em); /* Minimum line height
*/
    padding: max(0.75rem, 12px); /* Minimum touch target
*/
}
```

8.5 Converting Units Intelligently

Understanding Conversion Context

Unit conversion requires understanding the relationship between different measurement systems and their intended use cases.

Absolute to Relative Conversions

Converting fixed pixel values to flexible units:

#css

```css
/* Original pixel-based design */
.old-design {
    width: 960px;
    padding: 20px;
    font-size: 16px;
    margin: 40px auto;
}

/* Converted to flexible units */
.new-design {
    width: min(90%, 960px); /* Flexible with maximum */
    padding: clamp(1rem, 3vw, 2rem); /* Responsive padding */
    font-size: clamp(1rem, 2.5vw, 1.125rem); /* Scalable text */
    margin: clamp(2rem, 5vh, 4rem) auto; /* Responsive margins */
}
```

Creating Conversion Functions

Use CSS custom properties to maintain conversion relationships:

#css

```
:root {
    --base-font-size: 16px;
    --px-to-rem: calc(1rem / 16); /* Conversion factor */

    /* Converted values */
    --spacing-xs: calc(4 * var(--px-to-rem)); /* 4px ->
0.25rem */
    --spacing-sm: calc(8 * var(--px-to-rem)); /* 8px ->
0.5rem */
    --spacing-md: calc(16 * var(--px-to-rem)); /* 16px ->
1rem */
    --spacing-lg: calc(24 * var(--px-to-rem)); /* 24px ->
1.5rem */
    --spacing-xl: calc(32 * var(--px-to-rem)); /* 32px ->
2rem */
}
```

Smart Unit Selection Strategies

Choose units based on the element's purpose and behavior:

#css

```
.component-library {
    /* Borders: Always use px for precision */
    border: 1px solid #ddd;

    /* Spacing: Use rem for consistency */
```

```
    padding: 1rem 1.5rem;
    margin-bottom: 2rem;

    /* Typography: Mix rem and em strategically */
    font-size: 1rem; /* Base size in rem */
    line-height: 1.5; /* Unitless for proportional
scaling */

    /* Responsive elements: Use clamp() or viewport units
*/
    width: clamp(250px, 50vw, 400px);

    /* Decorative elements: Use em for scaling */
    border-radius: 0.25em;
    box-shadow: 0 0.125em 0.25em rgba(0,0,0,0.1);
}
```

Conversion Validation Techniques

Test conversions across different contexts:

#css

```
.conversion-test {
    /* Original design at 16px base */
    font-size: 1rem; /* 16px */
    padding: 0.75rem; /* 12px */
    margin: 1.5rem; /* 24px */

    /* Test at different base sizes */
    --test-small: 14px;
```

```
    --test-large: 20px;
}

/* Verify conversions maintain proportions */
@media (max-width: 480px) {
    html { font-size: 14px; }
}

@media (min-width: 1200px) {
    html { font-size: 18px; }
}
```

Migration Strategies

Gradual conversion from absolute to relative units:

#css

```
/* Phase 1: Maintain existing layout with CSS variables
*/
:root {
    --container-width: 960px;
    --header-height: 80px;
    --base-spacing: 20px;
}

/* Phase 2: Add responsive alternatives */
:root {
    --container-width: min(90%, 960px);
    --header-height: clamp(60px, 10vh, 80px);
    --base-spacing: clamp(1rem, 3vw, 1.5rem);
```

```
}

/* Phase 3: Full responsive implementation */
.migrated-component {
    width: var(--container-width);
    padding-top: var(--header-height);
    margin: var(--base-spacing);
}
```

Essential Tips

- **Always specify a base font size on the html element** to ensure rem units have a consistent reference point across different browsers and user settings.
- **Use unitless values for line-height** to maintain proportional spacing that scales naturally with font size changes, avoiding inheritance issues.
- **Combine min(), max(), and clamp() functions** with different unit types to create truly flexible layouts that work across all device sizes without media queries.
- **Test your designs with browser zoom levels from 50% to 200%** to ensure units scale appropriately and maintain usability at different magnification levels.
- **Avoid mixing too many different unit types** within a single component to maintain consistency and predictable behavior across different viewing contexts.

Actionable Strategies

- **Establish a spacing scale using rem units** based on multiples of your base font size (0.25rem, 0.5rem, 1rem, 1.5rem, 2rem) to create visual harmony throughout your design system.
- **Create CSS custom properties for commonly used measurements** and conversion factors to maintain consistency and enable easy global adjustments across your entire stylesheet.

- **Use calc() to combine fixed header heights with flexible content areas** ensuring full viewport utilization while maintaining precise layout control for navigation elements.
- **Implement clamp() for typography scaling** to eliminate the need for multiple media queries while ensuring text remains readable across all screen sizes and user preferences.
- **Leverage viewport units for hero sections and full-screen elements** while setting reasonable minimum and maximum constraints to prevent extreme scaling on very large or small screens.
- **Apply container queries with container-relative units** for component-level responsiveness that adapts to available space rather than viewport dimensions, creating more modular designs.
- **Use em units for component-internal spacing** that should scale with the component's font size, such as button padding, icon sizing, and border radius values that maintain visual proportions.

Chapter 9: Margins and Padding Mastery

Understanding margins and padding forms the cornerstone of effective CSS layout design. These two properties control the spacing around and within elements, determining how your content breathes on the page and how elements relate to each other spatially. Mastering these concepts allows you to create visually appealing, well-structured layouts that enhance user experience and readability.

9.1 Applying Margin and Padding Individually

Understanding the Box Model Foundation

Every HTML element exists within a rectangular box, consisting of four distinct areas: content, padding, border, and margin. The content area holds your text, images, or other elements. Padding creates space between the content and the border, while margin generates space outside the border, separating the element from its neighbors.

Individual Margin Properties

CSS provides four individual margin properties that correspond to each side of an element:

- `margin-top`: Controls space above the element
- `margin-right`: Controls space to the right of the element
- `margin-bottom`: Controls space below the element
- `margin-left`: Controls space to the left of the element

#css

```
.example-box {
    margin-top: 20px;
    margin-right: 15px;
    margin-bottom: 25px;
    margin-left: 10px;
    background-color: #e3f2fd;
```

```
    padding: 10px;
}
```

This approach offers precise control over spacing, allowing you to fine-tune the positioning of elements based on their specific requirements within your layout.

Individual Padding Properties

Similarly, padding can be controlled individually for each side:

- `padding-top`: Creates internal space at the top
- `padding-right`: Creates internal space on the right
- `padding-bottom`: Creates internal space at the bottom
- `padding-left`: Creates internal space on the left

#css

```
.content-card {
    padding-top: 30px;
    padding-right: 20px;
    padding-bottom: 30px;
    padding-left: 20px;
    background-color: #f5f5f5;
    border: 1px solid #ddd;
}
```

Practical Applications of Individual Properties

Individual margin and padding properties prove particularly useful when creating asymmetrical designs or when specific sides require different spacing values. For instance, a navigation menu might need extra padding on the left and right sides but minimal padding on the top and bottom.

#css

```css
.nav-item {
    padding-top: 8px;
    padding-right: 24px;
    padding-bottom: 8px;
    padding-left: 24px;
    margin-right: 5px;
    background-color: #007bff;
    color: white;
    border-radius: 4px;
}
```

Understanding Value Units

Margins and padding accept various unit types, each serving different purposes:

Absolute Units:

- `px` (pixels): Fixed size regardless of screen or parent element
- `pt` (points): Primarily used for print media
- `cm`, `mm`, `in`: Physical measurements

Relative Units:

- `em`: Relative to the element's font size
- `rem`: Relative to the root element's font size
- `%`: Relative to the parent element's dimensions
- `vh`, `vw`: Relative to viewport height and width

#css

```css
.responsive-element {
    margin-top: 2em;        /* Scales with font size */
```

```
    margin-right: 5%;        /* Scales with parent width
*/
    padding-left: 1.5rem;    /* Consistent across elements
*/
    padding-bottom: 10px;    /* Fixed pixel value */
}
```

9.2 Shorthand Notation Explained

The Power of Shorthand Properties

Shorthand notation provides an efficient method for setting multiple values simultaneously, reducing code repetition and improving maintainability. The margin and padding shorthand properties follow specific patterns that, once understood, significantly streamline your CSS writing process.

Single Value Shorthand

When you specify a single value, it applies to all four sides equally:

#css

```
.uniform-spacing {
    margin: 20px;      /* All sides get 20px margin */
    padding: 15px;     /* All sides get 15px padding */
}
```

This approach works well for elements requiring uniform spacing, such as buttons, cards, or containers where consistent spacing enhances visual harmony.

Two Value Shorthand

With two values, the first applies to top and bottom, while the second applies to left and right:

#css

```
.vertical-horizontal {
    margin: 30px 20px;     /* 30px top/bottom, 20px
left/right */
    padding: 15px 25px;    /* 15px top/bottom, 25px
left/right */
}
```

This pattern frequently appears in responsive design, where vertical spacing needs to differ from horizontal spacing to accommodate various screen sizes and reading patterns.

Three Value Shorthand

Three values follow the pattern: top, left/right, bottom:

#css

```
.three-value-example {
    margin: 20px 15px 30px;     /* 20px top, 15px
left/right, 30px bottom */
    padding: 10px 20px 15px;    /* 10px top, 20px
left/right, 15px bottom */
}
```

This configuration proves useful when the bottom spacing needs to differ from the top, while maintaining symmetrical left and right spacing.

Four Value Shorthand

Four values provide complete control, following clockwise order: top, right, bottom, left:

#css

```
.complete-control {
    margin: 10px 15px 20px 25px;    /* top, right, bottom, left */
    padding: 5px 10px 15px 8px;     /* top, right, bottom, left */
}
```

Remember the mnemonic "TRouBLe" (Top, Right, Bottom, Left) to recall the clockwise order.

Mixing Units in Shorthand

Shorthand properties allow mixing different units, providing flexibility for responsive designs:

#css

```
.mixed-units {
    margin: 2em 5% 1rem 20px;
    padding: 1vh 2vw 10px 1em;
}
```

Advanced Shorthand Techniques

You can combine shorthand with individual properties for fine-tuned control:

#css

```
.hybrid-approach {
```

```
    margin: 20px;              /* Set all sides to 20px */
    margin-bottom: 40px;       /* Override bottom margin */
    padding: 15px 25px;        /* Set vertical and
horizontal */
    padding-left: 35px;        /* Override left padding */
}
```

This technique allows you to establish base spacing values quickly, then customize specific sides as needed.

9.3 Collapsing Margins

Understanding Margin Collapse Behavior

Margin collapse represents one of CSS's most misunderstood concepts, yet mastering it prevents countless layout frustrations. When two or more margins meet, they don't simply add together as you might expect. Instead, they "collapse" into a single margin whose size equals the largest of the collapsing margins.

Vertical Margin Collapse

Vertical margin collapse occurs between adjacent block-level elements. Consider two paragraphs with different bottom and top margins:

#css

```
.first-paragraph {
    margin-bottom: 30px;
    background-color: #ffebee;
    padding: 10px;
}
```

```css
.second-paragraph {
    margin-top: 20px;
    background-color: #e8f5e8;
    padding: 10px;
}
```

Rather than creating 50px of space between these paragraphs (30px + 20px), margin collapse results in only 30px of space—the larger of the two margins.

Parent-Child Margin Collapse

Margin collapse also occurs between parent and child elements when no padding, border, or content separates their margins:

#css

```css
.parent-container {
    margin-top: 40px;
    background-color: #f0f0f0;
}

.child-element {
    margin-top: 60px;
    background-color: #fff;
    padding: 15px;
}
```

In this scenario, the child's larger margin (60px) collapses with the parent's margin (40px), resulting in a single 60px margin at the top of the parent container.

Empty Element Margin Collapse

Empty elements with no height, padding, or border experience margin collapse between their own top and bottom margins:

#css

```
.empty-element {
    margin-top: 25px;
    margin-bottom: 35px;
    /* No content, padding, or border */
}
```

The margins collapse into a single 35px margin (the larger value).

Preventing Margin Collapse

Several techniques prevent margin collapse when needed:

Adding Padding or Border:

#css

```
.parent-with-padding {
    padding-top: 1px;
    margin-top: 40px;
}

.parent-with-border {
    border-top: 1px solid transparent;
    margin-top: 40px;
}
```

Using Overflow Property:

#css

```
.overflow-container {
    overflow: hidden;
    margin-top: 40px;
}
```

Applying Display Properties:

#css

```
.flex-container {
    display: flex;
    flex-direction: column;
    margin-top: 40px;
}

.inline-block-element {
    display: inline-block;
    margin-top: 40px;
}
```

Strategic Use of Margin Collapse

Rather than fighting margin collapse, you can leverage it for consistent spacing:

#css

```
.content-section {
    margin-bottom: 2rem;
```

```
}

.content-section h2 {
    margin-top: 2rem;
    margin-bottom: 1rem;
}

.content-section p {
    margin-bottom: 1rem;
}
```

This approach ensures consistent spacing between sections while allowing natural content flow within each section.

Horizontal Margins and Inline Elements

Horizontal margins never collapse, and inline elements handle margins differently than block elements:

#css

```
.inline-element {
    display: inline;
    margin: 20px;  /* Only left and right margins apply
*/
}

.inline-block-element {
    display: inline-block;
    margin: 20px;  /* All margins apply */
}
```

9.4 Centering with Margin Auto

The Margin Auto Technique

The `margin: auto` property provides a powerful method for centering block-level elements horizontally within their containers. This technique calculates available space automatically and distributes it evenly on both sides of the element.

Basic Horizontal Centering

To center a block element horizontally, apply `margin: 0 auto`:

#css

```css
.centered-container {
    width: 600px;
    margin: 0 auto;
    background-color: #e3f2fd;
    padding: 20px;
}
```

The first value (0) sets top and bottom margins to zero, while `auto` distributes the remaining horizontal space equally between left and right margins.

Requirements for Margin Auto Centering

Margin auto centering requires specific conditions:

- **Block-level element**: The element must be block-level or block-like
- **Defined width**: The element must have a specified width less than its container
- **Sufficient container space**: The parent container must be wider than the element

#css

```css
.page-wrapper {
    max-width: 1200px;
    margin: 0 auto;
    padding: 0 20px;
}

.content-card {
    width: 80%;
    max-width: 800px;
    margin: 2rem auto;
    background-color: white;
    box-shadow: 0 2px 10px rgba(0, 0, 0, 0.1);
    padding: 2rem;
}
```

Centering with Flexbox Alternative

Modern CSS provides flexbox as an alternative centering method:

#css

```css
.flex-container {
    display: flex;
    justify-content: center;
    align-items: center;
    min-height: 100vh;
}

.flex-item {
```

```
    width: 400px;
    padding: 2rem;
    background-color: #f8f9fa;
}
```

Centering Multiple Elements

When centering multiple elements, consider their relationship:

#css

```
.gallery-container {
    max-width: 1000px;
    margin: 0 auto;
    padding: 2rem;
}

.gallery-item {
    width: 300px;
    margin: 1rem auto;
    display: block;
}

/* For inline-block elements */
.inline-gallery {
    text-align: center;
    max-width: 1000px;
    margin: 0 auto;
}

.inline-gallery-item {
```

```
    display: inline-block;
    width: 200px;
    margin: 0 10px 2rem;
}
```

Responsive Centering Techniques

Combine margin auto with responsive design principles:

#css

```
.responsive-center {
    width: 90%;
    max-width: 1200px;
    margin: 0 auto;
    padding: 0 1rem;
}

@media (min-width: 768px) {
    .responsive-center {
        width: 80%;
        padding: 0 2rem;
    }
}

@media (min-width: 1024px) {
    .responsive-center {
        width: 70%;
        padding: 0;
    }
}
```

Advanced Centering Scenarios

For complex layouts, combine margin auto with other positioning techniques:

#css

```
.modal-overlay {
    position: fixed;
    top: 0;
    left: 0;
    width: 100%;
    height: 100%;
    background-color: rgba(0, 0, 0, 0.5);
    display: flex;
    align-items: center;
    justify-content: center;
}

.modal-content {
    width: 90%;
    max-width: 500px;
    margin: 0 auto;
    background-color: white;
    border-radius: 8px;
    padding: 2rem;
}
```

9.5 Combining Margins and Padding Strategically

Creating Harmonious Spacing Systems

Strategic combination of margins and padding creates visual hierarchy, improves readability, and establishes consistent spacing patterns throughout your design. Understanding when to use margins versus padding determines the success of your layout's visual flow.

Establishing Spacing Hierarchies

Create systematic spacing using a consistent scale:

#css

```css
:root {
    --spacing-xs: 0.25rem;    /* 4px */
    --spacing-sm: 0.5rem;     /* 8px */
    --spacing-md: 1rem;       /* 16px */
    --spacing-lg: 1.5rem;     /* 24px */
    --spacing-xl: 2rem;       /* 32px */
    --spacing-xxl: 3rem;      /* 48px */
}

.card {
    margin-bottom: var(--spacing-xl);
    padding: var(--spacing-lg);
    background-color: white;
    border-radius: 8px;
    box-shadow: 0 2px 4px rgba(0, 0, 0, 0.1);
}

.card-header {
    margin-bottom: var(--spacing-md);
    padding-bottom: var(--spacing-sm);
```

```
    border-bottom: 1px solid #eee;
}

.card-content {
    margin-bottom: var(--spacing-lg);
}

.card-footer {
    padding-top: var(--spacing-sm);
    border-top: 1px solid #eee;
}
```

Component-Based Spacing Strategies

Design reusable components with internal padding and external margins:

#css

```
.button {
    padding: var(--spacing-sm) var(--spacing-lg);
    margin-right: var(--spacing-sm);
    background-color: #007bff;
    color: white;
    border: none;
    border-radius: 4px;
    cursor: pointer;
}

.button-group {
    margin-bottom: var(--spacing-lg);
}
```

```css
.button-group .button:last-child {
    margin-right: 0;
}

.form-field {
    margin-bottom: var(--spacing-lg);
}

.form-field label {
    display: block;
    margin-bottom: var(--spacing-xs);
    font-weight: 600;
}

.form-field input,
.form-field textarea {
    width: 100%;
    padding: var(--spacing-sm);
    border: 1px solid #ddd;
    border-radius: 4px;
}
```

Layout-Specific Spacing Combinations

Different layout patterns require specific margin and padding strategies:

Grid Layouts:

#css

```
.grid-container {
    display: grid;
    grid-template-columns: repeat(auto-fit, minmax(300px,
1fr));
    gap: var(--spacing-lg);
    padding: var(--spacing-lg);
    margin: 0 auto;
    max-width: 1200px;
}

.grid-item {
    padding: var(--spacing-lg);
    background-color: white;
    border-radius: 8px;
}
```

Article Layouts:

#css

```
.article-container {
    max-width: 800px;
    margin: 0 auto;
    padding: var(--spacing-xl) var(--spacing-lg);
}

.article-header {
    margin-bottom: var(--spacing-xxl);
    text-align: center;
}
```

```
.article-content h2 {
    margin-top: var(--spacing-xxl);
    margin-bottom: var(--spacing-lg);
}

.article-content p {
    margin-bottom: var(--spacing-lg);
    line-height: 1.6;
}

.article-content blockquote {
    margin: var(--spacing-xl) 0;
    padding: var(--spacing-lg);
    border-left: 4px solid #007bff;
    background-color: #f8f9fa;
}
```

Responsive Spacing Strategies

Adapt spacing for different screen sizes:

#css

```
.responsive-section {
    padding: var(--spacing-lg) var(--spacing-md);
    margin-bottom: var(--spacing-xl);
}

@media (min-width: 768px) {
    .responsive-section {
        padding: var(--spacing-xl) var(--spacing-lg);
```

```
        margin-bottom: var(--spacing-xxl);
    }
}

@media (min-width: 1024px) {
    .responsive-section {
        padding: var(--spacing-xxl) var(--spacing-xl);
    }
}
```

Negative Margins for Advanced Layouts

Use negative margins strategically for overlapping effects:

#css

```
.hero-section {
    background-color: #007bff;
    padding: var(--spacing-xxl) 0;
    margin-bottom: var(--spacing-xl);
}

.hero-card {
    background-color: white;
    padding: var(--spacing-xl);
    margin: 0 auto;
    margin-top: -2rem;  /* Negative margin for overlap */
    max-width: 600px;
    border-radius: 8px;
    box-shadow: 0 4px 20px rgba(0, 0, 0, 0.1);
}
```

Performance Considerations

Optimize spacing for better performance:

#css

```css
/* Use transform instead of margin for animations */
.animated-element {
    transition: transform 0.3s ease;
}

.animated-element:hover {
    transform: translateY(-4px);
}

/* Prefer margin-bottom over margin-top for better
collapse behavior */
.consistent-spacing {
    margin-bottom: var(--spacing-lg);
}
```

Essential Tips

- **Use relative units (rem, em) for scalable spacing** that adapts to different font sizes and device settings, creating more accessible and flexible designs that work across various user preferences.
- **Establish a consistent spacing scale early in your project** using CSS custom properties or variables, then stick to these predefined values throughout your stylesheet to maintain visual harmony and make global spacing adjustments easier.

- **Apply margins to separate elements from each other** and use padding to create breathing room within elements, following the principle that margins control external relationships while padding manages internal space.
- **Always test your spacing decisions across different screen sizes** using browser developer tools or responsive design testing tools to ensure your spacing choices work well on mobile devices, tablets, and desktop screens.
- **Remember that horizontal margins never collapse** unlike vertical margins, so you can reliably combine left and right margins from adjacent elements without worrying about unexpected spacing behavior.

Actionable Strategies

- **Create a spacing utility class system** with predefined margin and padding classes like `.m-sm`, `.p-lg`, `.mx-auto` to speed up development and maintain consistency across your entire project while reducing the need to write custom spacing rules.
- **Use margin-bottom consistently instead of alternating between margin-top and margin-bottom** to take advantage of margin collapse behavior and create more predictable spacing patterns that are easier to debug and maintain.
- **Implement a mobile-first approach to spacing** by starting with smaller spacing values for mobile devices and progressively increasing spacing for larger screens using media queries, ensuring optimal space usage across all device sizes.
- **Combine CSS Grid gap property with strategic padding** on individual grid items to create flexible, responsive layouts that automatically adjust spacing without requiring complex margin calculations or responsive breakpoint adjustments.
- **Use negative margins sparingly and purposefully** for creating overlapping effects, breaking out of container constraints, or achieving specific design requirements, but always document these instances clearly since they can affect layout flow in unexpected ways.
- **Leverage CSS custom properties for dynamic spacing** that can be adjusted based on user preferences, theme changes, or component states, allowing for more interactive and customizable spacing systems that respond to user needs.

Chapter 10: Borders and Outline Styling

Borders and outlines are fundamental design elements that define the visual boundaries of HTML elements, creating structure, hierarchy, and visual appeal in web layouts. This chapter provides comprehensive coverage of CSS border and outline properties, demonstrating how to create sophisticated visual effects and professional user interface components.

10.1 Basic Border Syntax and Styles

Understanding Border Fundamentals

CSS borders consist of three primary components: width, style, and color. These properties can be applied individually to each side of an element or collectively to all sides simultaneously. The border system provides granular control over element presentation, allowing developers to create precise visual boundaries.

Border Width Properties

Border width determines the thickness of the border line. The width can be specified using various units including pixels, ems, rems, or predefined keywords.

#css

```css
/* Specific width values */
.element-one {
    border-width: 1px;
}

.element-two {
    border-width: thin; /* Equivalent to 1px */
}

.element-three {
```

```
    border-width: medium; /* Equivalent to 3px */
}

.element-four {
    border-width: thick; /* Equivalent to 5px */
}

/* Individual side specifications */
.element-five {
    border-top-width: 2px;
    border-right-width: 4px;
    border-bottom-width: 6px;
    border-left-width: 8px;
}

/* Multiple value syntax */
.element-six {
    border-width: 2px 4px 6px 8px; /* top right bottom
left */
}

.element-seven {
    border-width: 2px 4px; /* top/bottom left/right */
}
```

Border Style Properties

The border style property defines the visual appearance of the border line. CSS provides numerous predefined styles that create different visual effects.

#css

```css
/* Solid borders */
.solid-border {
    border-style: solid;
    border-width: 3px;
    border-color: #333;
}

/* Dashed borders */
.dashed-border {
    border-style: dashed;
    border-width: 2px;
    border-color: #666;
}

/* Dotted borders */
.dotted-border {
    border-style: dotted;
    border-width: 4px;
    border-color: #999;
}

/* Double borders */
.double-border {
    border-style: double;
    border-width: 6px;
    border-color: #444;
}

/* Groove effect */
.groove-border {
```

```
    border-style: groove;
    border-width: 8px;
    border-color: #777;
}

/* Ridge effect */
.ridge-border {
    border-style: ridge;
    border-width: 8px;
    border-color: #555;
}

/* Inset effect */
.inset-border {
    border-style: inset;
    border-width: 6px;
    border-color: #888;
}

/* Outset effect */
.outset-border {
    border-style: outset;
    border-width: 6px;
    border-color: #aaa;
}

/* Individual side styles */
.mixed-styles {
    border-top-style: solid;
    border-right-style: dashed;
    border-bottom-style: dotted;
```

```
    border-left-style: double;
    border-width: 3px;
    border-color: #333;
}
```

Border Color Properties

Border colors can be specified using various color formats including hex values, RGB, RGBA, HSL, HSLA, and named colors. Color transparency allows for sophisticated visual effects.

#css

```
/* Solid colors */
.color-hex {
    border: 3px solid #ff6b6b;
}

.color-rgb {
    border: 3px solid rgb(255, 107, 107);
}

.color-rgba {
    border: 3px solid rgba(255, 107, 107, 0.7);
}

.color-hsl {
    border: 3px solid hsl(0, 100%, 71%);
}

.color-hsla {
```

```css
    border: 3px solid hsla(0, 100%, 71%, 0.8);
}

/* Named colors */
.color-named {
    border: 3px solid crimson;
}

/* Individual side colors */
.multi-color {
    border-width: 4px;
    border-style: solid;
    border-top-color: #ff4757;
    border-right-color: #3742fa;
    border-bottom-color: #2ed573;
    border-left-color: #ffa502;
}

/* Gradient-like effect with multiple elements */
.gradient-border-container {
    position: relative;
    padding: 20px;
}

.gradient-border-container::before {
    content: '';
    position: absolute;
    top: 0;
    left: 0;
    right: 0;
    bottom: 0;
```

```
    background: linear-gradient(45deg, #ff6b6b, #4ecdc4,
#45b7d1, #96ceb4);
    z-index: -1;
    margin: -3px;
}
```

Individual Border Side Properties

CSS provides precise control over each border side, enabling asymmetric designs and complex visual patterns.

#css

```
/* Top border only */
.top-border {
    border-top: 3px solid #e74c3c;
    padding: 15px;
}

/* Bottom border accent */
.bottom-accent {
    border-bottom: 4px solid #3498db;
    padding-bottom: 10px;
}

/* Left sidebar indicator */
.left-indicator {
    border-left: 5px solid #2ecc71;
    padding-left: 20px;
}
```

```css
/* Right edge highlight */
.right-highlight {
    border-right: 2px dashed #f39c12;
    padding-right: 15px;
}

/* Complex combination */
.complex-borders {
    border-top: 2px solid #e74c3c;
    border-right: 1px dashed #3498db;
    border-bottom: 3px double #2ecc71;
    border-left: 4px groove #f39c12;
    padding: 20px;
}
```

10.2 Border Shorthand Property

Understanding Shorthand Syntax

The border shorthand property combines width, style, and color into a single declaration, providing efficient and readable code. The shorthand follows a specific order: width, style, color.

#css

```css
/* Basic shorthand syntax */
.shorthand-basic {
    border: 2px solid #333;
}

/* Equivalent to: */
.longhand-equivalent {
```

```
    border-width: 2px;
    border-style: solid;
    border-color: #333;
}

/* Various shorthand combinations */
.shorthand-thick {
    border: 5px dashed #e74c3c;
}

.shorthand-thin {
    border: 1px dotted #3498db;
}

.shorthand-medium {
    border: 3px double #2ecc71;
}

.shorthand-transparent {
    border: 2px solid transparent;
}
```

Individual Side Shorthands

Each border side can utilize shorthand syntax independently, creating asymmetric designs with concise code.

#css

```
/* Individual side shorthands */
.top-shorthand {
```

```
    border-top: 3px solid #ff6b6b;
}

.right-shorthand {
    border-right: 2px dashed #4ecdc4;
}

.bottom-shorthand {
    border-bottom: 4px double #45b7d1;
}

.left-shorthand {
    border-left: 1px dotted #96ceb4;
}

/* Mixed shorthand and longhand */
.mixed-approach {
    border: 2px solid #ddd; /* Base border */
    border-top: 4px solid #e74c3c; /* Override top */
    border-left-color: #3498db; /* Override left color
only */
}

/* Card-like design with shorthand */
.card-design {
    border: 1px solid #e1e8ed;
    border-top: 3px solid #1da1f2;
    border-radius: 8px;
    padding: 20px;
    background-color: #fff;
    box-shadow: 0 2px 4px rgba(0, 0, 0, 0.1);
```

```
}
```

Advanced Shorthand Techniques

Shorthand properties can be combined with other CSS features to create sophisticated designs efficiently.

#css

```css
/* Conditional borders with CSS variables */
.dynamic-border {
    --border-color: #3498db;
    --border-width: 2px;
    --border-style: solid;
    border: var(--border-width) var(--border-style) var(--border-color);
}

.dynamic-border.error {
    --border-color: #e74c3c;
    --border-width: 3px;
}

.dynamic-border.success {
    --border-color: #2ecc71;
}

/* Hover effects with shorthand */
.interactive-border {
    border: 2px solid transparent;
    transition: border 0.3s ease;
```

```css
}

.interactive-border:hover {
    border: 2px solid #3498db;
}

/* Focus states for form elements */
.form-input {
    border: 1px solid #ddd;
    padding: 10px;
    border-radius: 4px;
    transition: border-color 0.2s ease;
}

.form-input:focus {
    border: 2px solid #3498db;
    outline: none;
}

/* Responsive border adjustments */
@media (max-width: 768px) {
    .responsive-border {
        border: 1px solid #ddd;
    }
}

@media (min-width: 769px) {
    .responsive-border {
        border: 3px solid #333;
    }
}
```

10.3 Rounded Corners with border-radius

Basic Border Radius Concepts

The border-radius property creates rounded corners by defining the radius of the circle used to round each corner. This property transforms sharp rectangular edges into smooth, curved corners.

#css

```css
/* Uniform radius on all corners */
.rounded-basic {
    border-radius: 10px;
    border: 2px solid #3498db;
    padding: 20px;
}

/* Different radius values */
.rounded-small {
    border-radius: 4px;
    border: 1px solid #ddd;
    padding: 15px;
}

.rounded-large {
    border-radius: 20px;
    border: 3px solid #e74c3c;
    padding: 25px;
}

.rounded-extreme {
```

```css
    border-radius: 50px;
    border: 2px solid #2ecc71;
    padding: 30px;
}

/* Circular elements */
.circle {
    width: 100px;
    height: 100px;
    border-radius: 50%;
    border: 3px solid #f39c12;
    display: flex;
    align-items: center;
    justify-content: center;
}
```

Individual Corner Control

Border-radius allows precise control over each corner individually, enabling asymmetric and creative designs.

#css

```css
/* Individual corner properties */
.custom-corners {
    border-top-left-radius: 20px;
    border-top-right-radius: 0px;
    border-bottom-right-radius: 20px;
    border-bottom-left-radius: 0px;
    border: 2px solid #9b59b6;
    padding: 20px;
```

```
}

/* Shorthand for individual corners */
.shorthand-corners {
    border-radius: 20px 0px 20px 0px; /* top-left top-
right bottom-right bottom-left */
    border: 2px solid #e67e22;
    padding: 20px;
}

/* Two-value shorthand */
.two-value-radius {
    border-radius: 15px 5px; /* top-left/bottom-right
top-right/bottom-left */
    border: 2px solid #1abc9c;
    padding: 20px;
}

/* Three-value shorthand */
.three-value-radius {
    border-radius: 20px 10px 5px; /* top-left top-
right/bottom-left bottom-right */
    border: 2px solid #34495e;
    padding: 20px;
}

/* Creative asymmetric designs */
.speech-bubble {
    border-radius: 20px 20px 20px 5px;
    border: 2px solid #3498db;
    padding: 15px;
```

```
    background-color: #ecf0f1;
    position: relative;
}

.speech-bubble::after {
    content: '';
    position: absolute;
    bottom: -10px;
    left: 20px;
    width: 0;
    height: 0;
    border-left: 10px solid transparent;
    border-right: 10px solid transparent;
    border-top: 10px solid #3498db;
}
```

Elliptical Border Radius

Border-radius supports elliptical curves by specifying horizontal and vertical radii separately, creating more sophisticated rounded shapes.

#css

```
/* Elliptical corners */
.elliptical-basic {
    border-radius: 50px / 25px; /* horizontal-radius / vertical-radius */
    border: 2px solid #e74c3c;
    padding: 20px;
    width: 200px;
    height: 100px;
```

```
}

/* Individual elliptical corners */
.elliptical-complex {
    border-top-left-radius: 40px 20px;
    border-top-right-radius: 20px 40px;
    border-bottom-right-radius: 40px 20px;
    border-bottom-left-radius: 20px 40px;
    border: 2px solid #2ecc71;
    padding: 20px;
    width: 250px;
    height: 120px;
}

/* Pill-shaped elements */
.pill-shape {
    height: 50px;
    border-radius: 25px;
    border: 2px solid #f39c12;
    padding: 10px 20px;
    display: inline-flex;
    align-items: center;
}

/* Oval shapes */
.oval-shape {
    width: 150px;
    height: 100px;
    border-radius: 50%;
    border: 3px solid #9b59b6;
    display: flex;
```

```
    align-items: center;
    justify-content: center;
}
```

Advanced Border Radius Techniques

Border-radius can be combined with other CSS properties to create sophisticated visual effects and interactive elements.

#css

```css
/* Animated border radius */
.morphing-shape {
    width: 100px;
    height: 100px;
    border: 3px solid #3498db;
    border-radius: 10px;
    transition: border-radius 0.5s ease;
}

.morphing-shape:hover {
    border-radius: 50%;
}

/* Percentage-based radius */
.percentage-radius {
    width: 200px;
    height: 150px;
    border-radius: 20% 30% 40% 10%;
    border: 2px solid #e67e22;
    background: linear-gradient(45deg, #ff6b6b, #4ecdc4);
```

```
}

/* Complex card designs */
.modern-card {
    border-radius: 12px;
    border: 1px solid rgba(0, 0, 0, 0.1);
    background: white;
    box-shadow: 0 4px 6px rgba(0, 0, 0, 0.1);
    overflow: hidden;
}

.modern-card-header {
    background: linear-gradient(135deg, #667eea 0%,
#764ba2 100%);
    padding: 20px;
    color: white;
    border-radius: 12px 12px 0 0;
}

.modern-card-body {
    padding: 20px;
}

/* Responsive border radius */
@media (max-width: 768px) {
    .responsive-radius {
        border-radius: 8px;
    }
}

@media (min-width: 769px) {
```

```
    .responsive-radius {
        border-radius: 16px;
    }
}
```

10.4 Outline vs Border Differences

Fundamental Differences

Outlines and borders serve different purposes in CSS layouts. While borders are part of the box model and affect element dimensions, outlines are drawn outside the element's border edge without affecting layout flow.

#css

```
/* Border affects layout */
.with-border {
    width: 200px;
    height: 100px;
    border: 5px solid #3498db;
    background-color: #ecf0f1;
    margin: 10px;
}

/* Outline doesn't affect layout */
.with-outline {
    width: 200px;
    height: 100px;
    outline: 5px solid #e74c3c;
    background-color: #ecf0f1;
    margin: 10px;
}
```

```
/* Comparison container */
.comparison-demo {
    display: flex;
    gap: 20px;
    align-items: flex-start;
}
```

Box Model Impact

The box model treats borders and outlines differently, which affects element positioning and spacing calculations.

#css

```
/* Border increases element size */
.border-box-demo {
    width: 200px;
    height: 100px;
    padding: 20px;
    border: 10px solid #2ecc71;
    background-color: #d5f4e6;
    box-sizing: content-box; /* Default behavior */
}

/* Border with border-box sizing */
.border-box-sizing {
    width: 200px;
    height: 100px;
    padding: 20px;
    border: 10px solid #f39c12;
```

```
    background-color: #fdf2e3;
    box-sizing: border-box; /* Includes border in
dimensions */
}

/* Outline never affects dimensions */
.outline-no-impact {
    width: 200px;
    height: 100px;
    padding: 20px;
    outline: 10px solid #9b59b6;
    background-color: #f4ecf7;
    /* Box-sizing doesn't affect outline */
}
```

Outline Properties and Syntax

Outlines share similar properties with borders but have unique characteristics and limitations.

#css

```
/* Basic outline properties */
.outline-basic {
    outline-width: 3px;
    outline-style: solid;
    outline-color: #e74c3c;
    padding: 15px;
}

/* Outline shorthand */
```

```
.outline-shorthand {
    outline: 2px dashed #3498db;
    padding: 15px;
}

/* Outline styles */
.outline-dotted {
    outline: 3px dotted #2ecc71;
    padding: 15px;
}

.outline-double {
    outline: 4px double #f39c12;
    padding: 15px;
}

.outline-groove {
    outline: 6px groove #9b59b6;
    padding: 15px;
}

/* Outline offset */
.outline-offset {
    outline: 2px solid #e67e22;
    outline-offset: 5px; /* Space between element and
outline */
    padding: 15px;
    background-color: #fdf2e3;
}

.outline-offset-negative {
```

```
    outline: 2px solid #1abc9c;
    outline-offset: -5px; /* Outline inside element */
    padding: 20px;
    background-color: #d5f9f6;
}
```

Accessibility and Focus States

Outlines play a crucial role in web accessibility, particularly for keyboard navigation and focus indicators.

#css

```
/* Default focus outline (don't remove without
replacement) */
.focusable-element {
    padding: 10px 15px;
    border: 1px solid #ddd;
    background-color: white;
    cursor: pointer;
}

.focusable-element:focus {
    outline: 2px solid #3498db;
    outline-offset: 2px;
}

/* Custom focus indicators */
.custom-focus {
    padding: 10px 15px;
    border: 2px solid #ecf0f1;
```

```
    background-color: white;
    transition: all 0.2s ease;
}

.custom-focus:focus {
    outline: none; /* Only remove if providing
alternative */
    border-color: #3498db;
    box-shadow: 0 0 0 3px rgba(52, 152, 219, 0.2);
}

/* Button focus states */
.button-focus {
    padding: 12px 24px;
    border: 2px solid #2ecc71;
    background-color: #2ecc71;
    color: white;
    border-radius: 6px;
    cursor: pointer;
    transition: all 0.2s ease;
}

.button-focus:focus {
    outline: 2px solid #27ae60;
    outline-offset: 3px;
}

.button-focus:hover {
    background-color: #27ae60;
    border-color: #27ae60;
}
```

```css
/* Form element focus states */
.form-focus {
    width: 100%;
    padding: 12px;
    border: 2px solid #bdc3c7;
    border-radius: 4px;
    font-size: 16px;
    transition: border-color 0.2s ease;
}

.form-focus:focus {
    outline: none;
    border-color: #3498db;
    box-shadow: 0 0 0 3px rgba(52, 152, 219, 0.2);
}
```

Practical Use Cases and Best Practices

Understanding when to use borders versus outlines enhances design effectiveness and user experience.

#css

```css
/* Card designs with borders */
.card-with-border {
    border: 1px solid #e1e8ed;
    border-radius: 8px;
    padding: 20px;
    background-color: white;
    margin-bottom: 20px;
```

```css
    box-shadow: 0 2px 4px rgba(0, 0, 0, 0.1);
}

/* Hover states with outlines */
.hover-outline {
    padding: 20px;
    background-color: #f8f9fa;
    border-radius: 6px;
    transition: outline 0.2s ease;
    cursor: pointer;
}

.hover-outline:hover {
    outline: 2px solid #3498db;
    outline-offset: 2px;
}

/* Debug outlines for development */
.debug-outline {
    outline: 1px solid red;
    outline-offset: -1px;
}

/* Combination techniques */
.border-outline-combo {
    border: 2px solid #ecf0f1;
    padding: 15px;
    border-radius: 8px;
    background-color: white;
    transition: all 0.3s ease;
}
```

```css
.border-outline-combo:hover {
    border-color: #3498db;
    outline: 2px solid rgba(52, 152, 219, 0.3);
    outline-offset: 2px;
}

/* Error states */
.error-state {
    border: 2px solid #e74c3c;
    outline: 2px solid rgba(231, 76, 60, 0.3);
    outline-offset: 1px;
    background-color: #fdedec;
}

/* Success states */
.success-state {
    border: 2px solid #2ecc71;
    outline: 2px solid rgba(46, 204, 113, 0.3);
    outline-offset: 1px;
    background-color: #eafaf1;
}
```

10.5 Creating Stylish UI Cards with Borders

Basic Card Structure

UI cards are fundamental components in modern web design, providing contained areas for related content. Effective card design combines borders, shadows, and spacing to create visual hierarchy.

#css

```css
/* Foundation card structure */
.card-foundation {
    border: 1px solid #e1e8ed;
    border-radius: 8px;
    background-color: white;
    padding: 0;
    margin-bottom: 20px;
    overflow: hidden;
    box-shadow: 0 2px 4px rgba(0, 0, 0, 0.1);
    transition: transform 0.2s ease, box-shadow 0.2s
ease;
}

.card-foundation:hover {
    transform: translateY(-2px);
    box-shadow: 0 4px 12px rgba(0, 0, 0, 0.15);
}

/* Card header */
.card-header {
    padding: 20px;
    border-bottom: 1px solid #e1e8ed;
    background-color: #f8f9fa;
}

.card-header h3 {
    margin: 0 0 5px 0;
    color: #2c3e50;
    font-size: 1.25rem;
}
```

```
.card-header p {
    margin: 0;
    color: #7f8c8d;
    font-size: 0.9rem;
}

/* Card body */
.card-body {
    padding: 20px;
}

/* Card footer */
.card-footer {
    padding: 15px 20px;
    border-top: 1px solid #e1e8ed;
    background-color: #f8f9fa;
    display: flex;
    justify-content: space-between;
    align-items: center;
}
```

Advanced Card Variations

Different card styles serve various design purposes and content types, from product showcases to information panels.

#css

```
/* Gradient border card */
.gradient-border-card {
    position: relative;
```

```
    background: white;
    border-radius: 12px;
    padding: 2px;
    background: linear-gradient(45deg, #ff6b6b, #4ecdc4,
#45b7d1, #96ceb4);
}

.gradient-border-card .card-content {
    background: white;
    border-radius: 10px;
    padding: 20px;
    height: 100%;
}

/* Elevated card design */
.elevated-card {
    border: none;
    border-radius: 16px;
    background: white;
    padding: 24px;
    box-shadow:
        0 1px 3px rgba(0, 0, 0, 0.12),
        0 1px 2px rgba(0, 0, 0, 0.24);
    transition: all 0.3s cubic-bezier(0.25, 0.8, 0.25,
1);
}

.elevated-card:hover {
    box-shadow:
        0 14px 28px rgba(0, 0, 0, 0.25),
        0 10px 10px rgba(0, 0, 0, 0.22);
```

```
    transform: translateY(-5px);
}

/* Material design card */
.material-card {
    border-radius: 4px;
    background: white;
    border: none;
    box-shadow: 0 2px 2px 0 rgba(0, 0, 0, 0.14),
                0 3px 1px -2px rgba(0, 0, 0, 0.12),
                0 1px 5px 0 rgba(0, 0, 0, 0.20);
    overflow: hidden;
    transition: box-shadow 0.3s ease;
}

.material-card:hover {
    box-shadow: 0 8px 10px 1px rgba(0, 0, 0, 0.14),
                0 3px 14px 2px rgba(0, 0, 0, 0.12),
                0 5px 5px -3px rgba(0, 0, 0, 0.20);
}

/* Neumorphism card */
.neumorphic-card {
    background: #f0f0f3;
    border: none;
    border-radius: 20px;
    padding: 30px;
    box-shadow:
        9px 9px 16px #a3a3a3,
        -9px -9px 16px #ffffff;
    transition: all 0.3s ease;
```

```css
}

.neumorphic-card:hover {
    box-shadow:
        inset 9px 9px 16px #a3a3a3,
        inset -9px -9px 16px #ffffff;
}

/* Glassmorphism card */
.glass-card {
    background: rgba(255, 255, 255, 0.25);
    border-radius: 16px;
    border: 1px solid rgba(255, 255, 255, 0.18);
    backdrop-filter: blur(10px);
    padding: 20px;
    box-shadow: 0 8px 32px 0 rgba(31, 38, 135, 0.37);
}
```

Interactive Card Components

Modern UI cards often include interactive elements that provide immediate feedback and enhanced user experience.

#css

```css
/* Clickable card states */
.interactive-card {
    border: 2px solid #e1e8ed;
    border-radius: 12px;
    background: white;
    padding: 20px;
```

```
    cursor: pointer;
    transition: all 0.3s ease;
    position: relative;
    overflow: hidden;
}

.interactive-card::before {
    content: '';
    position: absolute;
    top: 0;
    left: -100%;
    width: 100%;
    height: 100%;
    background: linear-gradient(90deg, transparent,
rgba(52, 152, 219, 0.1), transparent);
    transition: left 0.5s ease;
}

.interactive-card:hover {
    border-color: #3498db;
    transform: translateY(-3px);
    box-shadow: 0 6px 20px rgba(52, 152, 219, 0.2);
}

.interactive-card:hover::before {
    left: 100%;
}

.interactive-card:active {
    transform: translateY(-1px);
    box-shadow: 0 2px 8px rgba(52, 152, 219, 0.3);
```

```
}

/* Card with accent border */
.accent-card {
    border: 1px solid #e1e8ed;
    border-left: 4px solid #3498db;
    border-radius: 0 8px 8px 0;
    background: white;
    padding: 20px;
    margin-bottom: 16px;
    position: relative;
}

.accent-card.success {
    border-left-color: #2ecc71;
}

.accent-card.warning {
    border-left-color: #f39c12;
}

.accent-card.error {
    border-left-color: #e74c3c;
}

/* Feature card with icon */
.feature-card {
    border: 1px solid #e1e8ed;
    border-radius: 12px;
    background: white;
    padding: 24px;
```

```
    text-align: center;
    transition: all 0.3s ease;
    position: relative;
}

.feature-card::after {
    content: '';
    position: absolute;
    top: -1px;
    left: -1px;
    right: -1px;
    bottom: -1px;
    background: linear-gradient(45deg, #3498db, #2ecc71);
    border-radius: 12px;
    z-index: -1;
    opacity: 0;
    transition: opacity 0.3s ease;
}

.feature-card:hover::after {
    opacity: 1;
}

.feature-card:hover {
    border-color: transparent;
    transform: translateY(-2px);
    box-shadow: 0 8px 25px rgba(0, 0, 0, 0.15);
}

.feature-card-icon {
    width: 60px;
```

```
    height: 60px;
    margin: 0 auto 16px;
    background: #3498db;
    border-radius: 50%;
    display: flex;
    align-items: center;
    justify-content: center;
    color: white;
    font-size: 24px;
}
```

Card Layout Systems

Effective card layouts require consideration of spacing, alignment, and responsive behavior across different screen sizes.

#css

```
/* Grid-based card layout */
.card-grid {
    display: grid;
    grid-template-columns: repeat(auto-fit, minmax(300px,
1fr));
    gap: 24px;
    padding: 20px;
}

.card-grid-item {
    border: 1px solid #e1e8ed;
    border-radius: 8px;
    background: white;
```

```css
    overflow: hidden;
    transition: transform 0.2s ease;
}

.card-grid-item:hover {
    transform: scale(1.02);
}

/* Flexbox card layout */
.card-flex-container {
    display: flex;
    flex-wrap: wrap;
    gap: 20px;
    padding: 20px;
}

.card-flex-item {
    flex: 1 1 calc(33.333% - 20px);
    min-width: 280px;
    border: 1px solid #e1e8ed;
    border-radius: 8px;
    background: white;
    padding: 20px;
}

/* Masonry-style cards */
.card-masonry {
    column-count: 3;
    column-gap: 20px;
    padding: 20px;
}
```

```
.card-masonry-item {
    break-inside: avoid;
    margin-bottom: 20px;
    border: 1px solid #e1e8ed;
    border-radius: 8px;
    background: white;
    padding: 16px;
}

/* Card with image */
.image-card {
    border: 1px solid #e1e8ed;
    border-radius: 12px;
    background: white;
    overflow: hidden;
    transition: all 0.3s ease;
    max-width: 350px;
}

.image-card:hover {
    border-color: #3498db;
    box-shadow: 0 8px 25px rgba(52, 152, 219, 0.15);
}

.image-card-media {
    width: 100%;
    height: 200px;
    background: linear-gradient(135deg, #667eea 0%,
#764ba2 100%);
    position: relative;
```

```
    overflow: hidden;
}

.image-card-media::after {
    content: '';
    position: absolute;
    top: 0;
    left: 0;
    right: 0;
    bottom: 0;
    background: rgba(0, 0, 0, 0.1);
    transition: background 0.3s ease;
}

.image-card:hover .image-card-media::after {
    background: rgba(0, 0, 0, 0.2);
}

.image-card-content {
    padding: 20px;
}

/* Pricing card */
.pricing-card {
    border: 2px solid #e1e8ed;
    border-radius: 16px;
    background: white;
    padding: 0;
    text-align: center;
    position: relative;
    overflow: hidden;
```

```
    transition: all 0.3s ease;
}

.pricing-card.featured {
    border-color: #3498db;
    transform: scale(1.05);
}

.pricing-card.featured::before {
    content: 'Most Popular';
    position: absolute;
    top: 20px;
    right: -30px;
    background: #3498db;
    color: white;
    padding: 8px 40px;
    font-size: 12px;
    font-weight: bold;
    transform: rotate(45deg);
}

.pricing-card-header {
    background: linear-gradient(135deg, #667eea 0%,
#764ba2 100%);
    padding: 30px 20px;
    color: white;
}

.pricing-card-price {
    font-size: 3rem;
    font-weight: bold;
```

```
    margin: 0;
}

.pricing-card-period {
    font-size: 1rem;
    opacity: 0.8;
}

.pricing-card-body {
    padding: 30px 20px;
}

.pricing-card-feature {
    padding: 8px 0;
    border-bottom: 1px solid #f8f9fa;
}

.pricing-card-feature:last-child {
    border-bottom: none;
}

/* Testimonial card */
.testimonial-card {
    border: 1px solid #e1e8ed;
    border-radius: 12px;
    background: white;
    padding: 24px;
    position: relative;
    margin-top: 20px;
}
```

```
.testimonial-card::before {
    content: '"';
    position: absolute;
    top: -10px;
    left: 20px;
    font-size: 4rem;
    color: #3498db;
    line-height: 1;
    background: white;
    padding: 0 10px;
}

.testimonial-card-content {
    font-style: italic;
    margin-bottom: 20px;
    color: #2c3e50;
}

.testimonial-card-author {
    display: flex;
    align-items: center;
    gap: 12px;
}

.testimonial-card-avatar {
    width: 50px;
    height: 50px;
    border-radius: 50%;
    background: linear-gradient(45deg, #3498db, #2ecc71);
    display: flex;
    align-items: center;
```

```
    justify-content: center;
    color: white;
    font-weight: bold;
}

/* Dashboard card */
.dashboard-card {
    border: 1px solid #e1e8ed;
    border-radius: 8px;
    background: white;
    padding: 0;
    overflow: hidden;
}

.dashboard-card-header {
    padding: 16px 20px;
    border-bottom: 1px solid #e1e8ed;
    background: #f8f9fa;
    display: flex;
    justify-content: space-between;
    align-items: center;
}

.dashboard-card-title {
    margin: 0;
    font-size: 1.1rem;
    color: #2c3e50;
}

.dashboard-card-actions {
    display: flex;
```

```css
    gap: 8px;
}

.dashboard-card-body {
    padding: 20px;
}

.dashboard-card-metric {
    font-size: 2.5rem;
    font-weight: bold;
    color: #3498db;
    margin: 0 0 8px 0;
}

.dashboard-card-label {
    color: #7f8c8d;
    font-size: 0.9rem;
    margin: 0;
}

/* Responsive card adjustments */
@media (max-width: 768px) {
    .card-grid {
        grid-template-columns: 1fr;
        gap: 16px;
        padding: 16px;
    }

    .card-flex-item {
        flex: 1 1 100%;
        min-width: auto;
```

```
    }

    .card-masonry {
        column-count: 1;
    }

    .pricing-card.featured {
        transform: none;
    }

    .feature-card {
        padding: 20px;
    }
}

@media (max-width: 480px) {
    .elevated-card,
    .material-card,
    .neumorphic-card {
        margin: 10px;
        padding: 16px;
    }

    .dashboard-card-metric {
        font-size: 2rem;
    }

    .pricing-card-price {
        font-size: 2.5rem;
    }
}
```

Card Animation and Transitions

Smooth animations enhance user experience by providing visual feedback and creating engaging interactions.

#css

```css
/* Loading state animation */
.card-loading {
    border: 1px solid #e1e8ed;
    border-radius: 8px;
    background: white;
    padding: 20px;
    position: relative;
    overflow: hidden;
}

.card-loading::after {
    content: '';
    position: absolute;
    top: 0;
    left: -100%;
    width: 100%;
    height: 100%;
    background: linear-gradient(90deg, transparent,
rgba(255, 255, 255, 0.8), transparent);
    animation: loading-shimmer 1.5s infinite;
}

@keyframes loading-shimmer {
```

```
    0% { left: -100%; }
    100% { left: 100%; }
}

/* Flip card animation */
.flip-card {
    background-color: transparent;
    width: 300px;
    height: 200px;
    border: 1px solid #e1e8ed;
    border-radius: 8px;
    perspective: 1000px;
}

.flip-card-inner {
    position: relative;
    width: 100%;
    height: 100%;
    text-align: center;
    transition: transform 0.8s;
    transform-style: preserve-3d;
}

.flip-card:hover .flip-card-inner {
    transform: rotateY(180deg);
}

.flip-card-front,
.flip-card-back {
    position: absolute;
    width: 100%;
```

```
    height: 100%;
    backface-visibility: hidden;
    border-radius: 8px;
    display: flex;
    align-items: center;
    justify-content: center;
    padding: 20px;
    box-sizing: border-box;
}

.flip-card-front {
    background-color: #3498db;
    color: white;
}

.flip-card-back {
    background-color: #2ecc71;
    color: white;
    transform: rotateY(180deg);
}

/* Slide-in animation */
.slide-card {
    border: 1px solid #e1e8ed;
    border-radius: 8px;
    background: white;
    padding: 20px;
    opacity: 0;
    transform: translateY(30px);
    animation: slideInUp 0.6s ease forwards;
}
```

```css
.slide-card:nth-child(1) { animation-delay: 0.1s; }
.slide-card:nth-child(2) { animation-delay: 0.2s; }
.slide-card:nth-child(3) { animation-delay: 0.3s; }
.slide-card:nth-child(4) { animation-delay: 0.4s; }

@keyframes slideInUp {
    to {
        opacity: 1;
        transform: translateY(0);
    }
}

/* Pulsing effect */
.pulse-card {
    border: 2px solid #3498db;
    border-radius: 8px;
    background: white;
    padding: 20px;
    animation: pulse 2s infinite;
}

@keyframes pulse {
    0% {
        box-shadow: 0 0 0 0 rgba(52, 152, 219, 0.7);
    }
    70% {
        box-shadow: 0 0 0 10px rgba(52, 152, 219, 0);
    }
    100% {
        box-shadow: 0 0 0 0 rgba(52, 152, 219, 0);
```

```
    }
}
```

Essential Tips

- Always consider the box model impact when choosing between borders and outlines - borders affect layout flow while outlines do not, making outlines ideal for hover states and focus indicators that shouldn't shift content.
- Use consistent border-radius values throughout your design system to maintain visual harmony - establish a scale (4px, 8px, 12px, 16px) and stick to these predefined values across components.
- Leverage CSS custom properties for border colors and widths to create themeable designs that can adapt to different color schemes or user preferences without duplicating code.
- Test border and outline visibility across different backgrounds and ensure sufficient contrast ratios for accessibility - particularly important for focus indicators that must be visible to keyboard users.
- Combine subtle animations with border changes to create smooth, engaging transitions that provide immediate visual feedback without being distracting or overwhelming to users.

Actionable Strategies

- Implement a systematic approach to border usage by creating CSS utility classes for common border patterns, enabling consistent application across your entire project while maintaining flexibility for special cases.
- Create responsive border systems that adapt to different screen sizes - thicker borders work well on desktop but may overwhelm mobile interfaces, so adjust border widths using media queries.
- Use border gradients and multiple box-shadows to create sophisticated visual effects that stand out from standard flat designs, particularly effective for call-to-action elements and featured content.
- Establish a clear hierarchy using border weights and styles - primary elements get solid, thicker borders while secondary elements use lighter borders or dashed/dotted styles to create visual prioritization.

- Optimize performance by avoiding complex border-radius calculations on elements that animate frequently - instead, use transform properties or pre-calculate values to maintain smooth frame rates.
- Document your border design system with live examples and usage guidelines to ensure team consistency and make onboarding new developers more efficient and error-free.
- Test border implementations across different browsers and devices to identify rendering inconsistencies, particularly with advanced border-radius values and outline-offset properties that may behave differently across platforms.

Chapter 11: Flexbox Fundamentals

11.1 Introduction to Flexbox

Understanding Flexbox: The Modern Layout Solution

Flexbox, formally known as the Flexible Box Layout Module, represents a revolutionary approach to creating responsive and dynamic layouts in CSS. This powerful layout method provides developers with unprecedented control over the distribution, alignment, and sizing of elements within a container, solving many of the traditional challenges associated with CSS positioning and layout design.

The fundamental concept behind Flexbox revolves around the relationship between a parent container (flex container) and its direct children (flex items). When you apply `display: flex` to an element, it becomes a flex container, and all of its direct children automatically become flex items. This parent-child relationship forms the foundation of all Flexbox functionality.

The Evolution from Traditional Layout Methods

Before Flexbox, developers relied heavily on floats, positioning, and display properties like `inline-block` to create layouts. These methods often required complex calculations, clearfix hacks, and extensive media queries to achieve responsive designs. Flexbox eliminates many of these complications by providing a more intuitive and flexible approach to layout design.

Consider a simple three-column layout using traditional methods versus Flexbox:

Traditional Float Method:

#css

```
.container {
  width: 100%;
}


.column {
```

```
  float: left;
  width: 33.333%;
  padding: 20px;
  box-sizing: border-box;
}

.container::after {
  content: "";
  display: table;
  clear: both;
}
```

Flexbox Method:

#css

```css
.container {
  display: flex;
}

.column {
  flex: 1;
  padding: 20px;
}
```

The Flexbox approach is cleaner, more maintainable, and automatically handles equal-height columns without additional code.

Core Flexbox Concepts

Flex Container Activation

To activate Flexbox on an element, you apply the `display` property with either `flex` or `inline-flex` values:

#css

```
.flex-container {
  display: flex; /* Creates a block-level flex container
*/
}

.inline-flex-container {
  display: inline-flex; /* Creates an inline-level flex
container */
}
```

The difference between `flex` and `inline-flex` lies in how the container itself behaves in relation to surrounding elements. A `flex` container behaves like a block element, taking up the full width of its parent, while an `inline-flex` container behaves like an inline element, only taking up as much space as its content requires.

Flex Direction and Layout Orientation

Once a flex container is established, you can control the direction in which flex items are laid out using the `flex-direction` property:

#css

```
.container {
  display: flex;
  flex-direction: row; /* Default: items arranged
horizontally */
}
```

```css
.vertical-container {
  display: flex;
  flex-direction: column; /* Items arranged vertically */
}

.reverse-container {
  display: flex;
  flex-direction: row-reverse; /* Items arranged
horizontally in reverse order */
}

.column-reverse-container {
  display: flex;
  flex-direction: column-reverse; /* Items arranged
vertically in reverse order */
}
```

Real-World Application Example

Let's create a navigation bar that demonstrates basic Flexbox principles:

#html

```html
<nav class="navbar">
  <div class="logo">Brand Logo</div>
  <ul class="nav-links">
    <li><a href="#home">Home</a></li>
    <li><a href="#about">About</a></li>
    <li><a href="#services">Services</a></li>
    <li><a href="#contact">Contact</a></li>
```

```html
  </ul>
  <div class="auth-buttons">
    <button class="login-btn">Login</button>
    <button class="signup-btn">Sign Up</button>
  </div>
</nav>
```

#css

```css
.navbar {
  display: flex;
  align-items: center;
  justify-content: space-between;
  padding: 1rem 2rem;
  background-color: #333;
  color: white;
}

.logo {
  font-size: 1.5rem;
  font-weight: bold;
}

.nav-links {
  display: flex;
  list-style: none;
  gap: 2rem;
  margin: 0;
  padding: 0;
}
```

```
.nav-links a {
  color: white;
  text-decoration: none;
  transition: color 0.3s ease;
}

.nav-links a:hover {
  color: #ffd700;
}

.auth-buttons {
  display: flex;
  gap: 1rem;
}

.auth-buttons button {
  padding: 0.5rem 1rem;
  border: none;
  border-radius: 4px;
  cursor: pointer;
  transition: background-color 0.3s ease;
}

.login-btn {
  background-color: transparent;
  color: white;
  border: 1px solid white;
}

.signup-btn {
  background-color: #007bff;
```

```
  color: white;
}
```

This example demonstrates how Flexbox simplifies the creation of complex layouts with minimal code.

11.2 Main Axis vs Cross Axis

Understanding the Flexbox Coordinate System

The concept of axes is fundamental to mastering Flexbox. Unlike traditional CSS layout methods that rely on horizontal and vertical orientations, Flexbox introduces a more flexible coordinate system based on two perpendicular axes: the main axis and the cross axis.

The Main Axis: Primary Direction of Flow

The main axis represents the primary direction along which flex items are arranged within a flex container. The direction of the main axis is determined by the `flex-direction` property:

- When `flex-direction: row` (default), the main axis runs horizontally from left to right
- When `flex-direction: row-reverse`, the main axis runs horizontally from right to left
- When `flex-direction: column`, the main axis runs vertically from top to bottom
- When `flex-direction: column-reverse`, the main axis runs vertically from bottom to top

#css

```
.horizontal-container {
  display: flex;
  flex-direction: row; /* Main axis: horizontal */
```

```
}

.vertical-container {
  display: flex;
  flex-direction: column; /* Main axis: vertical */
}
```

The Cross Axis: Perpendicular to Main Axis

The cross axis always runs perpendicular to the main axis. Understanding this relationship is crucial for proper alignment and positioning of flex items:

- When the main axis is horizontal (row or row-reverse), the cross axis is vertical
- When the main axis is vertical (column or column-reverse), the cross axis is horizontal

Main Axis Properties and Control

justify-content: Main Axis Alignment

The `justify-content` property controls how flex items are distributed along the main axis:

#css

```
.container {
  display: flex;
  justify-content: flex-start; /* Default: items packed
at the start */
}

.center-main {
```

```
  display: flex;
  justify-content: center; /* Items centered along main axis */
}

.space-between {
  display: flex;
  justify-content: space-between; /* Equal space between items */
}

.space-around {
  display: flex;
  justify-content: space-around; /* Equal space around items */
}

.space-evenly {
  display: flex;
  justify-content: space-evenly; /* Equal space between and around items */
}

.flex-end {
  display: flex;
  justify-content: flex-end; /* Items packed at the end */
}
```

Practical Example: Button Group Layout
#html

```html
<div class="button-group">
  <button>Previous</button>
  <button>Next</button>
  <button>Cancel</button>
</div>
```

#css

```css
.button-group {
  display: flex;
  justify-content: space-between;
  padding: 1rem;
  border-top: 1px solid #ddd;
}

.button-group button {
  padding: 0.5rem 1rem;
  border: 1px solid #ccc;
  background-color: #f8f9fa;
  cursor: pointer;
  transition: background-color 0.2s ease;
}

.button-group button:hover {
  background-color: #e9ecef;
}
```

Cross Axis Properties and Control

align-items: Cross Axis Alignment for All Items

The `align-items` property controls how all flex items are aligned along the cross axis:

#css

```
.container {
  display: flex;
  height: 200px; /* Define height to see cross-axis
alignment */
  align-items: stretch; /* Default: items stretch to fill
container */
}

.center-cross {
  display: flex;
  height: 200px;
  align-items: center; /* Items centered along cross axis
*/
}

.flex-start-cross {
  display: flex;
  height: 200px;
  align-items: flex-start; /* Items aligned to cross axis
start */
}

.flex-end-cross {
  display: flex;
  height: 200px;
  align-items: flex-end; /* Items aligned to cross axis
end */
```

```
}

.baseline-cross {
  display: flex;
  height: 200px;
  align-items: baseline; /* Items aligned to their text baseline */
}
```

align-self: Individual Cross Axis Alignment

Individual flex items can override the container's `align-items` setting using `align-self`:

#css

```
.special-item {
  align-self: center; /* This item centers itself regardless of align-items */
}

.stretch-item {
  align-self: stretch; /* This item stretches regardless of align-items */
}
```

Comprehensive Axis Example: Card Layout

#html

```
<div class="card-container">
  <div class="card">
```

```html
    <div class="card-header">
      <h3>Product Title</h3>
      <span class="price">$99</span>
    </div>
    <div class="card-body">
      <p>Product description goes here...</p>
    </div>
    <div class="card-footer">
      <button class="btn-primary">Add to Cart</button>
      <button class="btn-secondary">View Details</button>
    </div>
  </div>
</div>
```

#css

```css
.card {
  display: flex;
  flex-direction: column;
  width: 300px;
  height: 400px;
  border: 1px solid #ddd;
  border-radius: 8px;
  overflow: hidden;
}

.card-header {
  display: flex;
  justify-content: space-between; /* Main axis: space
between title and price */
  align-items: center; /* Cross axis: center alignment */
```

```css
  padding: 1rem;
  background-color: #f8f9fa;
  border-bottom: 1px solid #ddd;
}

.card-header h3 {
  margin: 0;
  font-size: 1.2rem;
}

.price {
  font-weight: bold;
  color: #007bff;
  font-size: 1.1rem;
}

.card-body {
  flex: 1; /* Takes up remaining space */
  padding: 1rem;
  display: flex;
  align-items: flex-start; /* Content aligned to top */
}

.card-footer {
  display: flex;
  gap: 0.5rem;
  padding: 1rem;
  background-color: #f8f9fa;
  border-top: 1px solid #ddd;
}
```

```
.card-footer button {
  flex: 1; /* Equal width buttons */
  padding: 0.5rem;
  border: none;
  border-radius: 4px;
  cursor: pointer;
}

.btn-primary {
  background-color: #007bff;
  color: white;
}

.btn-secondary {
  background-color: #6c757d;
  color: white;
}
```

This example demonstrates how main and cross axes work together in both horizontal and vertical flex containers.

11.3 Flex Container Properties

Comprehensive Container Control

Flex container properties provide comprehensive control over how flex items behave within their container. These properties affect the overall layout, spacing, and behavior of all child elements collectively.

flex-direction: Establishing the Main Axis

The `flex-direction` property is fundamental as it establishes the main axis direction and influences how other properties behave:

#css

```
.row-container {
  display: flex;
  flex-direction: row; /* Default: left to right */
}

.row-reverse-container {
  display: flex;
  flex-direction: row-reverse; /* Right to left */
}

.column-container {
  display: flex;
  flex-direction: column; /* Top to bottom */
}

.column-reverse-container {
  display: flex;
  flex-direction: column-reverse; /* Bottom to top */
}
```

Practical Application: Responsive Navigation

#html

```
<nav class="responsive-nav">
  <div class="nav-brand">Logo</div>
  <ul class="nav-menu">
    <li>Home</li>
```

```html
    <li>About</li>
    <li>Services</li>
    <li>Contact</li>
  </ul>
</nav>
```

#css

```css
.responsive-nav {
  display: flex;
  flex-direction: row;
  padding: 1rem;
}

.nav-menu {
  display: flex;
  flex-direction: row;
  list-style: none;
  gap: 2rem;
  margin: 0;
  padding: 0;
}

/* Mobile responsive */
@media (max-width: 768px) {
  .responsive-nav {
    flex-direction: column;
  }

  .nav-menu {
    flex-direction: column;
```

```
    gap: 1rem;
    margin-top: 1rem;
  }
}
```

flex-wrap: Controlling Line Wrapping

The `flex-wrap` property determines whether flex items are forced onto a single line or can wrap onto multiple lines:

#css

```
.no-wrap-container {
  display: flex;
  flex-wrap: nowrap; /* Default: items stay on one line
*/
}

.wrap-container {
  display: flex;
  flex-wrap: wrap; /* Items wrap to new lines as needed
*/
}

.wrap-reverse-container {
  display: flex;
  flex-wrap: wrap-reverse; /* Items wrap in reverse order
*/
}
```

Advanced Wrapping Example: Image Gallery

#html

```html
<div class="gallery">
  <div class="image-card">Image 1</div>
  <div class="image-card">Image 2</div>
  <div class="image-card">Image 3</div>
  <div class="image-card">Image 4</div>
  <div class="image-card">Image 5</div>
  <div class="image-card">Image 6</div>
</div>
```

#css

```css
.gallery {
  display: flex;
  flex-wrap: wrap;
  gap: 1rem;
  padding: 1rem;
}

.image-card {
  flex: 1 1 300px; /* Grow, shrink, basis of 300px */
  min-width: 250px;
  height: 200px;
  background-color: #f0f0f0;
  border: 1px solid #ddd;
  border-radius: 8px;
  display: flex;
  align-items: center;
```

```
  justify-content: center;
  font-weight: bold;
  color: #666;
}
```

flex-flow: Shorthand for Direction and Wrap

The `flex-flow` property combines `flex-direction` and `flex-wrap` into a single declaration:

#css

```
.container {
  display: flex;
  flex-flow: row wrap; /* Same as flex-direction: row;
flex-wrap: wrap; */
}

.vertical-wrap {
  display: flex;
  flex-flow: column wrap;
}

.reverse-nowrap {
  display: flex;
  flex-flow: row-reverse nowrap;
}
```

justify-content: Main Axis Distribution

The `justify-content` property provides sophisticated control over how space is distributed along the main axis:

#css

```
.start-aligned {
  display: flex;
  justify-content: flex-start; /* Items packed at the
start */
}

.end-aligned {
  display: flex;
  justify-content: flex-end; /* Items packed at the end
*/
}

.center-aligned {
  display: flex;
  justify-content: center; /* Items centered */
}

.space-between {
  display: flex;
  justify-content: space-between; /* Space between items
*/
}

.space-around {
  display: flex;
  justify-content: space-around; /* Space around items */
}
```

```
.space-evenly {
  display: flex;
  justify-content: space-evenly; /* Even space
distribution */
}
```

Comprehensive Layout Example: Dashboard Header

#html

```
<header class="dashboard-header">
  <div class="header-left">
    <h1>Dashboard</h1>
    <span class="subtitle">Welcome back, John</span>
  </div>
  <div class="header-center">
    <input type="search" placeholder="Search..."
class="search-input">
  </div>
  <div class="header-right">
    <button class="notification-btn">🔔</button>
    <div class="user-avatar">JD</div>
  </div>
</header>
```

#css

```
.dashboard-header {
  display: flex;
  justify-content: space-between;
  align-items: center;
  padding: 1rem 2rem;
```

```
  background-color: white;
  border-bottom: 1px solid #e0e0e0;
  box-shadow: 0 2px 4px rgba(0,0,0,0.1);
}

.header-left {
  display: flex;
  flex-direction: column;
  align-items: flex-start;
}

.header-left h1 {
  margin: 0;
  font-size: 1.5rem;
  color: #333;
}

.subtitle {
  font-size: 0.9rem;
  color: #666;
  margin-top: 0.25rem;
}

.header-center {
  flex: 1;
  display: flex;
  justify-content: center;
  margin: 0 2rem;
}

.search-input {
```

```
  width: 100%;
  max-width: 400px;
  padding: 0.5rem 1rem;
  border: 1px solid #ddd;
  border-radius: 20px;
  font-size: 0.9rem;
}

.header-right {
  display: flex;
  align-items: center;
  gap: 1rem;
}

.notification-btn {
  background: none;
  border: none;
  font-size: 1.2rem;
  cursor: pointer;
  padding: 0.5rem;
  border-radius: 50%;
  transition: background-color 0.2s ease;
}

.notification-btn:hover {
  background-color: #f0f0f0;
}

.user-avatar {
  width: 40px;
  height: 40px;
```

```
  border-radius: 50%;
  background-color: #007bff;
  color: white;
  display: flex;
  align-items: center;
  justify-content: center;
  font-weight: bold;
  cursor: pointer;
}
```

align-items: Cross Axis Alignment

The `align-items` property controls cross-axis alignment for all flex items:

#css

```
.stretch-items {
  display: flex;
  align-items: stretch; /* Default: items stretch to fill container */
  height: 200px;
}

.center-items {
  display: flex;
  align-items: center; /* Items centered on cross axis */
  height: 200px;
}

.start-items {
  display: flex;
```

```
  align-items: flex-start; /* Items aligned to cross axis
start */
  height: 200px;
}

.end-items {
  display: flex;
  align-items: flex-end; /* Items aligned to cross axis
end */
  height: 200px;
}

.baseline-items {
  display: flex;
  align-items: baseline; /* Items aligned to text
baseline */
  height: 200px;
}
```

align-content: Multi-line Cross Axis Alignment

The `align-content` property aligns wrapped lines along the cross axis (only applies when `flex-wrap` is not `nowrap`):

#css

```
.content-start {
  display: flex;
  flex-wrap: wrap;
  align-content: flex-start; /* Lines packed at cross
axis start */
  height: 400px;
```

```
}

.content-center {
  display: flex;
  flex-wrap: wrap;
  align-content: center; /* Lines centered on cross axis
*/
  height: 400px;
}

.content-space-between {
  display: flex;
  flex-wrap: wrap;
  align-content: space-between; /* Space between lines */
  height: 400px;
}

.content-stretch {
  display: flex;
  flex-wrap: wrap;
  align-content: stretch; /* Lines stretch to fill
container */
  height: 400px;
}
```

gap: Modern Spacing Control

The `gap` property provides a clean way to add space between flex items:

#css

```
.gapped-container {
  display: flex;
  gap: 1rem; /* Equal gap between all items */
}

.custom-gaps {
  display: flex;
  row-gap: 1rem; /* Gap between rows */
  column-gap: 2rem; /* Gap between columns */
}

.responsive-gaps {
  display: flex;
  gap: clamp(0.5rem, 2vw, 2rem); /* Responsive gap */
}
```

11.4 Flex Item Properties

Individual Item Control

Flex item properties provide granular control over individual elements within a flex container. These properties allow specific items to behave differently from their siblings, creating sophisticated and flexible layouts.

flex-grow: Expansion Behavior

The `flex-grow` property determines how much a flex item should grow relative to other flex items when extra space is available:

#css

```
.container {
```

```
  display: flex;
  width: 600px;
}

.item-no-grow {
  flex-grow: 0; /* Default: doesn't grow */
  width: 100px;
  background-color: #ffeb3b;
}

.item-grow-1 {
  flex-grow: 1; /* Takes 1 part of available space */
  background-color: #4caf50;
}

.item-grow-2 {
  flex-grow: 2; /* Takes 2 parts of available space */
  background-color: #2196f3;
}
```

Practical Example: Responsive Sidebar Layout

#html

```
<div class="app-layout">
  <aside class="sidebar">Sidebar</aside>
  <main class="main-content">Main Content</main>
  <aside class="ads-panel">Ads</aside>
</div>
```

#css

```
.app-layout {
  display: flex;
  height: 100vh;
  gap: 1rem;
}

.sidebar {
  flex-grow: 0;
  width: 250px;
  background-color: #f4f4f4;
  padding: 1rem;
}

.main-content {
  flex-grow: 2; /* Takes twice as much space as ads panel
*/
  background-color: white;
  padding: 2rem;
  border: 1px solid #ddd;
}

.ads-panel {
  flex-grow: 1; /* Takes remaining space */
  width: 200px;
  background-color: #f9f9f9;
  padding: 1rem;
}

/* Mobile responsive */
@media (max-width: 768px) {
  .app-layout {
```

```
    flex-direction: column;
  }

  .sidebar,
  .ads-panel {
    flex-grow: 0;
    width: auto;
  }
}
```

flex-shrink: Compression Behavior

The `flex-shrink` property determines how much a flex item should shrink when space is limited:

#css

```
.container {
  display: flex;
  width: 300px; /* Smaller container to demonstrate
shrinking */
}

.no-shrink {
  flex-shrink: 0; /* Doesn't shrink */
  width: 150px;
  background-color: #f44336;
}

.normal-shrink {
  flex-shrink: 1; /* Default: normal shrinking */
```

```
  width: 150px;
  background-color: #ff9800;
}

.high-shrink {
  flex-shrink: 3; /* Shrinks 3 times faster */
  width: 150px;
  background-color: #9c27b0;
}
```

Advanced Shrinking Example: Navigation with Overflow

#html

```
<nav class="responsive-nav">
  <div class="nav-brand">Company Logo</div>
  <ul class="nav-links">
    <li><a href="#home">Home</a></li>
    <li><a href="#products">Products</a></li>
    <li><a href="#services">Services</a></li>
    <li><a href="#about">About Us</a></li>
    <li><a href="#contact">Contact</a></li>
  </ul>
  <div class="nav-actions">
    <button class="login-btn">Login</button>
  </div>
</nav>
```

#css

```
.responsive-nav {
  display: flex;
```

```css
  align-items: center;
  padding: 1rem;
  background-color: #333;
  color: white;
}

.nav-brand {
  flex-shrink: 0; /* Logo never shrinks */
  font-size: 1.2rem;
  font-weight: bold;
  min-width: 120px;
}

.nav-links {
  display: flex;
  flex-grow: 1;
  flex-shrink: 1; /* Can shrink when space is tight */
  justify-content: center;
  list-style: none;
  margin: 0;
  padding: 0;
  gap: 2rem;
}

.nav-links a {
  color: white;
  text-decoration: none;
  white-space: nowrap;
  padding: 0.5rem;
}
```

```
.nav-actions {
  flex-shrink: 0; /* Actions don't shrink */
  margin-left: 1rem;
}

.login-btn {
  padding: 0.5rem 1rem;
  background-color: #007bff;
  color: white;
  border: none;
  border-radius: 4px;
  cursor: pointer;
}
```

flex-basis: Initial Size Definition

The `flex-basis` property sets the initial main size of a flex item before free space is distributed:

#css

```
.container {
  display: flex;
}

.auto-basis {
  flex-basis: auto; /* Default: based on content size */
  background-color: #e1f5fe;
}

.fixed-basis {
```

```
  flex-basis: 200px; /* Fixed initial size */
  background-color: #f3e5f5;
}

.percentage-basis {
  flex-basis: 30%; /* Percentage of container */
  background-color: #e8f5e8;
}

.content-basis {
  flex-basis: content; /* Based on content size */
  background-color: #fff3e0;
}
```

Complex Example: Dashboard Cards

#html

```
<div class="dashboard">
  <div class="card stat-card">
    <h3>Total Sales</h3>
    <p class="stat-number">$24,567</p>
  </div>
  <div class="card chart-card">
    <h3>Monthly Revenue</h3>
    <div class="chart-placeholder">Chart goes here</div>
  </div>
  <div class="card activity-card">
    <h3>Recent Activity</h3>
    <ul class="activity-list">
      <li>New order received</li>
      <li>Payment processed</li>
```

```
      <li>Customer registered</li>
    </ul>
  </div>
</div>
```

#css

```
.dashboard {
  display: flex;
  gap: 1rem;
  padding: 1rem;
  flex-wrap: wrap;
}

.card {
  background-color: white;
  border-radius: 8px;
  padding: 1.5rem;
  box-shadow: 0 2px 8px rgba(0,0,0,0.1);
  border: 1px solid #e0e0e0;
}

.stat-card {
  flex-basis: 250px; /* Fixed width for stat cards */
  flex-grow: 0;
  flex-shrink: 0;
  text-align: center;
}

.stat-number {
  font-size: 2rem;
```

```
  font-weight: bold;
  color: #007bff;
  margin: 0.5rem 0 0 0;
}

.chart-card {
  flex-basis: 400px; /* Minimum width for chart */
  flex-grow: 2; /* Grows more than other cards */
  flex-shrink: 1;
}

.chart-placeholder {
  height: 200px;
  background-color: #f8f9fa;
  border: 2px dashed #dee2e6;
  display: flex;
  align-items: center;
  justify-content: center;
  margin-top: 1rem;
  border-radius: 4px;
}

.activity-card {
  flex-basis: 300px; /* Base width for activity */
  flex-grow: 1;
  flex-shrink: 1;
}

.activity-list {
  list-style: none;
  padding: 0;
```

```
  margin: 1rem 0 0 0;
}

.activity-list li {
  padding: 0.5rem 0;
  border-bottom: 1px solid #f0f0f0;
  font-size: 0.9rem;
  color: #666;
}

.activity-list li:last-child {
  border-bottom: none;
}
```

flex: The Ultimate Shorthand

The `flex` property combines `flex-grow`, `flex-shrink`, and `flex-basis` into a single, powerful declaration:

#css

```
.item-1 {
  flex: 1; /* Equivalent to: flex-grow: 1; flex-shrink:
1; flex-basis: 0%; */
}

.item-2 {
  flex: 2 1 300px; /* grow: 2, shrink: 1, basis: 300px */
}

.item-3 {
```

```
  flex: 0 0 auto; /* No grow, no shrink, auto basis */
}

.item-4 {
  flex: auto; /* Equivalent to: flex: 1 1 auto; */
}

.item-5 {
  flex: none; /* Equivalent to: flex: 0 0 auto; */
}
```

Real-World Example: Email Client Layout

#html

```
<div class="email-client">
  <nav class="sidebar">
    <ul class="folder-list">
      <li>Inbox (12)</li>
      <li>Sent</li>
      <li>Drafts (3)</li>
      <li>Trash</li>
    </ul>
  </nav>
  <div class="email-list">
    <div class="email-item">
      <strong>John Doe</strong>
      <span class="subject">Meeting Tomorrow</span>
      <span class="preview">Let's discuss the
project...</span>
    </div>
    <div class="email-item">
```

```
      <strong>Jane Smith</strong>
      <span class="subject">Budget Review</span>
      <span class="preview">Please find
attached...</span>
    </div>
  </div>
  <div class="email-content">
    <div class="email-header">
      <h2>Meeting Tomorrow</h2>
      <p>From: John Doe &lt;john@example.com&gt;</p>
    </div>
    <div class="email-body">
      <p>Hi there,</p>
      <p>Let's discuss the project details in tomorrow's
meeting...</p>
    </div>
  </div>
</div>
```

#css

```
.email-client {
  display: flex;
  height: 100vh;
  font-family: Arial, sans-serif;
}

.sidebar {
  flex: 0 0 200px; /* Fixed width sidebar */
  background-color: #f8f9fa;
  border-right: 1px solid #dee2e6;
```

```
  padding: 1rem;
}

.folder-list {
  list-style: none;
  padding: 0;
  margin: 0;
}

.folder-list li {
  padding: 0.75rem;
  cursor: pointer;
  border-radius: 4px;
  margin-bottom: 0.25rem;
  transition: background-color 0.2s ease;
}

.folder-list li:hover {
  background-color: #e9ecef;
}

.email-list {
  flex: 0 0 350px; /* Fixed width email list */
  border-right: 1px solid #dee2e6;
  overflow-y: auto;
}

.email-item {
  display: flex;
  flex-direction: column;
  padding: 1rem;
```

```
  border-bottom: 1px solid #f0f0f0;
  cursor: pointer;
  transition: background-color 0.2s ease;
}

.email-item:hover {
  background-color: #f8f9fa;
}

.email-item strong {
  margin-bottom: 0.25rem;
}

.subject {
  font-weight: 600;
  margin-bottom: 0.25rem;
  color: #495057;
}

.preview {
  font-size: 0.9rem;
  color: #6c757d;
  overflow: hidden;
  text-overflow: ellipsis;
  white-space: nowrap;
}

.email-content {
  flex: 1; /* Takes remaining space */
  display: flex;
  flex-direction: column;
```

```
  background-color: white;
}

.email-header {
  flex: 0 0 auto; /* Fixed height header */
  padding: 2rem;
  border-bottom: 1px solid #dee2e6;
  background-color: #f8f9fa;
}

.email-header h2 {
  margin: 0 0 0.5rem 0;
  color: #212529;
}

.email-header p {
  margin: 0;
  color: #6c757d;
  font-size: 0.9rem;
}

.email-body {
  flex: 1; /* Takes remaining space */
  padding: 2rem;
  overflow-y: auto;
}
```

align-self: Individual Cross Axis Control

The `align-self` property allows individual flex items to override the container's `align-items` setting:

#css

```
.container {
  display: flex;
  align-items: center; /* Default alignment for all items
*/
  height: 200px;
}

.item-start {
  align-self: flex-start; /* Overrides container
alignment */
  background-color: #ffcdd2;
}

.item-end {
  align-self: flex-end;
  background-color: #c8e6c9;
}

.item-stretch {
  align-self: stretch;
  background-color: #bbdefb;
}

.item-baseline {
  align-self: baseline;
  background-color: #f8bbd9;
  font-size: 2rem;
}
```

Advanced Example: Profile Card with Mixed Alignments

#html

```
<div class="profile-card">
  <div class="avatar">
    <img src="avatar.jpg" alt="Profile Picture">
  </div>
  <div class="profile-info">
    <h3>Sarah Johnson</h3>
    <p class="title">Senior Developer</p>
    <p class="bio">Passionate about creating amazing user
experiences...</p>
  </div>
  <div class="profile-actions">
    <button class="follow-btn">Follow</button>
    <button class="message-btn">Message</button>
  </div>
  <div class="profile-stats">
    <div class="stat">
      <span class="number">1.2k</span>
      <span class="label">Followers</span>
    </div>
    <div class="stat">
      <span class="number">543</span>
      <span class="label">Following</span>
    </div>
  </div>
</div>
```

#css

```
.profile-card {
  display: flex;
  align-items: center;
  gap: 1.5rem;
  padding: 2rem;
  background-color: white;
  border-radius: 12px;
  box-shadow: 0 4px 16px rgba(0,0,0,0.1);
  max-width: 800px;
  margin: 2rem auto;
}

.avatar {
  align-self: flex-start; /* Align to top */
  flex: 0 0 auto;
}

.avatar img {
  width: 80px;
  height: 80px;
  border-radius: 50%;
  object-fit: cover;
  border: 3px solid #e9ecef;
}

.profile-info {
  flex: 1;
  align-self: stretch; /* Full height */
  display: flex;
  flex-direction: column;
```

```css
  justify-content: center;
}

.profile-info h3 {
  margin: 0 0 0.5rem 0;
  font-size: 1.5rem;
  color: #212529;
}

.title {
  margin: 0 0 1rem 0;
  color: #007bff;
  font-weight: 600;
}

.bio {
  margin: 0;
  color: #6c757d;
  line-height: 1.5;
}

.profile-actions {
  align-self: center; /* Center vertically */
  display: flex;
  flex-direction: column;
  gap: 0.5rem;
}

.profile-actions button {
  padding: 0.5rem 1rem;
  border: none;
```

```
  border-radius: 6px;
  cursor: pointer;
  font-weight: 600;
  transition: all 0.2s ease;
}

.follow-btn {
  background-color: #007bff;
  color: white;
}

.message-btn {
  background-color: transparent;
  color: #007bff;
  border: 1px solid #007bff;
}

.profile-stats {
  align-self: flex-end; /* Align to bottom */
  display: flex;
  gap: 1rem;
}

.stat {
  text-align: center;
}

.stat .number {
  display: block;
  font-size: 1.2rem;
  font-weight: bold;
```

```
  color: #212529;
}

.stat .label {
  font-size: 0.8rem;
  color: #6c757d;
}
```

order: Visual Reordering

The `order` property allows you to change the visual order of flex items without altering the HTML structure:

#css

```
.container {
  display: flex;
}

.item-1 {
  order: 3; /* Appears third */
  background-color: #ffeb3b;
}

.item-2 {
  order: 1; /* Appears first */
  background-color: #4caf50;
}

.item-3 {
  order: 2; /* Appears second */
```

```
  background-color: #2196f3;
}
```

Responsive Reordering Example: Mobile-First Layout

#html

```html
<div class="content-layout">
  <main class="main-content">
    <h1>Main Article</h1>
    <p>This is the primary content...</p>
  </main>
  <aside class="sidebar">
    <h3>Related Links</h3>
    <ul>
      <li><a href="#">Link 1</a></li>
      <li><a href="#">Link 2</a></li>
    </ul>
  </aside>
  <nav class="navigation">
    <ul>
      <li><a href="#home">Home</a></li>
      <li><a href="#about">About</a></li>
      <li><a href="#contact">Contact</a></li>
    </ul>
  </nav>
</div>
```

#css

```css
.content-layout {
  display: flex;
```

```
  flex-direction: column;
  gap: 1rem;
  padding: 1rem;
}

/* Mobile-first: Navigation appears first */
.navigation {
  order: 1;
  background-color: #343a40;
  color: white;
  padding: 1rem;
  border-radius: 6px;
}

.navigation ul {
  display: flex;
  list-style: none;
  gap: 1rem;
  margin: 0;
  padding: 0;
  justify-content: center;
}

.navigation a {
  color: white;
  text-decoration: none;
  padding: 0.5rem;
}

.main-content {
  order: 2;
```

```css
  flex: 1;
  background-color: white;
  padding: 2rem;
  border-radius: 6px;
  box-shadow: 0 2px 8px rgba(0,0,0,0.1);
}

.sidebar {
  order: 3;
  background-color: #f8f9fa;
  padding: 1.5rem;
  border-radius: 6px;
  border: 1px solid #dee2e6;
}

.sidebar ul {
  list-style: none;
  padding: 0;
  margin: 1rem 0 0 0;
}

.sidebar li {
  margin-bottom: 0.5rem;
}

.sidebar a {
  color: #007bff;
  text-decoration: none;
}

/* Desktop: Reorder for optimal layout */
```

```
@media (min-width: 768px) {
  .content-layout {
    flex-direction: row;
  }

  .navigation {
    order: 1;
    flex: 0 0 200px;
  }

  .navigation ul {
    flex-direction: column;
    justify-content: flex-start;
  }

  .main-content {
    order: 2;
    flex: 1;
  }

  .sidebar {
    order: 3;
    flex: 0 0 250px;
  }
}
```

11.5 Common Flexbox Layout Patterns

Essential Layout Solutions

Flexbox excels at solving common layout challenges that have historically been difficult with CSS. These patterns represent tried-and-tested solutions for everyday design requirements.

Perfect Centering Pattern

Centering content both horizontally and vertically has traditionally been challenging, but Flexbox makes it effortless:

#css

```
.perfect-center {
  display: flex;
  justify-content: center; /* Horizontal centering */
  align-items: center; /* Vertical centering */
  height: 100vh; /* Full viewport height */
}
```

Advanced Centering: Modal Dialog

#html

```
<div class="modal-overlay">
  <div class="modal-dialog">
    <div class="modal-header">
      <h2>Confirm Action</h2>
      <button class="close-btn">&times;</button>
    </div>
    <div class="modal-body">
      <p>Are you sure you want to delete this item? This
action cannot be undone.</p>
    </div>
    <div class="modal-footer">
      <button class="btn-cancel">Cancel</button>
```

```
      <button class="btn-confirm">Delete</button>
    </div>
  </div>
</div>
```

#css

```
.modal-overlay {
  position: fixed;
  top: 0;
  left: 0;
  right: 0;
  bottom: 0;
  background-color: rgba(0, 0, 0, 0.5);
  display: flex;
  justify-content: center;
  align-items: center;
  z-index: 1000;
}

.modal-dialog {
  background-color: white;
  border-radius: 8px;
  box-shadow: 0 10px 40px rgba(0, 0, 0, 0.3);
  width: 90%;
  max-width: 500px;
  max-height: 90vh;
  display: flex;
  flex-direction: column;
  overflow: hidden;
}
```

```
.modal-header {
  display: flex;
  justify-content: space-between;
  align-items: center;
  padding: 1.5rem;
  border-bottom: 1px solid #dee2e6;
  background-color: #f8f9fa;
}

.modal-header h2 {
  margin: 0;
  color: #212529;
}

.close-btn {
  background: none;
  border: none;
  font-size: 1.5rem;
  cursor: pointer;
  color: #6c757d;
  width: 32px;
  height: 32px;
  display: flex;
  align-items: center;
  justify-content: center;
  border-radius: 4px;
  transition: background-color 0.2s ease;
}

.close-btn:hover {
```

```
  background-color: #e9ecef;
}

.modal-body {
  flex: 1;
  padding: 2rem 1.5rem;
  overflow-y: auto;
}

.modal-footer {
  display: flex;
  justify-content: flex-end;
  gap: 1rem;
  padding: 1.5rem;
  border-top: 1px solid #dee2e6;
  background-color: #f8f9fa;
}

.modal-footer button {
  padding: 0.5rem 1rem;
  border: none;
  border-radius: 4px;
  cursor: pointer;
  font-weight: 600;
  transition: all 0.2s ease;
}

.btn-cancel {
  background-color: #6c757d;
  color: white;
}
```

```css
.btn-confirm {
  background-color: #dc3545;
  color: white;
}
```

Holy Grail Layout Pattern

The Holy Grail layout features a header, footer, and three-column content area with a flexible center column:

#html

```html
<div class="holy-grail">
  <header class="header">Header Content</header>
  <div class="content">
    <nav class="left-sidebar">Left Navigation</nav>
    <main class="main-content">Main Content Area</main>
    <aside class="right-sidebar">Right Sidebar</aside>
  </div>
  <footer class="footer">Footer Content</footer>
</div>
```

#css

```css
.holy-grail {
  display: flex;
  flex-direction: column;
  min-height: 100vh;
}
```

```
.header {
  flex: 0 0 auto;
  background-color: #343a40;
  color: white;
  padding: 1rem 2rem;
  display: flex;
  justify-content: space-between;
  align-items: center;
}

.content {
  flex: 1;
  display: flex;
  gap: 1rem;
  padding: 1rem;
}

.left-sidebar {
  flex: 0 0 200px;
  background-color: #f8f9fa;
  padding: 1rem;
  border: 1px solid #dee2e6;
  border-radius: 6px;
}

.main-content {
  flex: 1;
  background-color: white;
  padding: 2rem;
  border: 1px solid #dee2e6;
  border-radius: 6px;
```

```css
  box-shadow: 0 2px 4px rgba(0,0,0,0.1);
}

.right-sidebar {
  flex: 0 0 250px;
  background-color: #f8f9fa;
  padding: 1rem;
  border: 1px solid #dee2e6;
  border-radius: 6px;
}

.footer {
  flex: 0 0 auto;
  background-color: #6c757d;
  color: white;
  padding: 2rem;
  text-align: center;
}

/* Responsive collapse */
@media (max-width: 768px) {
  .content {
    flex-direction: column;
  }

  .left-sidebar,
  .right-sidebar {
    flex: 0 0 auto;
  }
}
```

Card Grid Pattern

Responsive card grids that adapt to different screen sizes:

#html

```
<div class="card-grid">
  <div class="card">
    <img src="product1.jpg" alt="Product 1" class="card-image">
    <div class="card-content">
      <h3>Premium Headphones</h3>
      <p class="price">$199.99</p>
      <p class="description">High-quality wireless headphones with noise cancellation.</p>
      <button class="add-to-cart">Add to Cart</button>
    </div>
  </div>
  <div class="card">
    <img src="product2.jpg" alt="Product 2" class="card-image">
    <div class="card-content">
      <h3>Smart Watch</h3>
      <p class="price">$299.99</p>
      <p class="description">Feature-rich smartwatch with health monitoring.</p>
      <button class="add-to-cart">Add to Cart</button>
    </div>
  </div>
  <div class="card">
    <img src="product3.jpg" alt="Product 3" class="card-image">
```

```
    <div class="card-content">
      <h3>Wireless Speaker</h3>
      <p class="price">$89.99</p>
      <p class="description">Portable Bluetooth speaker with amazing sound quality.</p>
      <button class="add-to-cart">Add to Cart</button>
    </div>
  </div>
</div>
```

#css

```
.card-grid {
  display: flex;
  flex-wrap: wrap;
  gap: 1.5rem;
  padding: 2rem;
  justify-content: center;
}

.card {
  flex: 1 1 300px; /* Grow, shrink, 300px basis */
  max-width: 350px;
  min-width: 280px;
  background-color: white;
  border-radius: 12px;
  box-shadow: 0 4px 16px rgba(0,0,0,0.1);
  overflow: hidden;
  transition: transform 0.2s ease, box-shadow 0.2s ease;
  display: flex;
  flex-direction: column;
```

```
}

.card:hover {
  transform: translateY(-4px);
  box-shadow: 0 8px 24px rgba(0,0,0,0.15);
}

.card-image {
  width: 100%;
  height: 200px;
  object-fit: cover;
  background-color: #f8f9fa;
  display: flex;
  align-items: center;
  justify-content: center;
  color: #6c757d;
  font-size: 0.9rem;
}

.card-content {
  flex: 1;
  padding: 1.5rem;
  display: flex;
  flex-direction: column;
}

.card-content h3 {
  margin: 0 0 0.5rem 0;
  color: #212529;
  font-size: 1.2rem;
}
```

```
.price {
  margin: 0 0 1rem 0;
  font-size: 1.3rem;
  font-weight: bold;
  color: #007bff;
}

.description {
  margin: 0 0 1.5rem 0;
  color: #6c757d;
  line-height: 1.5;
  flex: 1;
}

.add-to-cart {
  padding: 0.75rem 1.5rem;
  background-color: #28a745;
  color: white;
  border: none;
  border-radius: 6px;
  cursor: pointer;
  font-weight: 600;
  transition: background-color 0.2s ease;
  align-self: flex-start;
}

.add-to-cart:hover {
  background-color: #218838;
}
```

Sticky Footer Pattern

A footer that sticks to the bottom of the viewport when content is short:

#html

```
<div class="page-wrapper">
  <header class="page-header">
    <h1>My Website</h1>
    <nav>Navigation</nav>
  </header>
  <main class="page-content">
    <h2>Welcome</h2>
    <p>This is the main content area...</p>
  </main>
  <footer class="page-footer">
    <p>&copy; 2025 My Website. All rights reserved.</p>
  </footer>
</div>
```

#css

```
.page-wrapper {
  display: flex;
  flex-direction: column;
  min-height: 100vh;
}

.page-header {
  flex: 0 0 auto;
  background-color: #007bff;
```

```
  color: white;
  padding: 2rem;
  display: flex;
  justify-content: space-between;
  align-items: center;
}

.page-content {
  flex: 1; /* Takes up remaining space, pushing footer down */
  padding: 2rem;
  background-color: #f8f9fa;
}

.page-footer {
  flex: 0 0 auto;
  background-color: #343a40;
  color: white;
  padding: 1rem;
  text-align: center;
}
```

Media Object Pattern

Perfect for comments, notifications, or any content with an image and accompanying text:

#html

```
<div class="media-object">
  <div class="media-image">
```

```
    <img src="avatar.jpg" alt="User Avatar">
  </div>
  <div class="media-content">
    <h4>John Doe</h4>
    <p class="timestamp">2 hours ago</p>
    <p>This is a comment or message that can be quite 
long and will wrap to multiple lines as needed. The image 
will stay aligned to the top.</p>
    <div class="media-actions">
      <button class="reply-btn">Reply</button>
      <button class="like-btn">Like</button>
    </div>
  </div>
</div>
```

#css

```
.media-object {
  display: flex;
  gap: 1rem;
  padding: 1rem;
  border-bottom: 1px solid #e9ecef;
}

.media-image {
  flex: 0 0 auto;
  align-self: flex-start;
}

.media-image img {
  width: 50px;
```

```
  height: 50px;
  border-radius: 50%;
  object-fit: cover;
}

.media-content {
  flex: 1;
  min-width: 0; /* Allows text to wrap properly */
}

.media-content h4 {
  margin: 0 0 0.25rem 0;
  color: #212529;
  font-size: 1rem;
}

.timestamp {
  margin: 0 0 0.5rem 0;
  font-size: 0.8rem;
  color: #6c757d;
}

.media-content p {
  margin: 0 0 1rem 0;
  line-height: 1.5;
  color: #495057;
}

.media-actions {
  display: flex;
  gap: 1rem;
```

```
}

.media-actions button {
  background: none;
  border: none;
  color: #007bff;
  cursor: pointer;
  font-size: 0.9rem;
  padding: 0.25rem 0;
  transition: color 0.2s ease;
}

.media-actions button:hover {
  color: #0056b3;
  text-decoration: underline;
}
```

Form Layout Pattern

Flexible form layouts that adapt to different screen sizes:

#html

```
<form class="flexible-form">
  <div class="form-row">
    <div class="form-group">
      <label for="firstName">First Name</label>
      <input type="text" id="firstName" name="firstName"
required>
    </div>
    <div class="form-group">
```

```
      <label for="lastName">Last Name</label>
      <input type="text" id="lastName" name="lastName"
required>
    </div>
  </div>
  <div class="form-row">
    <div class="form-group full-width">
      <label for="email">Email Address</label>
      <input type="email" id="email" name="email"
required>
    </div>
  </div>
  <div class="form-row">
    <div class="form-group">
      <label for="phone">Phone Number</label>
      <input type="tel" id="phone" name="phone">
    </div>
    <div class="form-group">
      <label for="company">Company</label>
      <input type="text" id="company" name="company">
    </div>
  </div>
  <div class="form-row">
    <div class="form-group full-width">
      <label for="message">Message</label>
      <textarea id="message" name="message"
rows="4"></textarea>
    </div>
  </div>
  <div class="form-actions">
    <button type="button" class="btn-
secondary">Cancel</button>
```

```
    <button type="submit" class="btn-primary">Send
Message</button>
  </div>
</form>
```

#css

```
.flexible-form {
  max-width: 600px;
  margin: 2rem auto;
  padding: 2rem;
  background-color: white;
  border-radius: 8px;
  box-shadow: 0 4px 16px rgba(0,0,0,0.1);
}

.form-row {
  display: flex;
  gap: 1rem;
  margin-bottom: 1.5rem;
}

.form-group {
  flex: 1;
  display: flex;
  flex-direction: column;
}

.form-group.full-width {
  flex: 1 1 100%;
}
```

```
.form-group label {
  margin-bottom: 0.5rem;
  font-weight: 600;
  color: #495057;
}

.form-group input,
.form-group textarea {
  padding: 0.75rem;
  border: 1px solid #ced4da;
  border-radius: 4px;
  font-size: 1rem;
  transition: border-color 0.2s ease, box-shadow 0.2s
ease;
}

.form-group input:focus,
.form-group textarea:focus {
  outline: none;
  border-color: #007bff;
  box-shadow: 0 0 0 3px rgba(0,123,255,0.25);
}

.form-actions {
  display: flex;
  justify-content: flex-end;
  gap: 1rem;
  margin-top: 2rem;
}
```

```
.form-actions button {
  padding: 0.75rem 1.5rem;
  border: none;
  border-radius: 4px;
  cursor: pointer;
  font-weight: 600;
  transition: all 0.2s ease;
}

.btn-primary {
  background-color: #007bff;
  color: white;
}

.btn-primary:hover {
  background-color: #0056b3;
}

.btn-secondary {
  background-color: #6c757d;
  color: white;
}

.btn-secondary:hover {
  background-color: #545b62;
}

/* Mobile responsive */
@media (max-width: 768px) {
  .form-row {
    flex-direction: column;
```

```
  }

  .form-actions {
    flex-direction: column-reverse;
  }

  .form-actions button {
    width: 100%;
  }
}
```

Essential Tips

- **Start with the container**: Always begin by applying `display: flex` to the parent element and understand how this affects the immediate children before focusing on individual item properties.
- **Visualize the axes**: Before writing any alignment properties, mentally identify where the main axis and cross axis are positioned based on your `flex-direction` setting. This prevents confusion when applying `justify-content` and `align-items`.
- **Use flex shorthand wisely**: The `flex` property is powerful but can be confusing. When in doubt, use explicit values like `flex: 1 0 auto` rather than just `flex: 1` to make your intentions clear.
- **Remember min-width matters**: Flex items have an implicit `min-width: auto`, which can prevent them from shrinking below their content size. Set `min-width: 0` when you need items to shrink smaller than their content.
- **Test with varying content**: Always test your flex layouts with different amounts of content - short text, long text, many items, few items - to ensure the layout remains stable and visually appealing in all scenarios.

Actionable Strategies

- **Create a flexbox testing environment**: Build a simple HTML page with adjustable flex properties using input controls or select dropdowns. This hands-on experimentation accelerates learning and helps you understand property interactions.
- **Implement the patterns progressively**: Start with basic centering and simple navigation bars, then gradually work toward complex layouts like dashboards and card grids. Build your complexity gradually rather than jumping to advanced patterns.
- **Study real-world websites**: Open developer tools on well-designed websites and examine how they use flexbox. Look for patterns in popular frameworks like Bootstrap or Tailwind CSS to understand industry best practices.
- **Build a component library**: Create reusable flex-based components for common elements like navigation bars, cards, forms, and modal dialogs. Having these templates ready saves time and ensures consistency across projects.
- **Practice responsive design**: Always consider how your flex layouts will behave on different screen sizes. Use media queries to adjust flex properties and create layouts that work seamlessly from mobile to desktop.
- **Debug systematically**: When flex layouts don't work as expected, use browser developer tools to inspect the computed flex properties. Add temporary background colors or borders

Chapter 12: CSS Grid System

12.1 Introduction to CSS Grid

CSS Grid represents a revolutionary approach to web layout design, providing developers with unprecedented control over two-dimensional layouts. Unlike Flexbox, which operates primarily along a single axis, CSS Grid excels at managing both rows and columns simultaneously, making it the ideal solution for complex layout requirements.

Understanding Grid Fundamentals

CSS Grid transforms any HTML element into a powerful layout container by applying `display: grid` or `display: inline-grid`. This declaration creates a grid container that establishes a new grid formatting context for its children, automatically converting them into grid items.

The grid system operates on a coordinate-based approach, where content placement occurs through explicit positioning or automatic flow algorithms. This methodology eliminates the need for complex float-based layouts or intricate positioning schemes that plagued earlier CSS techniques.

Grid vs. Other Layout Methods

Traditional layout methods often required creative workarounds and hacks to achieve desired results. CSS Grid eliminates these complications by providing native support for:

- **Overlapping elements** without absolute positioning
- **Equal-height columns** without JavaScript calculations
- **Complex asymmetrical layouts** with minimal code
- **Responsive design** through built-in flexibility
- **Content reordering** independent of HTML structure

Browser Support and Progressive Enhancement

CSS Grid enjoys excellent browser support across modern browsers, with over 95% global compatibility. For legacy browser support, Grid can be implemented progressively, allowing fallback layouts for older browsers while providing enhanced experiences for modern ones.

#css

```
/* Progressive enhancement approach */
.container {
  /* Fallback for older browsers */
  display: flex;
  flex-wrap: wrap;

  /* Grid for modern browsers */
  display: grid;
  grid-template-columns: repeat(3, 1fr);
  gap: 20px;
}
```

Grid Terminology

Understanding Grid requires familiarity with its specific terminology:

- **Grid Container**: The parent element with `display: grid`
- **Grid Items**: Direct children of the grid container
- **Grid Lines**: The dividing lines that create the grid structure
- **Grid Tracks**: The space between two adjacent grid lines
- **Grid Cells**: The intersection of a row and column
- **Grid Areas**: Rectangular areas spanning multiple cells

12.2 Grid Container and Grid Items

Creating Grid Containers

The foundation of any grid layout begins with establishing a grid container. The `display` property accepts two grid values:

#css

```
.grid-container {
  display: grid; /* Block-level grid container */
}

.inline-grid-container {
  display: inline-grid; /* Inline-level grid container */
}
```

The choice between `grid` and `inline-grid` depends on how the container should behave within its parent context. Block-level grid containers occupy the full width of their parent, while inline-grid containers only take up necessary space.

Grid Item Behavior

When an element becomes a grid container, its direct children automatically transform into grid items. This transformation triggers several important behaviors:

#css

```
.grid-container {
  display: grid;
  grid-template-columns: 1fr 2fr 1fr;
  grid-template-rows: 100px auto 100px;
}

.grid-item {
  /* Grid items can be explicitly positioned */
  grid-column: 2;
  grid-row: 1 / 3;
```

```
}
```

Grid items automatically participate in the grid formatting context, allowing them to be positioned using grid-specific properties. Unlike block elements, grid items don't create line breaks and can overlap when positioned explicitly.

Default Grid Behavior

Without explicit grid definitions, browsers create an implicit grid based on content requirements. This automatic behavior includes:

#css

```css
/* Default implicit grid behavior */
.auto-grid {
  display: grid;
  /* Implicit single column layout */
  /* Row height determined by content */
}
```

The implicit grid creates a single-column layout where each grid item occupies its own row. Row heights adjust automatically to accommodate content, while the single column spans the full container width.

Grid Item Properties

Grid items accept several positioning properties that control their placement and sizing:

#css

```css
.positioned-item {
```

```
  /* Column positioning */
  grid-column-start: 2;
  grid-column-end: 4;
  /* Shorthand: grid-column: 2 / 4; */

  /* Row positioning */
  grid-row-start: 1;
  grid-row-end: 3;
  /* Shorthand: grid-row: 1 / 3; */

  /* Area shorthand */
  grid-area: 1 / 2 / 3 / 4; /* row-start / col-start /
row-end / col-end */
}
```

Nested Grids

Grid items can themselves become grid containers, enabling complex nested layouts:

#css

```
.parent-grid {
  display: grid;
  grid-template-columns: 200px 1fr;
  gap: 20px;
}

.nested-grid {
  display: grid;
  grid-template-columns: repeat(2, 1fr);
```

```
  gap: 10px;
}
```

This nesting capability allows for sophisticated layout hierarchies while maintaining clean, semantic HTML structure.

12.3 Grid Template Columns and Rows

Defining Grid Tracks

Grid tracks define the size and number of columns and rows in your grid. The `grid-template-columns` and `grid-template-rows` properties accept various unit types and sizing functions.

Fixed Sizing

Fixed sizing uses absolute units like pixels, ems, or percentages:

#css

```css
.fixed-grid {
  display: grid;
  grid-template-columns: 200px 300px 150px;
  grid-template-rows: 100px 200px;
}
```

This approach provides precise control but lacks flexibility for responsive design.

Fractional Units (fr)

Fractional units distribute available space proportionally:

#css

```
.fractional-grid {
  display: grid;
  grid-template-columns: 1fr 2fr 1fr; /* 25% 50% 25%
distribution */
  grid-template-rows: 1fr 3fr; /* 25% 75% distribution */
}
```

Fractional units calculate remaining space after fixed-size tracks, making them ideal for flexible layouts.

Mixed Unit Types

Combining different unit types creates sophisticated layouts:

#css

```
.mixed-grid {
  display: grid;
  grid-template-columns: 200px 1fr 100px; /* Fixed-
Flexible-Fixed */
  grid-template-rows: auto 1fr auto; /* Content-Flexible-
Content */
}
```

The repeat() Function

The `repeat()` function simplifies repetitive track definitions:

#css

```
.repeated-grid {
```

```
  display: grid;
  /* Creates 5 equal columns */
  grid-template-columns: repeat(5, 1fr);

  /* Creates alternating pattern */
  grid-template-columns: repeat(3, 100px 200px);

  /* Mixed with other values */
  grid-template-columns: 200px repeat(3, 1fr) 100px;
}
```

Auto-Repeat Variations

The `repeat()` function includes automatic repetition options:

#css

```
.auto-repeat-grid {
  display: grid;
  /* Creates as many 200px columns as fit */
  grid-template-columns: repeat(auto-fit, 200px);

  /* Creates columns with minimum 200px, maximum 1fr */
  grid-template-columns: repeat(auto-fill, minmax(200px,
1fr));
}
```

Min-Max Sizing

The `minmax()` function defines flexible track sizes with constraints:

#css

```
.flexible-grid {
  display: grid;
  /* Columns: minimum 200px, maximum 1fr */
  grid-template-columns: repeat(3, minmax(200px, 1fr));

  /* Rows: minimum content size, maximum 300px */
  grid-template-rows: repeat(2, minmax(min-content,
300px));
}
```

Content-Based Sizing

Grid supports content-based sizing keywords:

#css

```
.content-grid {
  display: grid;
  grid-template-columns:
    min-content    /* Minimum width to fit content */
    max-content    /* Maximum width without wrapping */
    fit-content(300px); /* Content size capped at 300px
*/
}
```

Named Grid Lines

Grid lines can be named for easier reference:

#css

```
.named-grid {
  display: grid;
  grid-template-columns:
    [sidebar-start] 200px
    [sidebar-end main-start] 1fr
    [main-end];
  grid-template-rows:
    [header-start] 100px
    [header-end content-start] 1fr
    [content-end footer-start] 50px
    [footer-end];
}

.sidebar {
  grid-column: sidebar-start / sidebar-end;
  grid-row: content-start / content-end;
}
```

Implicit Grid Tracks

When grid items are placed outside the explicit grid, implicit tracks are created automatically:

#css

```
.implicit-grid {
  display: grid;
  grid-template-columns: repeat(3, 1fr);
  /* Only explicit columns defined */

  /* Control implicit row size */
```

```
  grid-auto-rows: 100px;

  /* Control implicit column size */
  grid-auto-columns: 200px;
}
```

12.4 Grid Gaps, Auto-Fit, and Auto-Fill

Understanding Grid Gaps

Grid gaps create space between grid tracks without affecting the overall grid structure or requiring margin calculations. The gap properties provide clean, consistent spacing throughout the grid.

Gap Property Syntax
#css

```
.gap-grid {
  display: grid;
  grid-template-columns: repeat(3, 1fr);

  /* Uniform gap for both rows and columns */
  gap: 20px;

  /* Different gaps for rows and columns */
  gap: 20px 30px; /* row-gap column-gap */

  /* Individual gap properties */
  row-gap: 20px;
  column-gap: 30px;
}
```

```

```

Gap Calculations

Gaps don't add to grid item sizes but create space between them:

#css

```css
.calculated-grid {
  display: grid;
  grid-template-columns: repeat(4, 1fr);
  gap: 20px;
  /* Each column gets: (container-width - 60px) / 4 */
  /* Gap total: 3 gaps × 20px = 60px */
}
```

Auto-Fit vs Auto-Fill

The `auto-fit` and `auto-fill` keywords work with `repeat()` to create responsive grids, but they behave differently when handling empty space.

Auto-Fill Behavior

`auto-fill` creates as many tracks as possible, maintaining empty tracks:

#css

```css
.auto-fill-grid {
  display: grid;
  grid-template-columns: repeat(auto-fill, minmax(200px,
1fr));
  gap: 20px;
}
```

In a 1000px container:

- Creates 4 columns at 200px minimum
- Leaves remaining 200px distributed among columns
- Maintains 4 columns even if only 2 items exist

Auto-Fit Behavior

`auto-fit` collapses empty tracks, allowing filled tracks to expand:

#css

```
.auto-fit-grid {
  display: grid;
  grid-template-columns: repeat(auto-fit, minmax(200px,
1fr));
  gap: 20px;
}
```

In a 1000px container with 2 items:

- Creates 2 columns
- Each column expands to fill available space
- Empty tracks collapse to zero width

Practical Applications

#css

```
/* Card layout that adapts to content */
.card-container {
  display: grid;
  grid-template-columns: repeat(auto-fit, minmax(300px,
1fr));
```

```
  gap: 20px;
  padding: 20px;
}

/* Gallery with consistent spacing */
.gallery {
  display: grid;
  grid-template-columns: repeat(auto-fill, minmax(250px,
1fr));
  gap: 15px;
}
```

Advanced Gap Techniques

Conditional Gaps

Gaps can be controlled with CSS custom properties and media queries:

#css

```
.responsive-gaps {
  display: grid;
  grid-template-columns: repeat(auto-fit, minmax(200px,
1fr));
  gap: var(--grid-gap, 20px);
}

@media (max-width: 768px) {
  .responsive-gaps {
    --grid-gap: 10px;
  }
}
```

Gap Alternatives

For more complex spacing needs, margin and padding can supplement gaps:

#css

```
.complex-spacing {
  display: grid;
  grid-template-columns: repeat(3, 1fr);
  gap: 20px;
}

.special-item {
  margin-top: 40px; /* Additional spacing for specific items */
}
```

Combining Auto-Sizing with Gaps

Auto-sizing combined with gaps creates highly responsive layouts:

#css

```
.flexible-cards {
  display: grid;
  grid-template-columns: repeat(auto-fit, minmax(280px, 1fr));
  gap: clamp(15px, 3vw, 30px); /* Responsive gap sizing */
  padding: clamp(15px, 3vw, 30px);
}
```

12.5 Grid Layout Use Cases

Dashboard Layouts

Grid excels at creating dashboard interfaces with multiple content areas:

#css

```css
.dashboard {
  display: grid;
  grid-template-areas:
    "header header header"
    "sidebar main widgets"
    "sidebar footer footer";
  grid-template-columns: 250px 1fr 300px;
  grid-template-rows: 80px 1fr 60px;
  gap: 20px;
  height: 100vh;
}

.header { grid-area: header; }
.sidebar { grid-area: sidebar; }
.main { grid-area: main; }
.widgets { grid-area: widgets; }
.footer { grid-area: footer; }
```

Magazine-Style Layouts

Complex editorial layouts benefit from Grid's precise positioning:

#css

```
.magazine-layout {
  display: grid;
  grid-template-columns: repeat(12, 1fr);
  grid-template-rows: repeat(8, 100px);
  gap: 15px;
}

.hero-article {
  grid-column: 1 / 8;
  grid-row: 1 / 5;
}

.feature-article {
  grid-column: 8 / 13;
  grid-row: 1 / 3;
}

.sidebar-content {
  grid-column: 8 / 13;
  grid-row: 3 / 6;
}
```

E-commerce Product Grids

Responsive product grids adapt to various screen sizes:

#css

```
.product-grid {
  display: grid;
```

```
  grid-template-columns: repeat(auto-fill, minmax(280px,
1fr));
  gap: 30px;
  padding: 30px;
}

.product-card {
  display: grid;
  grid-template-rows: 200px auto auto auto;
  gap: 15px;
  border: 1px solid #ddd;
  border-radius: 8px;
  overflow: hidden;
}

.product-image {
  grid-row: 1;
  background-size: cover;
  background-position: center;
}

.product-title {
  grid-row: 2;
  padding: 0 15px;
  font-weight: bold;
}

.product-price {
  grid-row: 3;
  padding: 0 15px;
  color: #e44d26;
```

```
}

.product-actions {
  grid-row: 4;
  padding: 15px;
}
```

Form Layouts

Grid simplifies complex form layouts:

#css

```
.form-grid {
  display: grid;
  grid-template-columns: repeat(2, 1fr);
  grid-template-rows: auto;
  gap: 20px;
  max-width: 600px;
}

.full-width {
  grid-column: 1 / -1;
}

.form-group {
  display: grid;
  gap: 5px;
}

.form-actions {
```

```
  grid-column: 1 / -1;
  display: grid;
  grid-template-columns: auto auto;
  gap: 15px;
  justify-content: end;
}
```

Card-Based Layouts

Flexible card systems adapt to content and screen size:

#css

```
.card-system {
  display: grid;
  grid-template-columns: repeat(auto-fit, minmax(320px, 1fr));
  gap: 25px;
  padding: 25px;
}

.card {
  display: grid;
  grid-template-rows: auto 1fr auto;
  border: 1px solid #e0e0e0;
  border-radius: 12px;
  overflow: hidden;
  transition: transform 0.2s;
}

.card:hover {
```

```
  transform: translateY(-5px);
  box-shadow: 0 10px 25px rgba(0,0,0,0.1);
}

.card-header {
  padding: 20px;
  background: linear-gradient(135deg, #667eea 0%, #764ba2
100%);
  color: white;
}

.card-content {
  padding: 20px;
  display: grid;
  gap: 15px;
}

.card-footer {
  padding: 20px;
  background: #f8f9fa;
  border-top: 1px solid #e9ecef;
}
```

Responsive Navigation

Grid creates flexible navigation systems:

#css

```
.navigation {
  display: grid;
```

```
  grid-template-columns: auto 1fr auto;
  align-items: center;
  gap: 20px;
  padding: 15px 30px;
  background: white;
  box-shadow: 0 2px 10px rgba(0,0,0,0.1);
}

.nav-menu {
  display: grid;
  grid-template-columns: repeat(auto-fit, minmax(100px,
auto));
  gap: 30px;
  list-style: none;
  margin: 0;
  padding: 0;
}

@media (max-width: 768px) {
  .navigation {
    grid-template-columns: auto auto;
    grid-template-rows: auto auto;
  }

  .nav-menu {
    grid-column: 1 / -1;
    grid-row: 2;
    grid-template-columns: 1fr;
    gap: 0;
    max-height: 0;
    overflow: hidden;
```

```
    transition: max-height 0.3s;
  }

  .nav-menu.active {
    max-height: 300px;
  }
}
```

Image Gallery Layouts

Grid enables sophisticated gallery arrangements:

#css

```
.gallery {
  display: grid;
  grid-template-columns: repeat(auto-fill, minmax(200px,
1fr));
  grid-auto-rows: 200px;
  gap: 15px;
  padding: 15px;
}

.gallery-item {
  border-radius: 8px;
  overflow: hidden;
  cursor: pointer;
  transition: transform 0.3s;
}

.gallery-item:hover {
```

```
  transform: scale(1.05);
}

/* Featured items span multiple cells */
.gallery-item.featured {
  grid-column: span 2;
  grid-row: span 2;
}

.gallery-item.wide {
  grid-column: span 2;
}

.gallery-item.tall {
  grid-row: span 2;
}
```

Essential Tips

- Start with simple grid layouts and gradually increase complexity as you become comfortable with grid properties and behaviors.
- Use browser developer tools to visualize grid lines and areas, making it easier to debug and understand your layouts.
- Combine CSS Grid with Flexbox strategically - use Grid for overall page layout and Flexbox for component-level alignment and distribution.
- Test your grid layouts across different screen sizes and devices to ensure responsive behavior works as expected.
- Name your grid lines and areas when creating complex layouts to improve code readability and maintenance.

Actionable Strategies

- Create a grid template library with common layout patterns that you can reuse across projects to speed up development.
- Implement progressive enhancement by starting with a flexible fallback layout before adding grid properties for modern browsers.
- Use CSS custom properties to create themeable grid systems where gap sizes, column counts, and breakpoints can be easily modified.
- Build responsive grids using `auto-fit` and `minmax()` to eliminate the need for media queries in many layout scenarios.
- Prototype complex layouts using grid-template-areas first, then convert to line-based positioning for production code when needed.
- Establish a consistent grid system across your entire project by defining standard column counts, gap sizes, and breakpoint behaviors.
- Document your grid patterns and naming conventions to ensure team consistency and easier maintenance of grid-based layouts.

Chapter 13: Float and Clear

The CSS float property represents one of the fundamental positioning mechanisms that shaped web layout design for over a decade. Originally designed to wrap text around images, float evolved into a powerful layout tool before modern alternatives like Flexbox and Grid emerged. Understanding float remains crucial for maintaining legacy code, troubleshooting existing layouts, and grasping the foundations of CSS positioning.

13.1 Float Left and Right

Understanding the Float Property

The float property removes an element from the normal document flow and positions it to the left or right side of its containing element. When an element floats, other content flows around it, creating the wrapping effect commonly seen with images and text.

#css

```
.float-left {
    float: left;
}

.float-right {
    float: right;
}

.no-float {
    float: none; /* Default value */
}
```

How Float Works

When you apply float to an element, several important changes occur:

- The element becomes a block-level element regardless of its original display type
- The element shrinks to fit its content width unless explicitly set
- Other elements flow around the floated element
- The parent container may collapse if it only contains floated children

#html

```
<div class="container">
    <img src="image.jpg" class="float-left" alt="Sample
image">
```

```
    <p>This paragraph text will wrap around the floated image, creating a natural flow that makes the content more readable and visually appealing.</p>
</div>
```

#css

```
.container {
    width: 600px;
    border: 1px solid #ccc;
    padding: 20px;
}

.float-left {
    float: left;
    width: 200px;
    height: 150px;
    margin: 0 20px 20px 0;
    border: 2px solid #333;
}
```

Float Direction Behavior

Left Float

Elements floated left move to the leftmost position available within their containing element. Multiple left-floated elements stack horizontally from left to right.

#css

```
.sidebar {
```

```
    float: left;
    width: 250px;
    background-color: #f0f0f0;
    padding: 20px;
    margin-right: 20px;
}

.content {
    /* Content naturally flows around the floated sidebar
*/
    background-color: #ffffff;
    padding: 20px;
}
```

Right Float

Right-floated elements position themselves at the rightmost available space. When multiple elements float right, they stack from right to left in the order they appear in the HTML.

#css

```
.advertisement {
    float: right;
    width: 300px;
    height: 250px;
    background-color: #ffffcc;
    border: 1px solid #cccc00;
    margin: 0 0 20px 20px;
}

.main-content {
```

```
    /* Text flows around the right-floated advertisement
*/
    line-height: 1.6;
    color: #333;
}
```

Stacking Floated Elements

Multiple floated elements in the same direction create horizontal stacks. Understanding this behavior helps create complex layouts.

#html

```
<div class="gallery">
    <div class="thumbnail">Image 1</div>
    <div class="thumbnail">Image 2</div>
    <div class="thumbnail">Image 3</div>
    <div class="thumbnail">Image 4</div>
</div>
```

#css

```
.gallery {
    width: 800px;
    border: 2px solid #ddd;
    padding: 20px;
}

.thumbnail {
    float: left;
    width: 180px;
```

```
    height: 120px;
    margin: 0 10px 10px 0;
    background-color: #eee;
    border: 1px solid #ccc;
    text-align: center;
    line-height: 120px;
}
```

Width Behavior with Float

Floated elements shrink to fit their content unless you specify a width. This behavior differs significantly from block elements, which naturally expand to fill available width.

#css

```
/* Without width specification */
.shrink-to-fit {
    float: left;
    background-color: #ffcccc;
    padding: 10px;
    /* Width automatically adjusts to content */
}

/* With explicit width */
.fixed-width {
    float: left;
    width: 300px;
    background-color: #ccffcc;
    padding: 10px;
}
```

13.2 Understanding the Clear Property

The Clear Property Fundamentals

The clear property prevents elements from appearing next to floated elements. It forces the cleared element to move below any preceding floated elements, effectively breaking the flow-around behavior.

#css

```css
.clear-left {
    clear: left; /* Clears left floats only */
}

.clear-right {
    clear: right; /* Clears right floats only */
}

.clear-both {
    clear: both; /* Clears both left and right floats */
}

.no-clear {
    clear: none; /* Default value - no clearing */
}
```

Clear Values and Their Effects

Clear: Left

This value moves the element below any left-floated elements but allows it to appear beside right-floated elements.

#html

```
<div class="container">
    <div class="left-float">Left Float</div>
    <div class="right-float">Right Float</div>
    <div class="clear-left">This clears left floats
only</div>
</div>
```

#css

```
.left-float {
    float: left;
    width: 200px;
    height: 100px;
    background-color: #ffcccc;
    margin-right: 20px;
}

.right-float {
    float: right;
    width: 200px;
    height: 100px;
    background-color: #ccffcc;
    margin-left: 20px;
}

.clear-left {
    clear: left;
    background-color: #ccccff;
    padding: 20px;
```

```
}
```

Clear: Right

This value clears right floats while allowing left floats to affect positioning.

#css

```
.clear-right {
    clear: right;
    background-color: #ffffcc;
    padding: 20px;
    /* Will move below right floats but can sit beside left floats */
}
```

Clear: Both

The most commonly used clear value, it moves the element below all floated elements regardless of direction.

#css

```
.clear-both {
    clear: both;
    background-color: #ffccff;
    padding: 20px;
    /* Moves below all floated elements */
}
```

Practical Clear Applications

Section Separators

Use clear to create distinct sections in your layout, ensuring each section starts below any floated content from previous sections.

#html

```html
<article>
    <section class="intro">
        <img src="author.jpg" class="author-photo">
        <p>Introduction text that wraps around the author
photo...</p>
    </section>

    <section class="main-content">
        <h2>Main Content</h2>
        <p>This section starts cleanly below the floated
image...</p>
    </section>
</article>
```

#css

```css
.author-photo {
    float: left;
    width: 100px;
    height: 100px;
    margin: 0 15px 15px 0;
    border-radius: 50%;
}

.main-content {
    clear: both;
```

```
    margin-top: 30px;
    padding-top: 20px;
    border-top: 2px solid #eee;
}
```

Footer Positioning

Ensure footers appear below all floated content using clear: both.

#css

```
.main-layout {
    width: 1000px;
    margin: 0 auto;
}

.sidebar {
    float: left;
    width: 300px;
}

.content {
    float: right;
    width: 680px;
}

.footer {
    clear: both;
    background-color: #333;
    color: white;
    padding: 40px 0;
    text-align: center;
```

```
    margin-top: 50px;
}
```

13.3 Float Issues and How to Fix Them

Container Collapse Problem

The most notorious float issue occurs when a container only contains floated children. Since floated elements leave the normal document flow, the parent container collapses to zero height.

Problem Demonstration

html

```
<div class="collapsed-container">
    <div class="float-child">Child 1</div>
    <div class="float-child">Child 2</div>
    <div class="float-child">Child 3</div>
</div>
<div class="next-element">This element may overlap
floated content</div>
```

#css

```
.collapsed-container {
    border: 3px solid red;
    /* Container height collapses to border thickness
only */
}

.float-child {
    float: left;
```

```
    width: 150px;
    height: 100px;
    background-color: #ccc;
    margin: 10px;
}
```

Solution 1: Clearfix Technique

The clearfix hack uses pseudo-elements to force container expansion.

#css

```css
.clearfix::after {
    content: "";
    display: table;
    clear: both;
}

/* Apply to containers with floated children */
.container-with-floats {
    /* Your existing styles */
}

.container-with-floats::after {
    content: "";
    display: table;
    clear: both;
}
```

Solution 2: Overflow Hidden

Setting overflow: hidden on the parent creates a new block formatting context, containing the floated elements.

#css

```css
.container-with-floats {
    overflow: hidden;
    /* This creates a block formatting context */
    border: 2px solid #333;
    padding: 20px;
}
```

Solution 3: Float the Container

Floating the parent container itself contains the floated children.

#css

```css
.floated-container {
    float: left;
    width: 100%;
    border: 2px solid #333;
    padding: 20px;
}
```

Text Wrapping Issues

Sometimes text wraps awkwardly around floated elements, creating undesirable layouts.

Problem and Solution

#html

```
<div class="article">
    <img src="image.jpg" class="article-image">
    <h2 class="article-title">Article Title That Might Be Too Long</h2>
    <p class="article-text">Article content that should wrap properly...</p>
</div>
```

#css

```
.article-image {
    float: left;
    width: 200px;
    height: 150px;
    margin: 0 20px 20px 0;
}

/* Prevent title from wrapping around image */
.article-title {
    clear: left;
    margin-top: 0;
    font-size: 24px;
    color: #333;
}

/* Allow text to wrap naturally */
.article-text {
    line-height: 1.6;
```

```
    color: #666;
}
```

Margin Collapse with Floated Elements

Floated elements don't participate in margin collapse, which can create unexpected spacing.

#css

```
.normal-element {
    margin-bottom: 20px;
}

.floated-element {
    float: left;
    margin-top: 20px;
    /* These margins don't collapse, creating 40px total space */
    width: 200px;
    height: 100px;
    background-color: #eee;
}

/* Solution: Use consistent spacing strategy */
.consistent-spacing > * {
    margin-bottom: 20px;
}

.consistent-spacing > *:last-child {
    margin-bottom: 0;
```

```
}
```

Z-Index Issues with Floated Elements

Floated elements can create stacking context problems.

#css

```
.dropdown-menu {
    position: relative;
    z-index: 1000;
}

.floated-sidebar {
    float: left;
    background-color: white;
    /* May appear above dropdown without proper z-index
management */
}

/* Solution: Establish stacking contexts */
.layout-container {
    position: relative;
    z-index: 1;
}

.dropdown-container {
    position: relative;
    z-index: 2;
}
```

13.4 Creating Layouts with Float

Two-Column Layout

Float enables creation of side-by-side column layouts with flexible content areas.

#html

```
<div class="two-column-layout">
    <aside class="sidebar">
        <h3>Sidebar Content</h3>
        <ul>
            <li>Navigation item 1</li>
            <li>Navigation item 2</li>
            <li>Navigation item 3</li>
        </ul>
    </aside>

    <main class="main-content">
        <h1>Main Content Area</h1>
        <p>This is the primary content area that adjusts to the remaining space after the sidebar is positioned.</p>
    </main>
</div>
```

#css

```
.two-column-layout {
    max-width: 1200px;
    margin: 0 auto;
    padding: 20px;
```

```
    background-color: #f9f9f9;
}

.sidebar {
    float: left;
    width: 300px;
    background-color: #333;
    color: white;
    padding: 30px 20px;
    margin-right: 30px;
}

.sidebar h3 {
    margin-top: 0;
    color: #fff;
    border-bottom: 2px solid #555;
    padding-bottom: 10px;
}

.sidebar ul {
    list-style: none;
    padding: 0;
}

.sidebar li {
    padding: 10px 0;
    border-bottom: 1px solid #555;
}

.main-content {
```

```
    overflow: hidden; /* Creates new block formatting context */
    background-color: white;
    padding: 30px;
    border-radius: 5px;
    box-shadow: 0 2px 5px rgba(0,0,0,0.1);
}
```

Three-Column Layout

Create complex three-column layouts using strategic float positioning.

#html

```
<div class="three-column-layout">
    <nav class="left-sidebar">
        <h3>Navigation</h3>
        <ul>
            <li><a href="#">Home</a></li>
            <li><a href="#">About</a></li>
            <li><a href="#">Services</a></li>
            <li><a href="#">Contact</a></li>
        </ul>
    </nav>

    <aside class="right-sidebar">
        <h3>Advertisement</h3>
        <div class="ad-placeholder">
            <p>Advertisement space</p>
        </div>
    </aside>
```

```
    <main class="center-content">
        <h1>Main Content</h1>
        <p>This center column contains the primary content and adjusts to fill the space between the two sidebars.</p>
    </main>
</div>
```

#css

```
.three-column-layout {
    max-width: 1200px;
    margin: 0 auto;
    padding: 20px;
    background-color: #f5f5f5;
}

.left-sidebar {
    float: left;
    width: 200px;
    background-color: #2c3e50;
    color: white;
    padding: 20px;
    margin-right: 20px;
}

.right-sidebar {
    float: right;
    width: 250px;
    background-color: #e74c3c;
```

```
    color: white;
    padding: 20px;
    margin-left: 20px;
}

.center-content {
    overflow: hidden; /* Creates new block formatting
context */
    background-color: white;
    padding: 30px;
    min-height: 400px;
    border-radius: 5px;
}

.left-sidebar ul {
    list-style: none;
    padding: 0;
    margin: 20px 0 0 0;
}

.left-sidebar li {
    margin-bottom: 10px;
}

.left-sidebar a {
    color: white;
    text-decoration: none;
    padding: 8px 0;
    display: block;
    border-bottom: 1px solid #34495e;
}
```

```
.ad-placeholder {
    background-color: #c0392b;
    padding: 20px;
    text-align: center;
    margin-top: 20px;
    border-radius: 3px;
}
```

Card-Based Layout

Use float to create responsive card grids that adapt to different screen sizes.

#html

```
<div class="card-container">
    <article class="card">
        <img src="image1.jpg" alt="Card image">
        <div class="card-content">
            <h3>Card Title 1</h3>
            <p>Brief description of the card content goes
here.</p>
            <a href="#" class="card-link">Read More</a>
        </div>
    </article>

    <article class="card">
        <img src="image2.jpg" alt="Card image">
        <div class="card-content">
            <h3>Card Title 2</h3>
```

```
            <p>Brief description of the card content goes
here.</p>
            <a href="#" class="card-link">Read More</a>
        </div>
    </article>

    <article class="card">
        <img src="image3.jpg" alt="Card image">
        <div class="card-content">
            <h3>Card Title 3</h3>
            <p>Brief description of the card content goes
here.</p>
            <a href="#" class="card-link">Read More</a>
        </div>
    </article>
</div>
```

#css

```
.card-container {
    max-width: 1200px;
    margin: 0 auto;
    padding: 20px;
}

.card-container::after {
    content: "";
    display: table;
    clear: both;
}
```

```
.card {
    float: left;
    width: calc(33.333% - 20px);
    margin: 0 10px 30px 10px;
    background-color: white;
    border-radius: 8px;
    box-shadow: 0 4px 8px rgba(0,0,0,0.1);
    overflow: hidden;
    transition: transform 0.3s ease;
}

.card:hover {
    transform: translateY(-5px);
    box-shadow: 0 8px 16px rgba(0,0,0,0.15);
}

.card img {
    width: 100%;
    height: 200px;
    object-fit: cover;
    display: block;
}

.card-content {
    padding: 20px;
}

.card h3 {
    margin: 0 0 15px 0;
    color: #333;
    font-size: 18px;
```

```
}

.card p {
    color: #666;
    line-height: 1.5;
    margin-bottom: 20px;
}

.card-link {
    color: #3498db;
    text-decoration: none;
    font-weight: bold;
    text-transform: uppercase;
    font-size: 14px;
}

.card-link:hover {
    color: #2980b9;
}

/* Responsive adjustments */
@media (max-width: 768px) {
    .card {
        width: calc(50% - 20px);
    }
}

@media (max-width: 480px) {
    .card {
        width: calc(100% - 20px);
    }
```

```
}
```

13.5 When to Use Float in Modern CSS

Legacy Support and Maintenance

Float remains important for maintaining existing codebases and supporting older browsers that lack modern layout features.

#css

```
/* Fallback approach for older browsers */
.layout-container {
    /* Float-based layout for older browsers */
}

.sidebar {
    float: left;
    width: 25%;
}

.main-content {
    float: right;
    width: 70%;
}

/* Modern layout enhancement */
@supports (display: grid) {
    .layout-container {
        display: grid;
        grid-template-columns: 1fr 3fr;
        gap: 2rem;
```

```
    }

    .sidebar,
    .main-content {
        float: none;
        width: auto;
    }
}
```

Text Wrapping Around Images

Float's original purpose remains highly relevant for editorial content where text should wrap around images.

#css

```
.article-content {
    max-width: 800px;
    margin: 0 auto;
    line-height: 1.8;
    font-size: 16px;
}

.article-image {
    float: left;
    width: 300px;
    height: auto;
    margin: 0 30px 20px 0;
    border-radius: 8px;
    box-shadow: 0 4px 8px rgba(0,0,0,0.1);
}
```

```css
.article-image.right {
    float: right;
    margin: 0 0 20px 30px;
}

/* Clear floats for new sections */
.article-section {
    clear: both;
    margin-top: 40px;
    padding-top: 30px;
    border-top: 1px solid #eee;
}
```

Quick Prototyping

Float provides rapid layout solutions for prototypes and temporary implementations.

#css

```css
/* Quick prototype navigation */
.prototype-nav {
    background-color: #333;
    padding: 0;
    overflow: hidden;
}

.prototype-nav li {
    float: left;
    list-style: none;
```

```
}

.prototype-nav a {
    display: block;
    color: white;
    padding: 15px 20px;
    text-decoration: none;
}

.prototype-nav a:hover {
    background-color: #555;
}
```

Browser Compatibility Requirements

When supporting Internet Explorer 8 and earlier versions, float provides reliable layout functionality.

#css

```
/* IE8-compatible layout */
.ie-compatible-grid {
    width: 100%;
}

.ie-compatible-grid::after {
    content: "";
    display: table;
    clear: both;
}
```

```
.grid-item {
    float: left;
    width: 23%;
    margin-right: 2.66%;
    background-color: #f0f0f0;
    padding: 20px;
    box-sizing: border-box;
}

.grid-item:nth-child(4n) {
    margin-right: 0;
}
```

Performance Considerations

Float can offer performance benefits in scenarios with many elements due to its simplicity compared to complex Grid or Flexbox calculations.

#css

```
/* Performance-optimized float layout */
.performance-grid {
    font-size: 0; /* Removes whitespace between inline-block alternatives */
}

.performance-item {
    float: left;
    width: 20%;
    font-size: 16px; /* Reset font size */
    background-color: #fff;
```

```
    border: 1px solid #ddd;
    padding: 15px;
    box-sizing: border-box;
}
```

Migration Strategy from Float to Modern CSS

When transitioning from float-based layouts to modern CSS, maintain backward compatibility while introducing enhancements.

#css

```
/* Progressive enhancement approach */
.enhanced-layout {
    /* Float fallback */
    overflow: hidden;
}

.enhanced-item {
    float: left;
    width: 50%;
    padding: 20px;
    box-sizing: border-box;
}

/* Flexbox enhancement */
@supports (display: flex) {
    .enhanced-layout {
        display: flex;
        flex-wrap: wrap;
    }
```

```
    .enhanced-item {
        float: none;
        flex: 1 1 50%;
    }
}

/* Grid enhancement */
@supports (display: grid) {
    .enhanced-layout {
        display: grid;
        grid-template-columns: repeat(auto-fit,
minmax(300px, 1fr));
        gap: 20px;
    }

    .enhanced-item {
        float: none;
        width: auto;
        flex: none;
        padding: 20px;
    }
}
```

Essential Tips

- Always use clearfix or overflow: hidden on containers with floated children to prevent collapse and maintain layout integrity across different browsers and content scenarios.

- Test float layouts thoroughly across multiple browsers, especially older versions of Internet Explorer, as float behavior can vary significantly and cause unexpected layout breaks.
- Consider float primarily for text wrapping around images and legacy browser support rather than primary layout structure in modern web development projects.
- Use percentage-based widths with float layouts to create responsive designs, but account for margin and padding calculations to prevent wrapping issues on smaller screens.
- Implement proper fallback strategies when using float as a backup for modern layout methods, ensuring graceful degradation while maintaining functional layouts across all browser versions.

Actionable Strategies

- Replace float-based grid systems with CSS Grid or Flexbox in new projects while maintaining float for specific use cases like image text wrapping and legacy browser compatibility requirements.
- Establish a consistent clearfix utility class in your CSS framework or reset stylesheet to apply to any container that houses floated elements, preventing layout collapse issues.
- Create a comprehensive browser testing matrix that includes older Internet Explorer versions when float layouts are necessary for project requirements or client specifications.
- Develop a systematic approach to migrating existing float layouts by identifying which components benefit from modern alternatives and which should retain float for functionality or compatibility.
- Document float usage patterns within your codebase, clearly marking where floats serve specific purposes versus where they exist as legacy code requiring future updates.
- Build responsive float layouts using CSS calc() functions and media queries to maintain precise control over element positioning across different screen sizes and device orientations.
- Implement performance monitoring for pages with extensive float usage, comparing rendering times against modern layout alternatives to make informed decisions about layout strategy updates.

Chapter 14: CSS Pseudo-Classes

CSS pseudo-classes represent one of the most powerful features for creating dynamic, interactive web experiences without relying on JavaScript. These special selectors allow you to style elements based on their state, position, or user interaction, transforming static HTML into engaging interfaces that respond to user behavior.

Pseudo-classes are preceded by a colon (:) and target elements in specific states or conditions. They enable developers to create sophisticated styling patterns that enhance user experience through visual feedback, improved accessibility, and interactive design elements.

14.1 Hover, Active, Focus

Understanding Interactive States

Interactive pseudo-classes form the foundation of user interface responsiveness. These states provide immediate visual feedback when users interact with elements, creating intuitive and accessible web experiences.

The :hover Pseudo-Class

The `:hover` pseudo-class activates when a user positions their cursor over an element. This state is crucial for indicating interactive elements and providing visual feedback.

#css

```css
/* Basic hover effect */
.button {
    background-color: #3498db;
    color: white;
    padding: 12px 24px;
    border: none;
    border-radius: 4px;
    cursor: pointer;
```

```
    transition: all 0.3s ease;
}

.button:hover {
    background-color: #2980b9;
    transform: translateY(-2px);
    box-shadow: 0 4px 8px rgba(0, 0, 0, 0.2);
}

/* Hover effects on navigation links */
.nav-link {
    color: #333;
    text-decoration: none;
    padding: 8px 16px;
    display: inline-block;
    position: relative;
    transition: color 0.3s ease;
}

.nav-link:hover {
    color: #e74c3c;
}

.nav-link::after {
    content: '';
    position: absolute;
    bottom: 0;
    left: 0;
    width: 0;
    height: 2px;
    background-color: #e74c3c;
```

```
    transition: width 0.3s ease;
}

.nav-link:hover::after {
    width: 100%;
}
```

Advanced Hover Techniques

Hover effects can be combined with other CSS properties to create sophisticated interactions:

#css

```
/* Image hover overlay */
.image-container {
    position: relative;
    overflow: hidden;
}

.image-overlay {
    position: absolute;
    top: 0;
    left: 0;
    right: 0;
    bottom: 0;
    background-color: rgba(0, 0, 0, 0.7);
    display: flex;
    align-items: center;
    justify-content: center;
    opacity: 0;
    transition: opacity 0.4s ease;
```

```
}

.image-container:hover .image-overlay {
    opacity: 1;
}

.image-container:hover img {
    transform: scale(1.1);
    transition: transform 0.4s ease;
}

/* Card hover effects */
.card {
    background: white;
    border-radius: 8px;
    box-shadow: 0 2px 4px rgba(0, 0, 0, 0.1);
    transition: all 0.3s ease;
}

.card:hover {
    transform: translateY(-8px);
    box-shadow: 0 12px 24px rgba(0, 0, 0, 0.15);
}
```

The :active Pseudo-Class

The `:active` pseudo-class applies styles when an element is being activated, typically during the moment a user clicks or taps an element.

#css

```
.button:active {
```

```
    transform: translateY(1px);
    box-shadow: 0 2px 4px rgba(0, 0, 0, 0.2);
    background-color: #1f618d;
}

/* Active states for different elements */
.link:active {
    color: #c0392b;
}

.checkbox:active {
    transform: scale(0.95);
}

/* Touch-friendly active states */
@media (hover: none) {
    .mobile-button:active {
        background-color: #2c3e50;
        transform: scale(0.98);
    }
}
```

The :focus Pseudo-Class

The `:focus` pseudo-class is essential for accessibility, styling elements when they receive keyboard focus or are selected for input.

#css

```
/* Form input focus styles */
.input-field {
    border: 2px solid #ddd;
```

```css
    padding: 12px;
    border-radius: 4px;
    transition: border-color 0.3s ease, box-shadow 0.3s
ease;
}

.input-field:focus {
    outline: none;
    border-color: #3498db;
    box-shadow: 0 0 0 3px rgba(52, 152, 219, 0.2);
}

/* Custom focus indicators */
.custom-button:focus {
    outline: 2px solid #e74c3c;
    outline-offset: 2px;
}

/* Focus within for container elements */
.form-group:focus-within {
    background-color: #f8f9fa;
    border-radius: 4px;
    padding: 8px;
}

/* Accessible skip links */
.skip-link {
    position: absolute;
    top: -40px;
    left: 6px;
    background: #000;
```

```
    color: white;
    padding: 8px;
    text-decoration: none;
    border-radius: 4px;
}

.skip-link:focus {
    top: 6px;
}
```

Combining Interactive States

Interactive pseudo-classes can be combined to create comprehensive user feedback systems:

#css

```
.interactive-element {
    background-color: #ecf0f1;
    color: #2c3e50;
    border: 2px solid transparent;
    padding: 12px 24px;
    cursor: pointer;
    transition: all 0.3s ease;
}

.interactive-element:hover {
    background-color: #d5dbdb;
    border-color: #95a5a6;
}
```

```
.interactive-element:active {
    background-color: #bdc3c7;
    transform: scale(0.98);
}

.interactive-element:focus {
    outline: none;
    border-color: #3498db;
    box-shadow: 0 0 0 3px rgba(52, 152, 219, 0.3);
}
```

14.2 First-child, Last-child, Nth-child

Structural Pseudo-Classes Overview

Structural pseudo-classes target elements based on their position within their parent container. These selectors provide powerful ways to style elements without adding additional classes or modifying HTML structure.

The :first-child Pseudo-Class

The `:first-child` pseudo-class selects the first child element of its parent:

#css

```
/* Style the first paragraph differently */
.content p:first-child {
    font-size: 1.2em;
    font-weight: bold;
    color: #2c3e50;
    margin-top: 0;
}
```

```css
/* First list item styling */
.menu li:first-child {
    border-top: none;
    border-radius: 8px 8px 0 0;
}

/* First card in a grid */
.card-grid .card:first-child {
    background: linear-gradient(135deg, #667eea 0%,
#764ba2 100%);
    color: white;
}

/* Navigation first item */
.navbar ul li:first-child a {
    margin-left: 0;
    padding-left: 0;
}
```

The :last-child Pseudo-Class

The `:last-child` pseudo-class targets the last child element:

#css

```css
/* Remove bottom margin from last paragraph */
.article p:last-child {
    margin-bottom: 0;
}

/* Last list item styling */
```

```css
.menu li:last-child {
    border-bottom: none;
    border-radius: 0 0 8px 8px;
}

/* Last breadcrumb item */
.breadcrumb li:last-child::after {
    content: none; /* Remove separator after last item */
}

/* Footer last element */
.footer-content > *:last-child {
    margin-bottom: 0;
}
```

The :nth-child() Pseudo-Class

The `:nth-child()` pseudo-class provides flexible targeting using mathematical expressions:

#css

```css
/* Every other row (zebra striping) */
.table tr:nth-child(even) {
    background-color: #f8f9fa;
}

.table tr:nth-child(odd) {
    background-color: white;
}

/* Every third item */
```

```
.gallery img:nth-child(3n) {
    margin-right: 0; /* Remove right margin every third
image */
}

/* First three items */
.featured-products .product:nth-child(-n+3) {
    border: 2px solid #e74c3c;
    position: relative;
}

.featured-products .product:nth-child(-n+3)::before {
    content: 'Featured';
    position: absolute;
    top: -10px;
    right: -10px;
    background: #e74c3c;
    color: white;
    padding: 4px 8px;
    border-radius: 4px;
    font-size: 0.8em;
}

/* Complex patterns */
.grid-item:nth-child(4n+1) {
    /* Every 4th item starting from 1st: 1, 5, 9, 13...
*/
    background-color: #3498db;
}

.grid-item:nth-child(4n+2) {
```

```
    /* Every 4th item starting from 2nd: 2, 6, 10, 14...
*/
    background-color: #e74c3c;
}

.grid-item:nth-child(4n+3) {
    /* Every 4th item starting from 3rd: 3, 7, 11, 15...
*/
    background-color: #f39c12;
}

.grid-item:nth-child(4n) {
    /* Every 4th item: 4, 8, 12, 16... */
    background-color: #27ae60;
}
```

Advanced Nth-child Patterns

#css

```
/* Skip first two, then every third */
.item:nth-child(n+3):nth-child(3n) {
    transform: scale(1.1);
}

/* Last 3 items */
.item:nth-last-child(-n+3) {
    opacity: 0.7;
}

/* All but first and last */
.item:not(:first-child):not(:last-child) {
```

```
    border-left: 1px solid #ddd;
    border-right: 1px solid #ddd;
}

/* Create responsive layouts */
@media (min-width: 768px) {
    .responsive-grid .item:nth-child(2n) {
        margin-right: 0;
    }
}

@media (min-width: 1024px) {
    .responsive-grid .item:nth-child(2n) {
        margin-right: 20px; /* Reset for larger screens
*/
    }

    .responsive-grid .item:nth-child(3n) {
        margin-right: 0;
    }
}
```

Practical Applications

Structural pseudo-classes excel in creating dynamic layouts and styling patterns:

#css

```
/* Timeline styling */
.timeline .event:nth-child(odd) {
    align-self: flex-start;
```

```
    text-align: right;
}

.timeline .event:nth-child(even) {
    align-self: flex-end;
    text-align: left;
}

/* Pricing table highlights */
.pricing-table .plan:nth-child(2) {
    transform: scale(1.05);
    z-index: 10;
    border: 3px solid #e74c3c;
}

.pricing-table .plan:nth-child(2)::before {
    content: 'Most Popular';
    position: absolute;
    top: -15px;
    left: 50%;
    transform: translateX(-50%);
    background: #e74c3c;
    color: white;
    padding: 5px 15px;
    border-radius: 15px;
    font-size: 0.9em;
}
```

14.3 Link and Visited States

Understanding Link States

Link pseudo-classes control the appearance of hyperlinks in different states, providing visual feedback about link status and user interaction history.

The :link Pseudo-Class

The `:link` pseudo-class targets unvisited links:

#css

```css
/* Basic link styling */
a:link {
    color: #3498db;
    text-decoration: none;
    border-bottom: 1px solid transparent;
    transition: all 0.3s ease;
}

/* Navigation links */
.nav a:link {
    color: #2c3e50;
    font-weight: 500;
    position: relative;
}

.nav a:link::after {
    content: '';
    position: absolute;
    bottom: -5px;
    left: 0;
    width: 0;
    height: 2px;
```

```
    background-color: #3498db;
    transition: width 0.3s ease;
}

/* External link indicators */
a[href^="http"]:link::after {
    content: '↗';
    font-size: 0.8em;
    margin-left: 4px;
    opacity: 0.7;
}
```

The :visited Pseudo-Class

The `:visited` pseudo-class styles previously visited links:

#css

```
a:visited {
    color: #8e44ad;
}

/* Subtle visited state for navigation */
.nav a:visited {
    color: #7f8c8d;
}

/* Article links with visited indicators */
.article-content a:visited {
    color: #9b59b6;
    background-color: rgba(155, 89, 182, 0.1);
```

```
    padding: 2px 4px;
    border-radius: 3px;
}

/* Breadcrumb visited styling */
.breadcrumb a:visited {
    color: #95a5a6;
    font-style: italic;
}
```

Security Considerations and Limitations

Due to privacy concerns, the `:visited` pseudo-class has limitations on which CSS properties can be modified:

#css

```
/* Allowed properties for :visited */
a:visited {
    color: #8e44ad;             /* ✓ Allowed */
    border-color: #8e44ad;      /* ✓ Allowed */
    background-color: #f3e5f5; /* ✓ Allowed */
    outline-color: #8e44ad;     /* ✓ Allowed */
}

/* Properties that won't work with :visited */
a:visited {
    /* font-size: 1.2em;        ✗ Not allowed */
    /* padding: 10px;           ✗ Not allowed */
    /* transform: scale(1.1); ✗ Not allowed */
```

```
    /* box-shadow: 0 2px 4px rgba(0,0,0,0.2); ✗ Not
allowed */
}
```

Link State Order (LVHA)

The correct order for link pseudo-classes follows the mnemonic "LoVe HAte" (Link, Visited, Hover, Active):

#css

```
/* Correct order for link states */
a:link {
    color: #3498db;
    text-decoration: none;
}

a:visited {
    color: #8e44ad;
}

a:hover {
    color: #e74c3c;
    text-decoration: underline;
}

a:active {
    color: #c0392b;
    transform: translateY(1px);
}
```

```css
/* Complex link styling with proper order */
.button-link:link {
    background-color: #3498db;
    color: white;
    padding: 12px 24px;
    border-radius: 4px;
    display: inline-block;
    transition: all 0.3s ease;
}

.button-link:visited {
    background-color: #8e44ad;
}

.button-link:hover {
    background-color: #2980b9;
    transform: translateY(-2px);
    box-shadow: 0 4px 8px rgba(0, 0, 0, 0.2);
}

.button-link:visited:hover {
    background-color: #7d3c98;
}

.button-link:active {
    transform: translateY(0);
    box-shadow: 0 2px 4px rgba(0, 0, 0, 0.2);
}
```

Advanced Link Styling Techniques

#css

```css
/* Animated underline effect */
.fancy-link {
    position: relative;
    color: #2c3e50;
    text-decoration: none;
    overflow: hidden;
}

.fancy-link::before {
    content: '';
    position: absolute;
    bottom: 0;
    left: -100%;
    width: 100%;
    height: 2px;
    background: linear-gradient(90deg, transparent,
#3498db, transparent);
    transition: left 0.5s ease;
}

.fancy-link:hover::before {
    left: 100%;
}

/* Link with icon transitions */
.icon-link {
    display: inline-flex;
    align-items: center;
```

```
    color: #3498db;
    text-decoration: none;
    transition: all 0.3s ease;
}

.icon-link::before {
    content: '→';
    margin-right: 8px;
    transform: translateX(-4px);
    opacity: 0;
    transition: all 0.3s ease;
}

.icon-link:hover::before {
    transform: translateX(0);
    opacity: 1;
}

.icon-link:hover {
    transform: translateX(8px);
}
```

14.4 Custom Checkbox/Radio Styling with Pseudo-Classes

The Challenge of Form Element Styling

Native form elements like checkboxes and radio buttons have limited styling options and inconsistent appearance across browsers. Pseudo-classes enable complete visual customization while maintaining accessibility and functionality.

Custom Checkbox Implementation
#css

```css
/* Hide the native checkbox */
.custom-checkbox input[type="checkbox"] {
    position: absolute;
    opacity: 0;
    cursor: pointer;
    width: 0;
    height: 0;
}

/* Create custom checkbox appearance */
.custom-checkbox {
    position: relative;
    display: inline-flex;
    align-items: center;
    cursor: pointer;
    font-size: 16px;
    user-select: none;
    padding: 8px 0;
}

.custom-checkbox .checkmark {
    position: relative;
    width: 20px;
    height: 20px;
    background-color: white;
    border: 2px solid #ddd;
    border-radius: 4px;
```

```
    margin-right: 12px;
    transition: all 0.3s ease;
}

/* Hover state */
.custom-checkbox:hover .checkmark {
    border-color: #3498db;
    background-color: #f8f9fa;
}

/* Checked state */
.custom-checkbox input:checked + .checkmark {
    background-color: #3498db;
    border-color: #3498db;
}

/* Checkmark icon */
.custom-checkbox .checkmark::after {
    content: '';
    position: absolute;
    display: none;
    left: 6px;
    top: 2px;
    width: 6px;
    height: 12px;
    border: solid white;
    border-width: 0 2px 2px 0;
    transform: rotate(45deg);
}

.custom-checkbox input:checked + .checkmark::after {
```

```
    display: block;
}

/* Focus state for accessibility */
.custom-checkbox input:focus + .checkmark {
    outline: 2px solid #3498db;
    outline-offset: 2px;
}

/* Disabled state */
.custom-checkbox input:disabled + .checkmark {
    background-color: #f5f5f5;
    border-color: #ddd;
    cursor: not-allowed;
}

.custom-checkbox input:disabled ~ .checkbox-label {
    color: #999;
    cursor: not-allowed;
}
```

Advanced Checkbox Variations

#css

```
/* Toggle switch style checkbox */
.toggle-switch {
    position: relative;
    display: inline-block;
    width: 50px;
    height: 24px;
}
```

```
.toggle-switch input {
    opacity: 0;
    width: 0;
    height: 0;
}

.toggle-slider {
    position: absolute;
    cursor: pointer;
    top: 0;
    left: 0;
    right: 0;
    bottom: 0;
    background-color: #ccc;
    border-radius: 24px;
    transition: 0.4s;
}

.toggle-slider::before {
    position: absolute;
    content: "";
    height: 18px;
    width: 18px;
    left: 3px;
    bottom: 3px;
    background-color: white;
    border-radius: 50%;
    transition: 0.4s;
}
```

```
.toggle-switch input:checked + .toggle-slider {
    background-color: #3498db;
}

.toggle-switch input:checked + .toggle-slider::before {
    transform: translateX(26px);
}

.toggle-switch input:focus + .toggle-slider {
    box-shadow: 0 0 0 3px rgba(52, 152, 219, 0.3);
}

/* Animated checkbox with bounce effect */
.bouncy-checkbox .checkmark {
    transform-origin: center;
    transition: all 0.3s cubic-bezier(0.68, -0.55, 0.265,
1.55);
}

.bouncy-checkbox input:checked + .checkmark {
    transform: scale(1.1);
}

.bouncy-checkbox .checkmark::after {
    animation: checkAnimation 0.3s ease 0.1s both;
}

@keyframes checkAnimation {
    0% {
        opacity: 0;
        transform: rotate(45deg) scale(0);
```

```
    }
    100% {
        opacity: 1;
        transform: rotate(45deg) scale(1);
    }
}
```

Custom Radio Button Implementation

#css

```
/* Custom radio button styling */
.custom-radio {
    position: relative;
    display: inline-flex;
    align-items: center;
    cursor: pointer;
    font-size: 16px;
    user-select: none;
    margin-bottom: 12px;
}

.custom-radio input[type="radio"] {
    position: absolute;
    opacity: 0;
    cursor: pointer;
}

.custom-radio .radio-mark {
    position: relative;
    width: 20px;
    height: 20px;
```

```
    background-color: white;
    border: 2px solid #ddd;
    border-radius: 50%;
    margin-right: 12px;
    transition: all 0.3s ease;
}

.custom-radio:hover .radio-mark {
    border-color: #3498db;
    background-color: #f8f9fa;
}

.custom-radio input:checked + .radio-mark {
    border-color: #3498db;
    background-color: white;
}

.custom-radio .radio-mark::after {
    content: '';
    position: absolute;
    display: none;
    top: 50%;
    left: 50%;
    width: 10px;
    height: 10px;
    border-radius: 50%;
    background-color: #3498db;
    transform: translate(-50%, -50%);
}

.custom-radio input:checked + .radio-mark::after {
```

```
    display: block;
}

/* Animated radio button */
.animated-radio .radio-mark::after {
    transform: translate(-50%, -50%) scale(0);
    transition: transform 0.3s cubic-bezier(0.68, -0.55,
0.265, 1.55);
}

.animated-radio input:checked + .radio-mark::after {
    transform: translate(-50%, -50%) scale(1);
}
```

Card-Style Selection Interface

#css

```
/* Radio button as selectable cards */
.card-radio {
    position: relative;
    margin-bottom: 16px;
}

.card-radio input[type="radio"] {
    position: absolute;
    opacity: 0;
    width: 0;
    height: 0;
}

.card-radio .radio-card {
```

```
    display: block;
    padding: 20px;
    border: 2px solid #e1e8ed;
    border-radius: 8px;
    background-color: white;
    cursor: pointer;
    transition: all 0.3s ease;
    position: relative;
}

.card-radio:hover .radio-card {
    border-color: #3498db;
    box-shadow: 0 2px 8px rgba(52, 152, 219, 0.1);
}

.card-radio input:checked + .radio-card {
    border-color: #3498db;
    background-color: #f8f9fa;
    box-shadow: 0 4px 12px rgba(52, 152, 219, 0.15);
}

.card-radio input:checked + .radio-card::after {
    content: '√';
    position: absolute;
    top: 12px;
    right: 12px;
    width: 24px;
    height: 24px;
    background-color: #3498db;
    color: white;
    border-radius: 50%;
```

```
    display: flex;
    align-items: center;
    justify-content: center;
    font-size: 14px;
    font-weight: bold;
}

.card-radio input:focus + .radio-card {
    outline: 2px solid #3498db;
    outline-offset: 2px;
}
```

14.5 Interactive Effects Without JavaScript

Pure CSS Interactions

CSS pseudo-classes enable sophisticated interactive effects that traditionally required JavaScript. These techniques improve performance and maintain functionality even when JavaScript is disabled.

Accordion/Collapse Interface

#css

```
/* CSS-only accordion */
.accordion-item {
    border: 1px solid #e1e8ed;
    border-radius: 4px;
    margin-bottom: 8px;
    overflow: hidden;
}
```

```
.accordion-toggle {
    position: absolute;
    opacity: 0;
    width: 0;
    height: 0;
}

.accordion-header {
    display: block;
    padding: 16px 20px;
    background-color: #f8f9fa;
    color: #2c3e50;
    font-weight: 600;
    cursor: pointer;
    user-select: none;
    position: relative;
    transition: background-color 0.3s ease;
}

.accordion-header::after {
    content: '+';
    position: absolute;
    right: 20px;
    top: 50%;
    transform: translateY(-50%);
    font-size: 20px;
    transition: transform 0.3s ease;
}

.accordion-toggle:checked + .accordion-header {
    background-color: #3498db;
```

```
    color: white;
}

.accordion-toggle:checked + .accordion-header::after {
    content: '-';
    transform: translateY(-50%) rotate(180deg);
}

.accordion-content {
    max-height: 0;
    overflow: hidden;
    transition: max-height 0.3s ease, padding 0.3s ease;
    background-color: white;
}

.accordion-toggle:checked ~ .accordion-content {
    max-height: 500px;
    padding: 20px;
}

/* Hover effects for accordion */
.accordion-header:hover {
    background-color: #e9ecef;
}

.accordion-toggle:checked + .accordion-header:hover {
    background-color: #2980b9;
}
```

Modal Dialog System

#css

```
/* CSS-only modal */
.modal-overlay {
    position: fixed;
    top: 0;
    left: 0;
    width: 100%;
    height: 100%;
    background-color: rgba(0, 0, 0, 0.5);
    display: flex;
    align-items: center;
    justify-content: center;
    opacity: 0;
    visibility: hidden;
    transition: all 0.3s ease;
    z-index: 1000;
}

.modal-toggle {
    display: none;
}

.modal-toggle:checked + .modal-overlay {
    opacity: 1;
    visibility: visible;
}

.modal-content {
```

```
    background: white;
    border-radius: 8px;
    padding: 30px;
    max-width: 500px;
    width: 90%;
    max-height: 80vh;
    overflow-y: auto;
    transform: scale(0.8);
    transition: transform 0.3s ease;
}

.modal-toggle:checked + .modal-overlay .modal-content {
    transform: scale(1);
}

.modal-close {
    position: absolute;
    top: 15px;
    right: 20px;
    font-size: 24px;
    cursor: pointer;
    color: #999;
    transition: color 0.3s ease;
}

.modal-close:hover {
    color: #333;
}

/* Modal trigger button */
.modal-trigger {
```

```
    background-color: #3498db;
    color: white;
    border: none;
    padding: 12px 24px;
    border-radius: 4px;
    cursor: pointer;
    transition: background-color 0.3s ease;
}

.modal-trigger:hover {
    background-color: #2980b9;
}
```

Tabbed Interface

#css

```
/* CSS-only tabs */
.tabs-container {
    width: 100%;
    margin: 20px 0;
}

.tab-input {
    display: none;
}

.tab-labels {
    display: flex;
    border-bottom: 2px solid #e1e8ed;
    margin-bottom: 20px;
}
```

```
.tab-label {
    flex: 1;
    padding: 15px 20px;
    background-color: #f8f9fa;
    border: 1px solid #e1e8ed;
    border-bottom: none;
    cursor: pointer;
    text-align: center;
    font-weight: 500;
    color: #6c757d;
    transition: all 0.3s ease;
    user-select: none;
}

.tab-label:not(:last-child) {
    border-right: none;
}

.tab-label:hover {
    background-color: #e9ecef;
    color: #495057;
}

.tab-input:checked + .tab-label {
    background-color: white;
    color: #3498db;
    border-bottom: 2px solid #3498db;
    transform: translateY(2px);
}
```

```
.tab-content {
    display: none;
    padding: 20px;
    background-color: white;
    border-radius: 0 0 8px 8px;
    animation: fadeIn 0.3s ease;
}

.tab-input:checked ~ .tab-content {
    display: block;
}

@keyframes fadeIn {
    from { opacity: 0; transform: translateY(10px); }
    to { opacity: 1; transform: translateY(0); }
}
```

Interactive Image Gallery

#css

```
/* CSS-only lightbox gallery */
.gallery {
    display: grid;
    grid-template-columns: repeat(auto-fit, minmax(200px,
1fr));
    gap: 16px;
    margin: 20px 0;
}

.gallery-item {
    position: relative;
```

```
    cursor: pointer;
    border-radius: 8px;
    overflow: hidden;
    transition: transform 0.3s ease;
}

.gallery-item:hover {
    transform: scale(1.05);
}

.gallery-item img {
    width: 100%;
    height: 200px;
    object-fit: cover;
    transition: filter 0.3s ease;
}

.gallery-item:hover img {
    filter: brightness(1.1);
}

/* Lightbox functionality */
.lightbox {
    position: fixed;
    top: 0;
    left: 0;
    width: 100%;
    height: 100%;
    background-color: rgba(0, 0, 0, 0.9);
    display: flex;
    align-items: center;
```

```
    justify-content: center;
    opacity: 0;
    visibility: hidden;
    transition: all 0.3s ease;
    z-index: 2000;
}

.lightbox-toggle {
    display: none;
}

.lightbox-toggle:checked + .lightbox {
    opacity: 1;
    visibility: visible;
}

.lightbox img {
    max-width: 90%;
    max-height: 90%;
    object-fit: contain;
    border-radius: 8px;
    transform: scale(0.8);
    transition: transform 0.3s ease;
}

.lightbox-toggle:checked + .lightbox img {
    transform: scale(1);
}

.lightbox-close {
    position: absolute;
```

```css
    top: 20px;
    right: 30px;
    color: white;
    font-size: 36px;
    cursor: pointer;
    transition: opacity 0.3s ease;
}

.lightbox-close:hover {
    opacity: 0.7;
}
```

Dropdown Menu System

#css

```css
/* Multi-level dropdown menu */
.dropdown {
    position: relative;
    display: inline-block;
}

.dropdown-toggle {
    background-color: #3498db;
    color: white;
    padding: 12px 20px;
    border: none;
    border-radius: 4px;
    cursor: pointer;
    display: flex;
    align-items: center;
    gap: 8px;
```

```
    transition: background-color 0.3s ease;
}

.dropdown-toggle::after {
    content: '▼';
    font-size: 12px;
    transition: transform 0.3s ease;
}

.dropdown:hover .dropdown-toggle {
    background-color: #2980b9;
}

.dropdown:hover .dropdown-toggle::after {
    transform: rotate(180deg);
}

.dropdown-menu {
    position: absolute;
    top: 100%;
    left: 0;
    background-color: white;
    min-width: 200px;
    box-shadow: 0 8px 16px rgba(0, 0, 0, 0.1);
    border-radius: 4px;
    overflow: hidden;
    opacity: 0;
    visibility: hidden;
    transform: translateY(-10px);
    transition: all 0.3s ease;
    z-index: 1000;
```

```
}

.dropdown:hover .dropdown-menu {
    opacity: 1;
    visibility: visible;
    transform: translateY(0);
}

.dropdown-item {
    display: block;
    padding: 12px 16px;
    color: #333;
    text-decoration: none;
    transition: background-color 0.3s ease;
    border-bottom: 1px solid #f0f0f0;
}

.dropdown-item:hover {
    background-color: #f8f9fa;
    color: #3498db;
}

.dropdown-item:last-child {
    border-bottom: none;
}

/* Nested dropdown */
.dropdown-item.has-submenu {
    position: relative;
}
```

```css
.dropdown-item.has-submenu::after {
    content: '►';
    position: absolute;
    right: 16px;
    top: 50%;
    transform: translateY(-50%);
    font-size: 12px;
}

.submenu {
    position: absolute;
    top: 0;
    left: 100%;
    background-color: white;
    min-width: 180px;
    box-shadow: 0 4px 8px rgba(0, 0, 0, 0.1);
    border-radius: 4px;
    overflow: hidden;
    opacity: 0;
    visibility: hidden;
    transform: translateX(-10px);
    transition: all 0.3s ease;
}

.dropdown-item:hover .submenu {
    opacity: 1;
    visibility: visible;
    transform: translateX(0);
}
```

Interactive Progress Indicators

#css

```
/* Animated progress bars */
.progress-container {
    width: 100%;
    background-color: #f0f0f0;
    border-radius: 25px;
    overflow: hidden;
    margin: 20px 0;
    cursor: pointer;
}

.progress-bar {
    height: 20px;
    background: linear-gradient(90deg, #3498db, #2ecc71);
    border-radius: 25px;
    width: 0%;
    transition: width 2s ease-in-out;
    position: relative;
    overflow: hidden;
}

.progress-container:hover .progress-bar {
    width: 100%;
}

.progress-bar::after {
    content: '';
    position: absolute;
```

```
    top: 0;
    left: 0;
    bottom: 0;
    right: 0;
    background-image: linear-gradient(
        -45deg,
        rgba(255, 255, 255, 0.2) 25%,
        transparent 25%,
        transparent 50%,
        rgba(255, 255, 255, 0.2) 50%,
        rgba(255, 255, 255, 0.2) 75%,
        transparent 75%,
        transparent
    );
    background-size: 50px 50px;
    animation: move 2s linear infinite;
}

@keyframes move {
    0% { background-position: 0 0; }
    100% { background-position: 50px 50px; }
}

/* Step-by-step progress indicator */
.stepper {
    display: flex;
    align-items: center;
    justify-content: space-between;
    margin: 40px 0;
    position: relative;
}
```

```
.stepper::before {
    content: '';
    position: absolute;
    top: 50%;
    left: 0;
    right: 0;
    height: 2px;
    background-color: #e1e8ed;
    z-index: 1;
}

.step {
    position: relative;
    z-index: 2;
    width: 40px;
    height: 40px;
    border-radius: 50%;
    background-color: #e1e8ed;
    display: flex;
    align-items: center;
    justify-content: center;
    color: #6c757d;
    font-weight: bold;
    cursor: pointer;
    transition: all 0.3s ease;
}

.step:hover {
    background-color: #3498db;
    color: white;
```

```
    transform: scale(1.1);
}

.step.completed {
    background-color: #27ae60;
    color: white;
}

.step.active {
    background-color: #3498db;
    color: white;
    animation: pulse 2s infinite;
}

@keyframes pulse {
    0% { box-shadow: 0 0 0 0 rgba(52, 152, 219, 0.7); }
    70% { box-shadow: 0 0 0 10px rgba(52, 152, 219, 0); }
    100% { box-shadow: 0 0 0 0 rgba(52, 152, 219, 0); }
}
```

Tooltip System
#css

```
/* CSS-only tooltips */
.tooltip {
    position: relative;
    display: inline-block;
    cursor: help;
}

.tooltip::before {
```

```
    content: attr(data-tooltip);
    position: absolute;
    bottom: 100%;
    left: 50%;
    transform: translateX(-50%);
    background-color: #333;
    color: white;
    padding: 8px 12px;
    border-radius: 4px;
    font-size: 14px;
    white-space: nowrap;
    opacity: 0;
    visibility: hidden;
    transition: all 0.3s ease;
    z-index: 1000;
    margin-bottom: 5px;
}

.tooltip::after {
    content: '';
    position: absolute;
    bottom: 100%;
    left: 50%;
    transform: translateX(-50%);
    border: 5px solid transparent;
    border-top-color: #333;
    opacity: 0;
    visibility: hidden;
    transition: all 0.3s ease;
}
```

```
.tooltip:hover::before,
.tooltip:hover::after {
    opacity: 1;
    visibility: visible;
}

/* Tooltip variations */
.tooltip-right::before {
    bottom: 50%;
    left: 100%;
    transform: translateY(50%);
    margin-left: 5px;
    margin-bottom: 0;
}

.tooltip-right::after {
    bottom: 50%;
    left: 100%;
    transform: translateY(50%);
    border: 5px solid transparent;
    border-right-color: #333;
    border-top-color: transparent;
}

.tooltip-error::before {
    background-color: #e74c3c;
}

.tooltip-error::after {
    border-top-color: #e74c3c;
}
```

```css
.tooltip-success::before {
    background-color: #27ae60;
}

.tooltip-success::after {
    border-top-color: #27ae60;
}
```

Performance Considerations

When implementing CSS-only interactions, consider these performance optimization techniques:

#css

```css
/* Use transform and opacity for animations */
.optimized-animation {
    transform: translateX(-100%);
    opacity: 0;
    transition: transform 0.3s ease, opacity 0.3s ease;
}

.trigger:hover .optimized-animation {
    transform: translateX(0);
    opacity: 1;
}

/* Use will-change for complex animations */
.complex-interaction {
    will-change: transform, opacity;
```

```
}

/* Debounce hover effects with transition delays */
.debounced-hover {
    transition: all 0.3s ease 0.1s;
}

.debounced-hover:hover {
    transition-delay: 0s;
}

/* Use hardware acceleration for smooth animations */
.hardware-accelerated {
    transform: translateZ(0);
    backface-visibility: hidden;
}
```

Essential Tips

- **Master the cascade order**: Always remember the LVHA order (Link, Visited, Hover, Active) for link states to prevent specificity conflicts and ensure expected behavior across all interactive states.
- **Combine pseudo-classes strategically**: Use multiple pseudo-classes together like `:nth-child(odd):hover` to create sophisticated targeting patterns that respond to both structural position and user interaction simultaneously.
- **Prioritize accessibility in custom form elements**: When styling checkboxes and radio buttons, always maintain keyboard navigation, screen reader compatibility, and clear focus indicators to ensure your custom designs remain usable for all users.
- **Leverage structural pseudo-classes for responsive design**: Use `:nth-child()` patterns to create responsive layouts that adapt to different

screen sizes without media queries, such as removing margins on specific items based on grid columns.

- **Test pseudo-class interactions across browsers**: Different browsers may handle pseudo-class combinations differently, especially with complex `:nth-child()` expressions and custom form element styling, so thorough cross-browser testing is essential.

Actionable Strategies

- **Create a comprehensive pseudo-class reference sheet** with common patterns like zebra striping, first/last child modifications, and interactive state combinations to speed up development and maintain consistency across projects.
- **Build a reusable component library** featuring custom-styled form elements, interactive buttons, and common UI patterns using pseudo-classes, ensuring consistent user experience and reducing development time.
- **Implement progressive enhancement principles** by starting with functional HTML forms and navigation, then layering pseudo-class enhancements that improve the experience without breaking core functionality.
- **Establish consistent hover and focus patterns** across your entire project by defining standard transition durations, color schemes, and interaction feedback styles that users can learn and predict.
- **Use CSS custom properties with pseudo-classes** to create themeable components where colors, sizes, and timing can be easily adjusted while maintaining the same interaction patterns throughout different contexts.
- **Optimize performance by minimizing repaints and reflows** in pseudo-class animations, focusing on transform and opacity changes rather than properties that trigger layout recalculations like width, height, and position.
- **Document your pseudo-class implementations thoroughly** including HTML structure requirements, accessibility considerations, and browser support notes to help team members understand and maintain complex interactive components.

Chapter 15: CSS Pseudo-Elements

Pseudo-elements represent virtual elements that don't exist in your HTML markup but can be created and styled through CSS. These powerful tools allow developers to insert content, style specific parts of elements, and create sophisticated visual effects without cluttering the HTML structure. Understanding pseudo-elements opens up numerous creative possibilities for enhancing user interfaces and creating polished designs.

15.1 ::before and ::after

Understanding Pseudo-Elements

The `::before` and `::after` pseudo-elements create virtual elements that appear as the first and last children of their parent element, respectively. These pseudo-elements must include the `content` property to be visible, even if the value is an empty string.

Basic Syntax and Implementation

#css

```css
.element::before {
    content: "";
    /* Additional styling properties */
}

.element::after {
    content: "";
    /* Additional styling properties */
}
```

The double colon notation (`::`) is the modern standard, though single colons (`:`) still work for backward compatibility. The `content` property is mandatory for these pseudo-elements to render.

Practical Examples with ::before

#css

```css
.quote::before {
    content: """;
    font-size: 2em;
    color: #666;
    position: relative;
    top: 0.1em;
    margin-right: 0.2em;
}

.notification::before {
    content: "⚠";
    color: #ff6b6b;
    font-weight: bold;
    margin-right: 8px;
}

.external-link::before {
    content: "🔗";
    margin-right: 5px;
    opacity: 0.7;
}
```

Implementing ::after for Visual Enhancements

#css

```
.card::after {
    content: "";
    position: absolute;
    bottom: 0;
    left: 0;
    width: 100%;
    height: 3px;
    background: linear-gradient(90deg, #ff6b6b, #4ecdc4);
}

.loading-text::after {
    content: "...";
    animation: dots 1.5s infinite;
}

@keyframes dots {
    0%, 20% { content: ""; }
    40% { content: "."; }
    60% { content: ".."; }
    80%, 100% { content: "..."; }
}
```

Positioning and Display Properties

Pseudo-elements are inline by default, but their display property can be modified. They can be positioned absolutely or relatively within their parent element.

#css

```
.container {
    position: relative;
}

.container::before {
    content: "";
    position: absolute;
    top: -10px;
    left: -10px;
    right: -10px;
    bottom: -10px;
    background: rgba(0, 0, 0, 0.1);
    z-index: -1;
    border-radius: 8px;
}
```

Creating Geometric Shapes

#css

```
.triangle::after {
    content: "";
    position: absolute;
    top: 100%;
    left: 20px;
    border: 10px solid transparent;
    border-top-color: #333;
}
```

```css
.circle::before {
    content: "";
    position: absolute;
    width: 20px;
    height: 20px;
    background: #ff6b6b;
    border-radius: 50%;
    top: -10px;
    right: -10px;
}
```

15.2 Styling the First Letter or Line

The ::first-letter Pseudo-Element

The `::first-letter` pseudo-element targets the first letter of the first line in a block-level element, enabling drop cap effects and special typography treatments.

#css

```css
.article-paragraph::first-letter {
    font-size: 3em;
    font-weight: bold;
    float: left;
    line-height: 1;
    margin-right: 8px;
    margin-top: 2px;
    color: #2c3e50;
    font-family: 'Georgia', serif;
}
```

Advanced First Letter Styling

#css

```
.fancy-paragraph::first-letter {
    font-size: 4em;
    float: left;
    line-height: 0.8;
    margin: 0.1em 0.1em 0 0;
    background: linear-gradient(45deg, #ff6b6b, #4ecdc4);
    -webkit-background-clip: text;
    -webkit-text-fill-color: transparent;
    background-clip: text;
    text-shadow: 2px 2px 4px rgba(0, 0, 0, 0.1);
}
```

The ::first-line Pseudo-Element

The `::first-line` pseudo-element styles the first line of text within a block-level element, automatically adjusting as the viewport or font size changes.

#css

```
.intro-text::first-line {
    font-weight: bold;
    color: #2c3e50;
    font-size: 1.1em;
    letter-spacing: 0.5px;
}
```

```
.poetry::first-line {
    font-style: italic;
    color: #7f8c8d;
    text-transform: uppercase;
    font-size: 0.9em;
}
```

Combining First Letter and First Line

#css

```
.elegant-text::first-letter {
    font-size: 2.5em;
    float: left;
    line-height: 1;
    margin-right: 6px;
    color: #e74c3c;
    font-family: 'Times New Roman', serif;
}

.elegant-text::first-line {
    font-weight: 600;
    color: #34495e;
    letter-spacing: 1px;
}
```

Responsive Typography with Pseudo-Elements

#css

```
.responsive-drop-cap::first-letter {
    font-size: 2em;
    float: left;
    line-height: 1;
    margin-right: 4px;
    color: #3498db;
}

@media (min-width: 768px) {
    .responsive-drop-cap::first-letter {
        font-size: 3em;
        margin-right: 8px;
    }
}

@media (min-width: 1200px) {
    .responsive-drop-cap::first-letter {
        font-size: 4em;
        margin-right: 12px;
    }
}
```

Limitations and Considerations

The `::first-letter` and `::first-line` pseudo-elements have specific limitations. They only work with block-level elements and have restricted CSS properties that can be applied to them.

#css

```
/* Valid properties for ::first-letter */
```

```css
.valid-first-letter::first-letter {
    font-properties: /* All font properties work */;
    color: #333;
    background: #f8f9fa;
    margin: 10px;
    padding: 5px;
    border: 1px solid #ddd;
    text-decoration: underline;
    text-transform: uppercase;
    line-height: 1.2;
    float: left;
    vertical-align: top;
}

/* Valid properties for ::first-line */
.valid-first-line::first-line {
    font-properties: /* All font properties work */;
    color: #333;
    background: #f8f9fa;
    word-spacing: 2px;
    letter-spacing: 1px;
    text-decoration: underline;
    text-transform: uppercase;
    line-height: 1.4;
    vertical-align: baseline;
}
```

15.3 Inserting Decorative Content

Content Property Variations

The `content` property accepts various types of values, including strings, Unicode characters, counters, and attribute values, enabling rich decorative possibilities.

#css

```
.badge::before {
    content: "NEW";
    background: #e74c3c;
    color: white;
    font-size: 0.8em;
    padding: 2px 6px;
    border-radius: 3px;
    margin-right: 8px;
    font-weight: bold;
}

.price::before {
    content: "$";
    font-weight: bold;
    color: #27ae60;
}

.email::before {
    content: "✉ ";
    color: #3498db;
}
```

Using Unicode and Special Characters

#css

```css
.star-rating::before {
    content: "★★★★★";
    color: #f39c12;
    font-size: 1.2em;
}

.checkmark::before {
    content: "✓";
    color: #27ae60;
    font-weight: bold;
    margin-right: 5px;
}

.arrow-right::after {
    content: "→";
    margin-left: 5px;
    color: #3498db;
    font-weight: bold;
}
```

Attribute-Based Content

Pseudo-elements can display attribute values using the `attr()` function, creating dynamic content based on HTML attributes.

#css

```css
.tooltip {
    position: relative;
}
```

```
.tooltip::after {
    content: attr(data-tooltip);
    position: absolute;
    bottom: 100%;
    left: 50%;
    transform: translateX(-50%);
    background: #2c3e50;
    color: white;
    padding: 8px 12px;
    border-radius: 4px;
    font-size: 0.9em;
    white-space: nowrap;
    opacity: 0;
    pointer-events: none;
    transition: opacity 0.3s ease;
}

.tooltip:hover::after {
    opacity: 1;
}

.link-external[href^="http"]::after {
    content: " (" attr(href) ")";
    font-size: 0.8em;
    color: #7f8c8d;
}
```

Counter-Based Decorative Elements

CSS counters enable automatic numbering and can be used creatively with pseudo-elements.

#css

```css
.numbered-list {
    counter-reset: item-counter;
}

.numbered-item {
    counter-increment: item-counter;
    position: relative;
    padding-left: 40px;
    margin-bottom: 15px;
}

.numbered-item::before {
    content: counter(item-counter);
    position: absolute;
    left: 0;
    top: 0;
    background: #3498db;
    color: white;
    width: 25px;
    height: 25px;
    border-radius: 50%;
    display: flex;
    align-items: center;
    justify-content: center;
    font-weight: bold;
    font-size: 0.9em;
}
```

Image and Gradient Backgrounds

#css

```
.decorative-header::before {
    content: "";
    position: absolute;
    top: 0;
    left: 0;
    right: 0;
    height: 4px;
    background: linear-gradient(90deg,
        #ff6b6b 0%,
        #4ecdc4 25%,
        #45b7d1 50%,
        #96ceb4 75%,
        #ffeaa7 100%);
}

.card-accent::after {
    content: "";
    position: absolute;
    top: 10px;
    right: 10px;
    width: 40px;
    height: 40px;
    background: url('data:image/svg+xml;utf8,<svg
xmlns="http://www.w3.org/2000/svg" viewBox="0 0 24 24"
fill="%23ff6b6b"><path d="M12 2l3.09 6.26L22 9.27l-5 4.87
```

```
1.18 6.88L12 17.77l-6.18 3.25L7 14.14 2 9.27l6.91-1.01L12
2z"/></svg>') no-repeat center;
    background-size: contain;
}
```

Complex Decorative Patterns

#css

```
.pattern-background::before {
    content: "";
    position: absolute;
    top: 0;
    left: 0;
    right: 0;
    bottom: 0;
    background-image:
        radial-gradient(circle at 25% 25%, transparent
20%, rgba(52, 152, 219, 0.1) 21%),
        radial-gradient(circle at 75% 75%, transparent
20%, rgba(231, 76, 60, 0.1) 21%);
    background-size: 40px 40px;
    z-index: -1;
}
```

15.4 Animating Pseudo-Elements

Basic Pseudo-Element Animations

Pseudo-elements can be animated using CSS transitions and keyframe animations, creating engaging visual effects without additional HTML elements.

#css

```
.animated-button {
    position: relative;
    overflow: hidden;
    background: #3498db;
    color: white;
    padding: 12px 24px;
    border: none;
    border-radius: 4px;
    cursor: pointer;
    transition: color 0.3s ease;
}

.animated-button::before {
    content: "";
    position: absolute;
    top: 0;
    left: -100%;
    width: 100%;
    height: 100%;
    background: linear-gradient(90deg, transparent,
rgba(255, 255, 255, 0.3), transparent);
    transition: left 0.5s ease;
}

.animated-button:hover::before {
    left: 100%;
}
```

Loading and Progress Animations

#css

```
.loading-spinner::after {
    content: "";
    width: 20px;
    height: 20px;
    border: 2px solid #f3f3f3;
    border-top: 2px solid #3498db;
    border-radius: 50%;
    animation: spin 1s linear infinite;
    display: inline-block;
    margin-left: 10px;
}

@keyframes spin {
    0% { transform: rotate(0deg); }
    100% { transform: rotate(360deg); }
}

.progress-bar {
    position: relative;
    background: #ecf0f1;
    height: 8px;
    border-radius: 4px;
    overflow: hidden;
}
```

```
.progress-bar::after {
    content: "";
    position: absolute;
    top: 0;
    left: 0;
    height: 100%;
    width: 0%;
    background: linear-gradient(90deg, #3498db, #2ecc71);
    border-radius: 4px;
    animation: progress 3s ease-in-out infinite;
}

@keyframes progress {
    0% { width: 0%; }
    50% { width: 70%; }
    100% { width: 100%; }
}
```

Hover Animations and Transitions

#css

```
.hover-underline {
    position: relative;
    text-decoration: none;
    color: #2c3e50;
    transition: color 0.3s ease;
}

.hover-underline::after {
```

```
    content: "";
    position: absolute;
    bottom: -2px;
    left: 0;
    width: 0;
    height: 2px;
    background: #e74c3c;
    transition: width 0.3s ease;
}

.hover-underline:hover {
    color: #e74c3c;
}

.hover-underline:hover::after {
    width: 100%;
}

.scale-effect {
    position: relative;
    transform-origin: center;
    transition: transform 0.3s ease;
}

.scale-effect::before {
    content: "";
    position: absolute;
    top: 50%;
    left: 50%;
    width: 0;
    height: 0;
```

```
    background: rgba(52, 152, 219, 0.2);
    border-radius: 50%;
    transform: translate(-50%, -50%);
    transition: width 0.3s ease, height 0.3s ease;
}

.scale-effect:hover::before {
    width: 100%;
    height: 100%;
}
```

Pulsing and Breathing Effects

#css

```
.pulse-notification::before {
    content: "";
    position: absolute;
    top: -5px;
    right: -5px;
    width: 12px;
    height: 12px;
    background: #e74c3c;
    border-radius: 50%;
    animation: pulse 2s infinite;
}

@keyframes pulse {
    0% {
        transform: scale(1);
```

```
        opacity: 1;
    }
    50% {
        transform: scale(1.3);
        opacity: 0.7;
    }
    100% {
        transform: scale(1);
        opacity: 1;
    }
}

.breathing-glow::after {
    content: "";
    position: absolute;
    top: -2px;
    left: -2px;
    right: -2px;
    bottom: -2px;
    background: linear-gradient(45deg, #ff6b6b, #4ecdc4,
#45b7d1, #96ceb4);
    border-radius: 8px;
    z-index: -1;
    animation: breathe 3s ease-in-out infinite;
    filter: blur(4px);
}

@keyframes breathe {
    0%, 100% {
        opacity: 0.5;
        transform: scale(1);
```

```
    }
    50% {
        opacity: 0.8;
        transform: scale(1.02);
    }
}
```

Text Animation Effects

#css

```
.typewriter {
    position: relative;
    font-family: 'Courier New', monospace;
}

.typewriter::after {
    content: "|";
    position: absolute;
    right: -2px;
    color: #2c3e50;
    animation: blink 1s infinite;
}

@keyframes blink {
    0%, 50% { opacity: 1; }
    51%, 100% { opacity: 0; }
}

.glitch-text {
```

```
    position: relative;
    color: #fff;
}

.glitch-text::before,
.glitch-text::after {
    content: attr(data-text);
    position: absolute;
    top: 0;
    left: 0;
    width: 100%;
    height: 100%;
}

.glitch-text::before {
    animation: glitch-1 2s infinite;
    color: #ff0000;
    z-index: -1;
}

.glitch-text::after {
    animation: glitch-2 2s infinite;
    color: #00ff00;
    z-index: -2;
}

@keyframes glitch-1 {
    0%, 14%, 15%, 49%, 50%, 99%, 100% {
        transform: translate(0);
    }
    15%, 49% {
```

```
        transform: translate(-2px, 0);
    }
}

@keyframes glitch-2 {
    0%, 20%, 21%, 62%, 63%, 99%, 100% {
        transform: translate(0);
    }
    21%, 62% {
        transform: translate(2px, 0);
    }
}
```

15.5 Pseudo-elements in Button Design

Basic Button Enhancements

Pseudo-elements transform ordinary buttons into visually appealing interactive elements without requiring additional markup.

#css

```
.modern-button {
    position: relative;
    background: #3498db;
    color: white;
    border: none;
    padding: 12px 24px;
    border-radius: 6px;
    cursor: pointer;
    font-size: 16px;
    font-weight: 500;
```

```
    transition: all 0.3s ease;
    overflow: hidden;
}

.modern-button::before {
    content: "";
    position: absolute;
    top: 0;
    left: -100%;
    width: 100%;
    height: 100%;
    background: linear-gradient(90deg, transparent,
rgba(255, 255, 255, 0.2), transparent);
    transition: left 0.6s ease;
}

.modern-button:hover {
    transform: translateY(-2px);
    box-shadow: 0 8px 25px rgba(52, 152, 219, 0.3);
}

.modern-button:hover::before {
    left: 100%;
}
```

Icon Integration with Pseudo-Elements

#css

```
.icon-button {
```

```
    position: relative;
    background: #2ecc71;
    color: white;
    border: none;
    padding: 12px 24px 12px 45px;
    border-radius: 25px;
    cursor: pointer;
    font-size: 16px;
    transition: all 0.3s ease;
}

.icon-button::before {
    content: "→";
    position: absolute;
    left: 15px;
    top: 50%;
    transform: translateY(-50%);
    font-size: 18px;
    font-weight: bold;
    transition: transform 0.3s ease;
}

.icon-button:hover {
    background: #27ae60;
    padding-left: 50px;
}

.icon-button:hover::before {
    transform: translateY(-50%) translateX(5px);
}
```

```
.download-button {
    position: relative;
    background: #9b59b6;
    color: white;
    border: none;
    padding: 14px 50px 14px 24px;
    border-radius: 4px;
    cursor: pointer;
    font-size: 16px;
    transition: background 0.3s ease;
}

.download-button::after {
    content: "⬇";
    position: absolute;
    right: 18px;
    top: 50%;
    transform: translateY(-50%);
    font-size: 16px;
    transition: transform 0.3s ease;
}

.download-button:hover {
    background: #8e44ad;
}

.download-button:hover::after {
    transform: translateY(-50%) translateY(3px);
}
```

Gradient and Border Effects

#css

```
.gradient-border-button {
    position: relative;
    background: white;
    color: #333;
    border: none;
    padding: 14px 28px;
    border-radius: 8px;
    cursor: pointer;
    font-size: 16px;
    font-weight: 600;
    transition: color 0.3s ease;
}

.gradient-border-button::before {
    content: "";
    position: absolute;
    top: -2px;
    left: -2px;
    right: -2px;
    bottom: -2px;
    background: linear-gradient(45deg, #ff6b6b, #4ecdc4,
#45b7d1, #96ceb4);
    border-radius: 10px;
    z-index: -1;
    transition: opacity 0.3s ease;
    opacity: 0;
}
```

```
.gradient-border-button:hover {
    color: #fff;
}

.gradient-border-button:hover::before {
    opacity: 1;
}

.neon-button {
    position: relative;
    background: transparent;
    color: #00ff88;
    border: 2px solid #00ff88;
    padding: 12px 24px;
    border-radius: 4px;
    cursor: pointer;
    font-size: 16px;
    font-family: 'Courier New', monospace;
    text-transform: uppercase;
    letter-spacing: 1px;
    transition: all 0.3s ease;
}

.neon-button::before {
    content: "";
    position: absolute;
    top: 0;
    left: 0;
    right: 0;
    bottom: 0;
```

```
    background: #00ff88;
    opacity: 0;
    z-index: -1;
    transition: opacity 0.3s ease;
}

.neon-button::after {
    content: "";
    position: absolute;
    top: -4px;
    left: -4px;
    right: -4px;
    bottom: -4px;
    border: 1px solid #00ff88;
    border-radius: 4px;
    opacity: 0;
    transition: opacity 0.3s ease;
}

.neon-button:hover {
    color: #000;
    box-shadow: 0 0 20px #00ff88;
}

.neon-button:hover::before {
    opacity: 1;
}

.neon-button:hover::after {
    opacity: 1;
}
```

Loading States and Feedback

#css

```
.loading-button {
    position: relative;
    background: #3498db;
    color: white;
    border: none;
    padding: 12px 24px;
    border-radius: 4px;
    cursor: pointer;
    font-size: 16px;
    transition: background 0.3s ease;
    min-width: 120px;
}

.loading-button.loading {
    background: #bdc3c7;
    cursor: not-allowed;
    color: transparent;
}

.loading-button.loading::after {
    content: "";
    position: absolute;
    top: 50%;
    left: 50%;
    width: 16px;
```

```
    height: 16px;
    margin: -8px 0 0 -8px;
    border: 2px solid #ecf0f1;
    border-top: 2px solid #3498db;
    border-radius: 50%;
    animation: button-spin 1s linear infinite;
}

@keyframes button-spin {
    0% { transform: rotate(0deg); }
    100% { transform: rotate(360deg); }
}

.success-button {
    position: relative;
    background: #2ecc71;
    color: white;
    border: none;
    padding: 12px 24px;
    border-radius: 4px;
    cursor: pointer;
    font-size: 16px;
    transition: all 0.3s ease;
}

.success-button.success {
    background: #27ae60;
}

.success-button.success::before {
    content: "✓";
```

```
    position: absolute;
    left: 8px;
    top: 50%;
    transform: translateY(-50%);
    font-size: 18px;
    font-weight: bold;
    animation: checkmark-appear 0.5s ease;
}

@keyframes checkmark-appear {
    0% {
        opacity: 0;
        transform: translateY(-50%) scale(0);
    }
    100% {
        opacity: 1;
        transform: translateY(-50%) scale(1);
    }
}
```

Advanced Interactive Effects

#css

```
.ripple-button {
    position: relative;
    background: #e74c3c;
    color: white;
    border: none;
    padding: 14px 28px;
```

```
    border-radius: 4px;
    cursor: pointer;
    font-size: 16px;
    overflow: hidden;
    transition: background 0.3s ease;
}

.ripple-button::before {
    content: "";
    position: absolute;
    top: 50%;
    left: 50%;
    width: 0;
    height: 0;
    border-radius: 50%;
    background: rgba(255, 255, 255, 0.3);
    transform: translate(-50%, -50%);
    transition: width 0.6s ease, height 0.6s ease;
}

.ripple-button:active::before {
    width: 300px;
    height: 300px;
}

.magnetic-button {
    position: relative;
    background: #9b59b6;
    color: white;
    border: none;
    padding: 16px 32px;
```

```
    border-radius: 50px;
    cursor: pointer;
    font-size: 16px;
    font-weight: 600;
    transition: all 0.3s cubic-bezier(0.23, 1, 0.32, 1);
    transform-style: preserve-3d;
}

.magnetic-button::before {
    content: "";
    position: absolute;
    top: 0;
    left: 0;
    right: 0;
    bottom: 0;
    background: linear-gradient(135deg, rgba(255, 255,
255, 0.1), transparent);
    border-radius: 50px;
    opacity: 0;
    transition: opacity 0.3s ease;
}

.magnetic-button:hover {
    transform: perspective(1000px) rotateX(-10deg)
rotateY(5deg) translateZ(10px);
    box-shadow: 0 20px 40px rgba(155, 89, 182, 0.4);
}

.magnetic-button:hover::before {
    opacity: 1;
}
```

Essential Tips

- Always include the `content` property when using `::before` and `::after`, even if it's an empty string, as these pseudo-elements won't render without it.
- Use `position: relative` on parent elements when positioning pseudo-elements absolutely to ensure proper containment and positioning context.
- Remember that pseudo-elements inherit from their parent element, so properties like `color`, `font-family`, and `font-size` will cascade down unless explicitly overridden.
- Leverage the `z-index` property strategically with pseudo-elements to control layering, especially when creating overlays, backgrounds, or decorative elements that should appear behind or in front of content.
- Consider performance implications when animating pseudo-elements - use `transform` and `opacity` for smooth animations rather than properties that trigger layout recalculations like `width`, `height`, or `top`.

Actionable Strategies

- Create a consistent naming convention for pseudo-element classes that clearly indicates their purpose, such as `.card--highlight::after` or `.button--loading::before`.
- Build a library of reusable pseudo-element components for common design patterns like tooltips, badges, loading states, and decorative accents that can be applied across projects.
- Test pseudo-element implementations across different browsers and devices, paying special attention to mobile responsiveness and touch interactions.
- Combine pseudo-elements with CSS custom properties (variables) to create themeable components that can easily adapt to different design systems and color schemes.
- Document your pseudo-element usage patterns and create style guides that explain when and how to use different pseudo-element techniques within your team or organization.

- Optimize pseudo-element animations by using `will-change` property when appropriate and removing it after animations complete to improve performance.
- Implement fallback styles for older browsers that may not fully support certain pseudo-element features, ensuring graceful degradation of your designs.

www.ingramcontent.com/pod-product-compliance
Lightning Source LLC
La Vergne TN
LVHW072119210926
848482LV00027B/689